CRIME LAW AND POLICE SCIENCE

By the same auther

1. *Banker's Safety : Methods and Techniques*
2. *United Nations and Indian Mysticism : Parrallels on Human Rights and Police*

About the Author

Criminologist Dr. James Vadackumchery has twenty-five years of teaching police officers of all ranks in criminology, law, police science and correction. He is a noted author of nearly four dozen authoritative and authentic books in the areas of police, crime and justice. He has authored books in criminal justice, victim justice, human rights justice, juvenile justice, gender justice, equal justice, enforcement crimes and criminology. His theory – James's Law on police interrogation – is widely applied in police work and he is a guest faculty in universities and national institutes of higher learning.

Dr. Vadackumchery is B.A (Criminology & Forensic Science), M.A. (Criminology and Forensic Science) and LL.B. in law. He received his Ph.D. in criminal justice from the University of Kerala. He has published hundreds of articles exposing 600 areas of justice administration and miscarriage of justice.

He is married to Mary and they have two daughters –Neethu and Neethi.

CRIME LAW AND POLICE SCIENCE

JAMES VADACKUMCHERY

CONCEPT PUBLISHING COMPANY, NEW DELHI - 110059

ISBN 81-7022-995-2

First Published 1986
Revised Edition, 2003

Published and Printed by

Ashok Kumar Mittal
Concept Publishing Company
A/15-16, Commercial Block, Mohan Garden,
NEW DELHI -110059 (India)

Phones : 25351460, 25351794
Fax : 091-11-25357103
E-mail : publishing@conceptpub.com

JACOB and *MARY*, my *PARENTS*
to whom
I owe much of what
I am able to do today.

PREFACE TO THE SECOND EDITION

I am simply taken up by the interest shown by police officers, crime investigators, lawyers, prosecutors, magistrates, judges and private detectives to study scientific investigation of crimes. Many of them pressured me to bring out the second edition of the book *Crime, Law and Police Science*. Crimes have been on the increase and they are indeed very complex now. Traditional methods of investigation and interrogation cannot and will not yield results in these days. Criminal cases are acquitted in large numbers. Scientific investigation of crimes is the only solution to reduce the rate of acquittals. Professionalism is what is required. The crude and questionable methods and tactics of interrogation are of no real utility when human rights of the suspects, detinues and the incarcerated are recognised. This book, I hope, is an answer to many problems which the police investigators face today.

August 9, 2002 **Dr. James Vadackumchery**

PREFACE TO THE FIRST EDITION

Books on *Science and Crime Investigation* by foreign experts are available in plenty. But the laws, procedures and modalities of investigation in other countries are, to some extent, different from what they are in India. Hence a book based on Indian needs becomes all the more essential.

All throughout this book, a number of decisions made by Indian courts have been quoted. Since a new Code of Criminal Procedure was enacted in 1973, the decided cases before 1973 have references to sections of law contained in the Criminal Procedure Code that was in existence before 1973. The reader is, therefore, cautioned to bear this fact in mind when he appreciates the case laws quoted in this book.

The author feels it to be his proud honour to dedicate this book, most respectfully, at the feet of his affectionate parents. They could successfully transmit sublime values and a vision in life among their children. They are thoughtfully remembered here. Again, the author wants to put it on record the invaluable assistance which he received from his wife, *Mary*, particularly at a time when numerous other family and academic engagements seemed already have claimed her time and energies. She has been an indefatigable aid to the author at all stages during his preparation of this title. The services of his wife and his little, but understanding daughters –*Neethu* and *Neethi* are gratefully acknowledged.

Finally, the author wants to make it clear that the opinions expressed in this book do not reflect the views of the Union Government, State Governments and Police Departments. They are the personal views of the author. The responsibility for the shortcomings, if any, in this book is that of the author alone.

September, 1986 **Dr. James Vadackumchery**
Trivandrum

CONTENTS

CONTENTS

1

CRIME LAW AND CRIMINAL LIABILITY

Crime are those acts or omissions involving breach of a duty to which by the law of a country a sanction is attached by way of punishment in the public interest, and for which the ordinary remedy is by indictment[1]. Section 2 (n) of the Code of Criminal Procedure, 1973 (Act No. 2 of 1974) defines offence as "any act or omission made punishable by any law for the time being in force and includes any act in respect of which a complaint may be made under section 20 of the Cattle Trespass Act, 1871 (1 of 1871)". In the Indian Penal Code, 1860 (Act No. XLV of 1860), section 40 reads:[2] ["Except in the[3] (chapters) and sections mentioned in Cls. 2 and 3 of this section, the word "offence" denotes a thing made punishable by this Code].

In Chapter IV [4], (Chapter V-A) and in the following sections, namely sections[5] 64, 65, 66,[6] (67), 71, 109, 110, 112, 114, 115, 116, 117, 187, 194, 195, 203, 211, 213, 214, 221, 222, 223, 224, 225, 327, 328, 329, 330, 331, 347, 348, 388, 389 and 445, the word "offence" denotes a thing punishable under this Code, or under any special or local law as hereinafter defined.

And in sections 141, 176, 177, 201, 202, 212, 216 and 441, the word "offence" has the same meaning when the thing punishable under the special or local law is punishable under such law with imprisonment for a term of six months or upwards, whether with or without fine."

The definition for offence in the Procedure Code and the same in the Penal Code shows that the scope of the definition in the former is wider than the same in the latter. This is so because the Precedure Code is meant for the "trial of all offences under and without the Code", while the Penal Code "has to define the term with strict reference to its future use" in the Penal Code itself.[7]

Elements of an Offence

An offence consists of three elements or ingredients. They are 1. The act, 2. *Mens rea*, and 3. The harmful consequence of the act.

The Act

The act in the Indian penal law refers to the bare physical act—i.e., "the muscular change and what might be called the concomitant circumstances, such as for example, the instrument employed and as including no part of its consequences, not even the target of the act".[8] Hence the word act (*actus*) "connotes a '*deed*', a physical result of human conduct".[9] The conduct refers to both commissions and omissions. The most important aspect to be considered here is to look whether or not such deeds are legally prohibited. If only such deeds are legally prohibited they become crimes. Hence the acts of people protected by the provisions of law under the chapter on General Exceptions in the Indian Penal Code, 1860 are not crimes. In such instances, the man who caused the harm is deemed to be not guilty.

Mens rea

The maxim, *Et actus non facit reum nisi mens sit rea*, is recognised in Indian Jurisprudence. The *actus* (deed) and the *mental processes* (mens) of the actor at the time he commits the act are important. This maxim "recognizes that there are two necessary elements in crime, a physical element and a mental element".[10] In other words, the crime-doer must have done an act which is prohibited by the law and at the same time he must have a "legally reprehensible state of mind".[11] In Mul Chandra Pal *vs.* State, it has been accepted that "the well established rule is that unless a statute clearly or by necessary implications rules out *mens rea* as a constituent part of crime, the deponent could not be held guilty of an offence under a criminal law unless he has guilty mind".[12] But there may arise a case when the object of the Act and the language employed in it might reasonably entitle the Court to think that proof of guilty mind is not essential to the proof of crime.[13] It goes therefore without saying that one cannot find '*mens rea*' in the involuntary acts of people —e.g., if harms resulted from a man's movement during intoxication, somniambulism etc. In this context writes Kenney:

> Once it had been admitted that some degree of wickedness was a requisite in criminal guilt, it followed logically that *mens rea* must eventually become a subjective matter of an increasingly subtle kind. It is not enough to be satisfied that an accused person's conduct was voluntary since there may still be no moral blame if voluntary action does result in harm, provided that the harm was not contemplated……a man should not be punished unless he had been aware that what he was doing might lead to mischievous results; he must have had foresight of the consequences of his conduct. The nature of the precise circumstances, the foresight of which attracts criminal guilt, is fixed by law and varies from crime to crime. But whatever they may be for the particular crime, foresight of them is the common requirement for all, and it is this subjective element of foresight which now a days constitutes *mens rea*".[14]

Malice aforethought, intention, recklessness and negligence etc., are said to be the elements of *mens rea.* In Indian law, for example, homicide can be either culpable homicide amounting to murder or not amounting to murder. In this case *malice aforethought* is defined as "the freely formed intentions of a man to pursue a course of conduct which he realizes will or may bring about the death of some person".[15] This concept of *malice aforethought* explains well all of the following attitudes of human mind, namely :

1. Intention to kill the particular person, who, infact, was killed.
2. Intention to kill a particular person, but not the one who actually was killed. For example, A, lays sticks and turf over a pit with the intention of thereby causing the death of B or with the knowledge that death is likely to be thereby caused. Z, believing the ground to be firm, treads on it, falls in and is killed. Here A had no intention to take the life of Z. At the same time he had the intention to kill (*mens rea*), and infact he killed a person (*actus reus*).[16]
3. Intention to cause such bodily injury as is likely to cause death.
4. The knowledge that he is likely by such act to cause death.

The *malice aforethought* can be either express or implied. *Express malice* is seen in cases where there is a definite intention to kill, and *implied malice* is seen in cases where the intention was to cause only hurt or grievous hurt, but it so happened that death resulted from it. In such cases *implied malice* is found as every man is presumed to know the consequence of his acts. Remember that here the term *malice aforethought* is a term used to explain the mental element necessary in the offence of culpable homicide.

Intention means to keep in mind a specific purpose to arrive at a desired and specified aim or goal. In the context of crime, intention is used "to donote the state of mind of a man who not only foresees but also wills the possible consequence of his conduct".[17] It does not necessarily mean that every person should always forsee all the possible consequence of his act. But when a man shoots at another, it would be quite obvious that he foresees both the victim's death and also he desires for it. The same principle is applicable in the case of omissions too, for instance, if man knowingly abstains from food until he dies, it is very plain that he intended his death and also desired for the same. Hence it can be rightly said that "there cannot be intention unless there is also foresight".[18]

'Intention' is different from 'motives'. The ulterior intention may be called the motive. For instance, a man shoots at a tiger—here the immediate intention may be to kill the tiger but the motive (ultimate intention) may be to prevent the danger of having a tiger in the vicinity of the house. Hence in Molu *vs.* State of Haryana, the Supreme Court observed: Motive pales into insignificance when there is direct evidence, but assumes importance, when the case depends on circumstantial evidence. Often the motive is shrouded in mystery and it is very difficult to locate the same".[19] Again in Rajinder Kumar *vs.* State of Punjab, the Supreme Court observed : "It often happens that only the culprit himself knows what moved him to a certain course of action".[20] Hence the discovery of the true motive for a crime is not imperative in every case.[21] It is not incumbent on the prosecution to prove the motive for the crime.[22] In Ediga Anamma *vs.* State of Andhra Pradesh, the Supreme Court said, "Motive by itself is not much, particularly in the absence of direct evidence, but in the company of other facts it plays probative role".[23] Therefore, "the fact that the apparent motive was too flimsy is no reply to the unshaken testimony of creditable and natural eye-witnesses who had no motive whatsoever to implicate the appellant falsely".[24]

Recklessness is otherwise called rashness. Secion 304-A I.P.C. deals with the causing of death by rash or negligent act. Here the man who is reckless in his act may prefer that the contemplated event shall not happen, or he may not care whether it happens or not; but in either case he does not *desire* it to happen and therefore does not act with the purpose that it shall happen.[25] Here one must remember that "intention cannot exist without foresight but foresight can exist without intention".[26] Hence a man who is reckless is actually running a risk, at the same time he necessarily foresees or ought to foresee the possibility of the risk or danger. The risk comes to him as a surprise. Here comes the question of *negligence*. "The difference between recklessness and negligence is the difference between advertence and inadvertence" says Kenney. He further argues :

> "Negligence must also be carefully distinguished from neglect. This word neglect does not indicate specific attitude of mind, but states a matter of objective fact, which may be produced either by intention or by negligence. Thus a man who has neglected to feed his animal may have done so (a) consciously and purposely because, for example, he did not want to take the trouble; or on the other hand (b) negligently, in that he simply forgets to feed it. Again, if a man, being aware that the brakes or wheels of his motor car are defective, yet takes it on the road well knowing that with it in that condition he may cause injury to some person, and if such injury is thereby caused then this will be a case of harm brought about not by his negligence but by his wilful neglect and recklessness." This would imply that there are only two states of mind which constitutes, '*mens rea*' and they are nothing but intention and recklessness.

Mens rea in statutory offences

Justice Subba Rao, in State of Maharashtra *vs.* M.H. George observed : "It is a well settled principle of common law that *mens rea* is an essential ingredient of a criminal offence. Doubtless a Statute can exclude that element, but it is a sound rule of construction adopted in England and also accepted in India to construe a statutory provision creating an offence in conformity with the common law rather than against it unless the statute expressly or by necessary implication excluded *mens rea*. To put it differently, there is a presumption that *mens rea* is an essential ingredient of a statutory offence; but this may be rebutted by the express words of a Statute creating the offence or by necessary implication. But the mere fact that the object of a Statute is to promote welfare activities or to eradicate grave social evils is in itself not decisive of questions whether the elements of guilty mind is excluded from the ingredients of the offence. It is also necessary to enquire whether a Statute by putting a person under strict liability helps him to assist the State in the enforcement of the law: can he do anything to promote the observance of law ? A person who does not know that gold cannot be brought into India without a license or is not bringing into India any gold at all cannot possibly do anything to promote the observance of the law. *Mens rea* by necessary implication can be excluded from a statute only where it is absolutely clear that the implementation of the object of a Statute would otherwise be defeated and its exclusion enables those put under strict liability by their act or omissions to assist the promotion of the law. The nature of *mens rea* that will be implied in a Statute creating an offence depends upon the object of the Act and the provisions thereof".[27]

The harmful conseqence of the Act

The maxim-*nullum crimen sine poena* —no crime without punishment—means that people cannot be punished for acts which are not punished or punishable under the law in force. Society punishes a man under law if he has done some act which has harmful consequences to the society or individuals or both. This does not mean that all acts which have harmful consequences are punished in law. If the individual has a legally recognised defence or justification for the act (mistake of fact, consent, intoxication, etc.), he cannot be punished. This is the reason why the dictum *Nulla Poena Sine Lego* —no punishment without law—is recognized in criminal justice administration.

In criminal law an "individual is treated as if he were autonomous, but in fact an act which harms an individual also harms the groups in which he has membership".[28] Sutherland and Cressey argue: "There must be a casual relation between the legally forbidden harms and the voluntary misconduct".[29] For instance, to convict an individual of murder, it must be proved that the person actually stabbed the victim or behaved in some other way that led directly to the death of the victim. It is necessary to prove that the harmful consequences was the effect of the alleged offender's act.

Classification of Crimes in Indian Law

Crimes in Indian law are classified in respect to their atrocity as *cognizable* and *non-cognizable*. The more serious ones are called cognizable crimes and therefore a cognizable offence means an offence for which a police officer may, in accordance with the First Schedule of the Code of Criminal Procedure, 1973 or under any other law for the time being in force, arrest without warrant and logically it follows that a non-cognizable offence is one in which a police officer cannot arrest the crime-doer without a warrant from a Magistrate. The more serious cognizable crimes are punished with death, life sentence or confinement in prisons or fine and the less serious ones (especially the non-cognizable ones) are punished with imprisonment or fine or both. As a classification of crime this may not be very useful except for effective police action when a crime is reported.

Crimes are frequently classified for statistical purposes as crimes against the State, against persons, against property, against document etc. Infact, the Indian Penal Code, 1860 has classified crimes under these heads (see Table 1.1).

The classification of crimes in the Indian Penal Code has been done as early as 1860. The Code defines offences in several categories and embodies the substantial criminal law of the Country. In the changed socio-economic and political melieu of the Country, critics on the Code are doubtful about the effectiveness of the criminal laws and their classification to combat the emerging patterns of crimes and their unchecked growth. In Mobarik Ali, *vs.* State of Bombay, the Supreme Court observed: "The notions of criminal jurisdiction have very considerably changed during a period of nearly a century that has passed since the Penal Code was inscribed on the Statute Book. It is legitimate to construe the Code with reference to the modern needs whenever this is permissible unless there is anything in the Code or in any particular section of the Code to indicate to the contrary".[30]

Table 1.1 : Classification of Crimes Under the Indian Penal Code, 1860

Sl No.	Crimes	Total Penal Sections
1.	Abetment	11
2.	Criminal Conspiracy	13
3.	Offences against the State	12
4.	Offences relating to the Army, Navy and Air Force	9
5.	Offences against the public tranquility	18
6.	Offences by or relating to the public servants	17
7.	Offences relating to elections	5
8.	Contempt of the lawful authority of public servants	19
9.	False evidence and offences against public justice	39
10.	Offences relating to coins and government stamps	34
11.	Offences relating to weights and measures	4
12.	Offences affecting the public health, safety, convenience, decency and morals	27
13.	Offences relating to religion	5
14.	Offences affecting the human body	51
15.	Offences against property	70
16.	Offences relating to documents and to property marks	26
17.	Criminal breach of contracts of service	1
18.	Offences relating to marriage	9
19.	Offences relating to defamation	3
20.	Criminal intimidation, insult and annoyance	7
21.	Attempts to commit offences	1

The Penal Code of India has, besides chapters on definitions, punishments and general exceptions, twenty one chapters dealing with various categories of crimes. A significant feature of the Code is that several categories are created for one and the same offence, e.g., there are as many as thirteen different offences in house-trespass (Sections 448 – 460 I.P.C.) and in some instances provisions in the Code overlap one another.[31]

Some of the traditional offences affecting the human body, property, public tranquility, public health, safety, convenience, decency and morals are dealt with in four chapters in the Penal Code.

Vadackumchery has found that 95.45 per cent of the cases during 1979 in Kerala were registered under various sections in those chapters. This implies that 4.55 per cent of the cases only attracted the provisions from the rest of the chapters in the Code.[32]

Code of Criminal Procedure, 1973

The Code of Criminal Procedure, 1973 (Act 2 of 1974) provides a mechanism for the treatment of offences against substantive criminal laws. The actual procedure in the Code is dealt with in Chapters on trials (Chapters XVIII, XIX, XX, XXI, XXIV), appeals (Chapter XXIX), references and revision (Chapter XXXI). Certain provisions in the Code are on substantive criminal laws. In addition, there are chapters on evidence in inquiries and trials (Chapter XXIII), execution, suspension, remission and commutation of sentences (Chapter XXXII), bail and bonds, sentences (Chapter XXXIII), disposal of property (Chapter XXXIV) etc. The provisions in the Code regarding procedure are obligatory and not merely directory. The Code classifies offences into two categories – cognizable and non-cognizable. All offences under the Indian Penal Code, 1860, whether cognizable or not are given in tabular form in the First Schedule of the Code of Criminal Procedure, 1973. The Schedule also indicates whether or not the offence is to be tried as a summons or warrant case, is bailable or non-bailable compoundable or non-compoundable and the penalty stipulated for the offence together with the Court by which it is triable.[33]

The Indian Evidence Act, 1872

The Indian Evidence Act, 1872 (Act 1 of 1872) applies to both civil and criminal cases. The Act is meant to assist the proceedings of courts of law in the investigation of facts submitted for their decision. The evidence adduced before the courts can be of two kinds: parole evidence consisting of viva-voce examination of witnesses and written or documentary evidence. Part I of the Act deals with the relevancy of facts including admissions and confessions. James Stephen in his introduction to the Indian Evidence

Act writes: "the law of Evidence determines (i) what sort of facts may be proved in order to establish the existence of that which is defined by the substantive law as conclusive, (ii) what sort of proof is to be given to those facts; (iii) who is to give it, and (iv) how it is to be given".[34] Chapter III in Part II of the Act is about facts which need not be proved. Chapter IV treats oral evidence. Chapter V deals with documentary evidence. Chapter VI contains provisions regarding exclusion of oral evidence by documentary evidence. Part III of the Act concerns the production and effect of evidence, i.e., burden of proof, estoppel, examination of witnesses and finally improper admission and rejection of evidence.

Cognizable Cases

In a cognizable crime, the investigation starts when the commission of such an offence is reported to an officer in-charge of a police station. Cognizable cases, as stated earlier, are those shown as: (i) cognizable in the First Schedule of the Code of Criminal Procedure, 1973; (ii) Cases which are endorsed by competent magistrates under section 202 of the Code of Criminal Procedure' 1973; (iii) those referred to the police for investigation by magistrates under section 156 (3) of the Cr. P.C., 1973, (iv) suicides and accidental or suspicious deaths, fires, missing of persons, missing of cattle and all other occurrences where there is reason to suspect the commission of a cognizable offence; (v) non-cognizable cases endorsed to the police by magistrates for inquiry and investigation; (vi) cases under sections 107 to 110 of the Code of Criminal Procedure, 1973 after it has been determined to put them before a Magistrate; and (vii) reports made to magistrates with a view to action being taken under section 144 or under section 145 of the Criminal Procedure Code, 1973.

The police officers have the power to arrest the suspects without warrant in cognizable cases by virtue of sections 41, 42, 60, 129(2), 151 and 432 Cr. P.C., 1973 and the provisions in various other central and state enactments.

Criminal Liability

"In certain circumstances a person may be (a) entirely excused from criminal responsibility for legally prohibited harm which has resulted from his conduct; and in certain other circumstances he may be (b) excused merely from punishment for the commission of such harm".[35] But in both instances there should be some legal provision expressly exempting the person committing the harm. The grounds which can be advanced by the individual who has committed a legally forbidden deed for getting exemption from penalty are given, as stated earlier, under General Exceptions in Chapter IV of the Indian Penal Code, 1860. This chapter dealing with exceptions to criminal liability contains altogether 32 sections and they can be classified as :

1 Where there is absence of criminal intent – Sections 81, 82, 83, 84, 85, 86, 92, 93 and 94 I.P.C.
2 Cases of accident —Section 80 I.P.C.
3 Mistake of fact —Sections 76, 79 I.P.C.
4 Acts done by consent —Sections 87, 88, 89, 90 I.P.C.
5 Triviality —Section 95 I.P.C.
6 Act done in exercise of the right of the private defence—Sections 95, 96, 97, 98, 99, 100, 101, 103, 104, 105 and 106 I.P.C.
7 Privileged acts —Sections 77 and 78 I.P.C.

"All these cases, though variously classified and described are really cases in which there is absence of criminal intent. There is only one case dealt with in section 95, in which provision is made for exemption in spite of the presence of criminal intent, the act committed being so inconsiderable as to be negligible".[36] The provisions under the General Exceptions are applicable to all offences under special and local laws.[37]

(a) *Absence of Criminal Intent*

Section 81, I.P.C. reads: "Nothing is an offence merely by reasons of its being done with the knowledge that it is likely to cause harm if it be done without any criminal intention to cause harm, and in good faith for the purpose of preventing or avoiding other harm to person or property.

Explanation – It is a question of fact in such a case whether the harm to be prevented or avoided was of such a nature and so imminent as to justify or excuse the risk of doing the act with the knowledge that it was likely to cause harm".

This section gives legislative sanction to the doctrine of necessity. In other words, the law permits the doing of an evil so that good may result from such transactions. To avoid or prevent a greater or more severe evil, the person is permitted to inflict a lesser evil. Cecil Turner in this context writes :

> "When the defence of "necessity" is set up it will be found that this really means that the accused person with freedom of choice before him, had preferred to act in the way he did act, thus performing an *actus reus,* rather than in another way with different results. The dilemma which faced the man have been a cruel one, either alternative leading to serious harm.... There is really no escape from the dilemma in many cases and the situation is not alleviated by loose use of the word necessity".[38]

Necessity may create the law and at times will supersede rules. In such situations whatever is just and reasonable will also be legal.[39] For example, the illustration given in the I.P.C. is that A, in a great fire, pulls down houses in order to prevent the conflagration from spreading. He does this with the intention in good faith of saving human life or property. Here, if it be found that the harm to be prevented was of such a nature and so imminent as to excuse A's act. A is not guilty of the offence. It must be remembered here that necessity *vincit legem* and all good involves some sacrifice and hardship.

(b) *Acts of Infants*

In all cases, competent age, sanity, and some degree of freedom from coercion etc. are presumed to be essential to criminality.[40] Sections 82 and 83 I.P.C. deal with the criminal responsibility of children in Indian Law. According to law, "Nothing is an offence which is done by a child under seven years of age"[41] and "Nothing is an offence which is done by a child above seven years of age and under twelve, who has not attained sufficient maturity of understanding to judge of the nature and consequences of his conduct on that occasion".[42]

When the doctrine of *mens rea* has been accepted in criminal jurisprudence as an essential ingredient in crimes, it became necessary to exempt children from criminal liability. Accordingly the law in India is that a child under seven years of age is incapable of *mens rea* or criminal intent and therefore he is called "doli incapax". But this presumption weakens when the child grows in age and therefore section 83 I.P.C. attaches only a qualified criminal liability to children above seven and below twelve years of age. In such cases, it is necessary to look into the child's behaviour and see whether or not it had attained sufficient maturity of understanding to judge the nature and consequence of its conduct on that occasion. This exemption granted in favour of children extends to all offences under special and local laws as well.[43] Under the Juvenile Justice (Care and Protection of Children) Act- 2000 in India and other special laws applicable to children, action can be initiated against delinquent children. Infact, the above Acts deal not only with delinquent children, but also with neglected and uncontrollable children.

(c) *Mistake of Fact and Mistake of Law*

Section 76 I.P.C. reads: "Nothing is an offence which is done by a person who is, or who by reason of a mistake of fact and not by reason of a mistake of law in good faith believes himself to be bound by law to do it" and section 79 I.P.C. is that "Nothing is an offence which is done by any person who is justified by law, or who by reason of a mistake of fact and not by reason of a mistake of law in good faith, believes himself to be justified by law, in doing it".

The well known maxim: *ignorantia facit excusat; ignorantia juris non excusat* — ignorance of fact excuses; ignorance of law does not excuse —is a ground here for the non-liability for criminal action. But the mistake must be real. A, a police officer arrests B thinking or believing that he is C wherein B and C are identical twins. Here the officer is committing an honest mistake and he is excused for the harm caused. The mistake negatives *mens rea* and *actus reus*. Another condition is that the mistake must be reasonable one. And finally, "the mistake however resonable, must not relate to matters of law but to matters of fact".[44] For, the maxims are *ignorantia juris, quod quisque tenetur scire neminem excusat* – i.e., ignorance of law, which every man is presumed to know, excuses no one, and *ignoram corum quo escire tenetur non excusat* – ignorance of those things which one is bound to know, excuses not. Ignorance of law can not be therefore made a defence, for, if it were so, it would be a loop-hole for offenders to escape and ultimately lead to variety of complications. However, the word 'law' used here refers to the general law of the Country and the principle applies to all laws, bye-laws, rules and regulations having force of law.[45]

Section 79 I.P.C. speaks of *'acts justified by law'*. An act is justified by law if it is warranted, validated and made blameless by law.[46]

(d) *Intoxication*

How far 'intoxication' exempts people from criminal responsibility? Section 85 I.P.C. reads: "Nothing is an offence which is done by a person who, at the time of doing it is, by reason of intoxication, incapable of knowing the nature of the act, or that he is doing what is either wrong, or contrary to law: provided that the thing which intoxicated him was administered to him without his knowledge or against his will". Here it can be seen that the person has been intoxicated through no fault of his and therefore the law gives him full exemptive effect. The section makes it clear that the drink must have been administered to him without his knowledge or against his will. The result of the intoxication has been that the person intoxicated became "incapable of knowing the nature of the act or that he is doing what is either wrong or contrary to law". Any person who gets himself intoxicated voluntarily cannot claim the benefit of this section. For, section 86 I.P.C. makes it very clear that in such instances the person who is intoxicated voluntarily is presumed to have the same knowledge as he would have had if he had not been intoxicated. The law cannot permit voluntary drunkenness as a plea to get immunity, for, in such cases the leniency will be more misused by people. The law exempts people and declares them immune to their criminal acts if they have been intoxicated without their consent or against their will, because the law attaches *'dementia offectata'* — temporary insanity to such persons and it so happened for no fault of theirs. When does this state occur? This state takes place when a man is made to drink "through stratagem or the fraud of another or through ignorance or coercion practiced by his friend or foe, when a person is dragged by his enemies or given to eat or drink such a thing as causes frenzy, or his unskillful physician gives him an intoxicant to drink, in all of which cases the person intoxicated may be said to have been free agent, and therefore, not responsible for the consequence of his act".[47] Drugs and drinks come under the operation of this law.

(e) *Unsoundness of mind*

"Nothing is an offence which is done by a person who, at the time of doing it, by reason of unsoundness of mind is incapable of knowing the nature of the act or that he is doing what is either wrong or contrary to law" —reads section 84 I.P.C.

In a discussion on insanity as a ground for immunity, it is necessary to study the *M' Naghten Answers* in English legal history. In the case of Daniel M' Naghten (in 1843), the judges in England made very anthoritative pronouncements with respect to persons afflicted with insane delusions and their criminal acts. The principle may be summed up as:[48]

(i) "Every man is presumed to be sane, and to possess a

sufficient degree of reason to be responsible for his crimes, until the contrary be proved to the satisfaction of a jury.

(ii) To establish a defence on the ground of insanity, it must be clearly proved that, at the time of committing the act, the party accused was labouring under such defect of reason, from disease of the mind, as not to know the nature and quality of the act he was doing or, if he did know it, that he did not know he was doing what was wrong".

Section 84 I.P.C. has incorporated this view of unsoundness of mind in Indian law. Unsoundness of mind is applicable not only to *insanity proper* (like psychosis), but also to cases of mental retardation (morons, imbeciles and idiots whose development of intelligence has been arrested)—in other words to lunatics as well as mentally deficient people. In all such cases, the point to be proved is whether or not the person can be viewed as legally insane as described in section 84 I.P.C. i.e., at the time of doing the act, is he by reason of unsoundness of mind, incapable of knowing the nature of the act or that he is doing what is either wrong or contrary to law.

Legal insanity is not the same as medical insanity and moral insanity. The courts are concerned with only legal insanity,[49] and what is meant by legal insanity is explained in section 84 I.P.C. For instance, people suffering from manias (such as nymphomania, kleptomania etc.) it is seen, have got an understanding into the nature of their acts – but they suffer from irresistible impulses i.e., obsessive-compulsive reactions to such a degree that they may be morally insane or even medically insane but cannot be treated as legally insane.

(f) *Privileged Acts*

Sections 77 and 78 I.P.C. relate to privileged acts of judges when acting judicially and to acts done pursuant to the judgement or order of a Court. Here they are judicial acts and immunity is attached to such acts. These deeds are legal when done lawfully for the advancement of justice and in such instances the deeds do not constitute *punishable acts.*

(g) *Accidents and Acts of Triviality*

Section 80 I.P.C. deals with cases of accident wherein a person is exempted from criminal liability in cases of accident or misfortune. In such instances the *mens rea* is not there and it must be proved that the person was doing a lawful act, in a lawful manner, by lawful means and with proper care and caution. The absence of criminal intention and criminal knowledge should be there to get the benefit of section 80 I.P.C. The legal dictum is that "no act is *per se* criminal unless the actor did it with criminal intent" – *actus non facit reum, nisi mens sit rea* – The act itself does not make a man guilty unless his intentions were so.

Dealing with accident and misfortune, Sir Hari Singh Gour writes:

> "Now, in the first place what is an accident? Literally, the term means only the befalling of an event. In ordinary parlance it means an event that takes place without one's foreseen expectation. And this is substantially the sense in which the term has been used here.
>
> It means here not only an event, or a thing which occurs, for every occurrence in not an accident. An accident is an occurrence out of the ordinary course which no man of ordinary prudence could anticipate or provide against. A misfortune is only accident with attendant evil consequences. Now as the words "accident" as well as "misfortune" are here used necessarily in the sense of implying injury to another, the word "misfortune" differs from "accident" in that while the latter involves only injury to another the former causes injury as much to the author as to another unconnected with the act".

Section 95 I.P.C. concerns with acts of triviality. i.e., "nothing is an offence by reason that it causes, or that it is intended to cause or that it is known to be likely to cause any harm, if that harm is so slight that no person of ordinary sense and temper would complain of such harm". This law recognizes the maxim *de minimis non curat lex* – i.e., 'law does not care about trifles'. Sir Hari Singh Gour in his Penal Law of India enumerates a number of examples to illustrate this further. He writes :

> "As our definitions are framed it is theft to dip a pen in another man's ink; mischief to crumble one of his wafers; an assault to cover him with a cloud of dust by riding past him; hurt to incommode him by pressing against him in getting into a carriage. There are innumerable acts without performing which men cannot live together in society-acts which all men constantly do and suffer in turns and which it is desirable that they should do and suffer in turns —yet which differ only in degree from crimes".

(h) *Acts done by Consent*

Sections 87, 88, 89 and 90 I.P.C. relate to acts done by consent. Indian law recognizes it, in some instances, as a good defence to the causing of harm. The principle is the outcome of the acceptance of the doctrine —No one will consent to that which is harmful to his interests. Sir James Stephen defines consent in law to mean "a consent freely given by a rational and sober person so situated as to be able to form a rational opinion upon the matter to which he consents".[50] He continues: "Consent is said to be given freely when it is not procured by force, fraud or threats of whatever nature". Consent can be either express or implied. A consent is said to be *"implied"* if it is used to signify:

(a) a consent by acts and conduct —e.g. a modest girl may even signify her consent to her lover's proposal by uttering 'no' thereby denoting 'yes' or when you ask a pen to a friend, he may not say anything back, but his silence can be treated as to signify his consent.

(b) Consent presumed though never given or in any way signified —e.g., A and B are friends. A goes to B's house and puts on B's shirt with the intention of returning it. Here A presumes the consent of B.[51]

But illegal acts cannot be justified on the ground of consent. Section 87 I.P.C. reads: "Nothing which is not intended to cause death, or grievous hurt, and which is not known by the doer to be likely to cause death, or grievous hurt, is an offence by reason of any harm which it may cause or be intended by the doer to cause, to any person, above eighteen years of age, who has given consent, whether express or implied, to suffer that harm, or by reason of any harm which it may be known by the doer to be likely to cause to any such person who has consented to take the risk of that harm". Here it is necessary that the consent must be given by the person suffering the harm and he must be above eighteen years of age. The intention and knowledge of the person causing the harm are important considerations in such instances. If the offence is of a public character, the consent given by the party suffering the harm is not treated as a consent at all —e.g., offences relating to army, navy and air-force or those affecting public tranquillity or offences by or relating to the public servants. For example, in case of illegal gratification, if at all the money is received by consent, it will not mitigate or negativate the criminal liability of the crime-doer.

Section 88 I.P.C. relates to acts not intended to cause death, done by consent in *good faith* for person's benefit —i.e. "Nothing which is not intended to cause death is an offence by reason of any harm which it may cause, or be intended by the doer to cause, or be known by the doer to be likely to cause, to any person for whose benefit it is done in good faith, and who has given a consent, whether express or implied to suffer that harm, or to take the risk of that harm". In this section, unintentional causing of grievous hurt or death is made justifiable in law. Here the act is done in *good faith* for the benefit of the person injured by the act. Surgeons and medical officers can claim immunity for their acts done in good faith. No doubt the section has wider applicability. At the same time, no one can perform the act in good faith for the benefit of another under this section without obtaining the consent of the person for whom the help is extended. The consent here need not be express. It can be implied as well. The intention of the person working for the benefit of another is given due consideration in the applicability of the scope of this section. It is not right to think that a surgeon desires harm to be inflicted of his patients, although he may know that harm is likely to be caused by the surgical operation. But the harm is, in fairness, to be treated as one intended for the benefit of the patient unless the contrary is proved. The consent on the part of the patient and good faith on the part of the surgeon are interdependent.

Section 89 I.P.C. concerns itself with acts done in *good faith* for benefit of a child or an insane person, by or by consent of guardian. The guardian or other person similarly positioned can inflict harm either himself or through some one else. But in such situations, the consent of the guardian or person similarly situated should be given. The infliction of harm should be: *(i) done in good faith; (ii) for benefit of the person; (iii) and it is not an act which is immoral or illegal.* Thus the *'de jure* or *de facto'* guardians can give consent for the benefit of a person under twelve years of age or of unsound mind and the benefit contemplated here is the personal *temporal benefit* of the child or the person of unsound mind. Spiritual benefits, e.g., sacrificing the innocent child to the deity if at all it is for the benefit of the child according to the guardian, cannot be justified under the law.

Section 90 I.P.C. speaks of consent known to be given under fear or under misconception of facts. In such cases the consent given is not deemed as *'consent'* for the purpose of law. Misconception may arise from fraud or misrepresentation of the fact. It is observed "where consent is obtained by duress, fraud or misrepresentation, there is not even the freedom of will necessary for consent".[52] Mere submission is not treated as consent in law. Similarly the consent given by a person who, from unsoundness of mind or intoxication, cannot understand the nature and consequence of that to which he gives his consent and the consent given by a child under twelve years of age (in the case of a child, unless the contrary appears from the context) are not considered as *'consent'* in law. Section 91 I.P.C. says that "the exceptions in sections 87, 88 and 89 do not extend to acts which are offences independently of any harm which they may cause or be intended to cause, or be known to be likely to cause, to the person giving the consent or on whose behalf the consent is given". For example the consent of an individual to obscene publications, indecent exhibitions and public nuisances has no effect on criminal responsibility of the person guilty of them.[53] Sir Hari Singh Gour in this context writes :

> "The section is a recognition of the two great sub-divisions of crime, public offences and private offences. Such are the offences against the state, or its various departments or its currency or revenue offences intended to produce public commotion or disturbance, acts intended to interfere with public convenience or to corrupt public morals which are all punishable regardless of the consent of any person who may have been incidently affected by them".

(i) *Act of Necessity*

Acts of necessity includes acts done without criminal intent. Earlier in this chapter, section 81 I.P.C. has been treated in detail. Here sections 92, 93 and 94 I.P.C. are discussed. Section 92 deals with cases of emergency and the illustrations given under section 92 I.P.C. sufficiently prove the nature of emergency warranted in the situation. The interference in such situations of emergency is to save life or property or both and not to imperil it and the purpose is to do more good than harm. Prompt assistance and immediate relief needed in such situations do not necessitate the obtaining of consent from the person who suffers harm. Similarly 93 I.P.C. is about the harm caused by communication made in good faith. The illustration given under section 93 I.P.C. is an example of a communication made by a surgeon in good faith to a sinking patient who dies in consequence of the shock. Here the doctor may be under the painful and hard necessity of communicating to his patient a timely warning about his fast approaching death. And it was, no doubt, done in good faith and it has to be deemed necessary for the benefit of the ailing patient. Therefore no offence is committed.

Section 94 I.P.C. deals with acts which a person is compelled to do by threats. Compulsion can be *(i) over powering physical compulsion, (ii) superior orders, (iii) threats, (iv) necessity,* and *(v) marital coercion [in English law.].* According to the Indian law, no complusion can justify murder and offences against the State punishable with death (see section 121 and section 300 I.P.C.). Here the person who claims the benefit of this section should have to show that he was not a voluntary agent at the time he committed the offence and also that he had no alternative left with him but to do or die. The complusion can be physical or moral. "Necessity, short of the threat of the death, does not excuse a crime" – says Gour, and there should have been reasonable apprehension of instant death provided that the person did not voluntarily expose himself to the constraint.

(j) *Acts done in Private Defence*

According to section 96 I.P.C. nothing is an offence which is done in the exercise of the right of private defence. This is a right essentially of defence and it can be exercised at actual or imminent danger. It should, on no account, be exercised in a spirit of revenge.

"Section 97 I.P.C. reads:

> Every person has a right subject to the restrictions contained in section 99 to defend :
>
> First —His own body, and the body of any other person, against any offence affecting the human body;
>
> Secondly —The property, whether movable or immovable, of himself, or of any other person against any act which is an offence falling under the definition of theft, robbery, mischief or criminal trespass, or which is an attempt to commit theft, robbery, mischief or criminal trespass".

Section 99 sets out limitations on the right of private defence i.e., the right does not arise if there is time to have recourse to the protection of the public authorities and also the right does not extend to the infliction of more harm than is necessary for the purpose of defence. Again if death is caused, the person exercising the right of private defence must be under reasonable apprehension of death or grievous hurt to himself or to those whom he has to offer protection. In the case of property, the danger must be of such a character, as is specified in section 103 I.P.C. Regarding the commencement and continuance of the right of private defence of the body and the same of the property the laws are given under sections 102 and 105 I.P.C. respectively.

The onus of proof when right of private defence is pleaded rests with the accused in the case. Here section 105, Indian Evidence Act makes an exception to the general rule regarding burden of proof in the accusatorial system of criminal justice that prevails in India. This section reads that the onus of proving the existence of the circumstances bringing the case within any of the general exceptions in the Indian Penal Code, or with any special exception or proviso contained in any other part of the Code or in any other Law, shall be on the accused and the Court shall presume the absence of such circumstances.

Section 106 I.P.C. permits a person to run the risk of harming innocent persons (in case of extreme necessity) in order to save himself from deadly assault or fatal injury.

Case-Laws —Variations in Liability*

1. The general exceptions in Chapter IV of the Penal Code are applicable not only to offences under the Penal Code, but also to offences under special or local laws.[54]
2. The section in the chapter – General Exceptions – applies to mistakes of a fact and not to mistakes of law.[55]
3. Mistake of law ordinarily means mistakes as to existence or otherwise of any law on a relevant subject as well as mistakes as to what the law is.[56]
4. Of course the "law" as used in this connection means the general law of the land. But the rule applies equally to all laws, bye-laws, rules and regulations having the force of law[57] (see section 76 I.P.C.)
5. It is a cardinal principle of criminal law that unless the State, either clearly or by necessary implication, rules out *mens*

* See Gour's *Penal Law of India*, Law Publishers, Allahabad 1982.

rea as a constituent part of a crime, an accused should not be found guilty of an offence against the criminal law unless he has got a guilty mind.[58]

6. Sir Hari Singh Gour in his Penal Law of India writes: "Where for instance, a man kills a man believing him to be a ghost,[59] a father kills his own son believing him to be a tiger[60], a hunter mistakes a man for an animal and fires, his mistake may be as much due to defective vision as to defective intellect. In either case there was no *mens rea* —there was a mistake and, therefore, it may be no crime.
7. It is however settled that an error on mixed question of law and fact is treated as a mistake of fact. If the accused is misled into this error of fact on account of an error of law, his mistake shall be treated as a mistake of fact rather than of law.[61]
8. Obedience to an illegal order can only be used in mitigation of punishment.[62]
9. A person who knowingly obeys an illegal order abets the illegal act of his superior and as the latter so is the former without any justification.[63]
10. A Magistrate or other person acting in a judicial capacity is not liable for acts done within his jurisdiction, but he is liable to an action for false imprisonment if he unlawfully commits a person to prison in a matter in which he has no jurisdiction, provided that he has knowledge or the means of knowledge of the facts which show that he has no jurisdiction.[64]
11. An officer charged with the duty to arrest must be in possession of his authority. For, under the Code of Criminal Procedure, it is obligatory on him to notify the substance of the warrant to the person to be arrested and if so required to show him the warrant, and the same rule would appear to apply to an arrest made in execution of a civil process.[65]
12. If, therefore, a person attempts to arrest another under a warrant not in his possession, he may plead this section[66] as a defence to a charge of wrongful confinement or wrongful restraint; but the person arrested has then also the right of private defence, and he cannot be punished, if he resists his seizure or escapes from custody.[67]

13. The occupier of land may cut off the overhanging branches of his neighbour's trees, or sever roots which have spread from these trees into his own land. It is one of the "General Exceptions" recognized by the Indian Penal Code that when a person is justified by law in doing an act the commission of that act cannot amount to an offence.[68]
14. When an accused in a spirit of bravado or of recklessness struck a blow on the vulnerable part of the deceased as a result of which the man died, and the accused in his trial under section 80 read with section 302 I.P.C. pleaded in his defence that there was no intention on his part to commit murder of the man and the death was caused by accident or by chance it was held that this plea of accident or his lack of intention to murder did not take the cause out of the offence of murder.[69]
15. The respondent fired at the object from a distance of 152 feet; and to the horror of all, this was followed by the cry of a human being in pain. The respondent in examination admitted that he had fired at the object with the gun, because he was under the impression that it was the hyena which had been seen in the vicinity of his quarters on the previous day. He also pointed out that at the time of the shooting, rain was falling, and in defence he added that he had not expected a human being to be at the place in question and the object at which he aimed had a brown covering. The respondent had, therefore, no reason to suppose that the object might well be a man who has grazing cattle or cutting grass. It was held that the amount of care and circumspection taken by the respondent was that which a prudent and reasonable man would consider to be adequate upon all the circumstances of the case. The whole affair was a pure accident and he was protected by the provisions of section 80 of the Indian Panel Code. The fact that he used an unlicensed gun would not deprive him to the benefit of that immunity.[70]
16. Intention, however, is not capable of positive proof. It can only be implied from overt acts. As a general rule, every man is presumed to intend the necessary or the natural and

probable consequences of his acts and this presumption of law will prevail unless from a consideration of all the evidence the Court entertains a reasonable doubt whether such an intention existed. This presumption, however, is not conclusive, nor alone sufficient to justify a conviction and should be supplemented by other testimony.[71]

17. Absence of motive is a factor to be considered in determining the guilt of the accused.[72]
18. Motive becomes vitally important in a case depending on circumstantial evidence although it may not be important in a case depending on direct evidence.[73]
19. Proof of motive must be assigned a minor place in a criminal trial and its importance should not be exaggerated.[74]
20. Though a boy of 12 is physically incapable of committing the offence of rape, he can nevertheless be held guilty of an attempt to commit it.[75]
21. When a plea of insanity is set up the Court has to consider whether at the time of commission of the offence, the accused, by reason of unsoundness of mind, was incapable of knowing the nature of the act or that he was doing what was either wrong or contrary to law. The crucial point of time for ascertaining the state of the mind of the accused is the time when the offence was committed. Whether the accused was in such a state of mind as to be entitled to the benefit of section 84 of the Penal Code can only be established from the circumstances which preceded, attended and followed the crime.[76]
22. Every man is presumed to be sane and to possess sufficient degree of reason to be responsible for his acts unless the contrary is proved. To establish insanity it must be clearly proved that at the time of committing the act the party is labouring under such defect of reason as not to know the nature and quality of the act which he is committing —that is, the physical nature and quality as distinguished from the moral – or, if he does know the nature and quality of the act he is committing, that he does not know that he is doing wrong.[77]

23. It is necessary for the application of section 84 I.P.C. to show (1) that the accused was of unsound mind; (2) that he was of unsound mind at the time he did the act and not merely before or after the act; and (3) as a result of unsoundness of mind he was incapable of knowing the nature of the act or that he was doing what was either wrong or contrary to law. It is therefore applicable to every person mentally diseased who *ipso facto* is exempted from criminal responsibility.[78]
24. A man may be suffering from some form of insanity in the sense in which the term is used by medical men but may not be suffering from unsoundness of mind as described in section 84 I.P.C.[79]
25. Drunkenness is never an excuse, but when drunkenness becomes a disease, it is then a defence, not because, it is drunkenness but because it is a disease.[80]
26. In order to relieve a person of criminal responsibility, it must produce a disease of the mind such as *delirium tremens.*[81]
27. Voluntary drunkenness is an excuse only as regards *"intention"* so that it is a complete excuse in crimes requiring the presence of an *"intention"* to complete crime.[82]
28. The fact that the accused was in an excited state as the result of having partaken of liquor in his house. This in itself is no excuse, but it may be taken into consideration when the question of sentence is considered, especially when the quarrel was started by the deceased himself.[83]
29. So where a person consented to the performance of a surgical operation upon himself with great reluctance, the only information communicated to him being that if he submitted to it, he would be cured, the court held that a person could, hardly be said to accept a risk of which he was not aware and that, therefore, there was no case for exceptional treatment unless it were shown that the patient was aware of the risk and accepted it.[84]
30. A misrepresentation as to the intention of a person stating the purpose for which the consent is asked is a misrepresentation of a *"fact"* within the meaning of section 3 of the Evidence Act.[85]

31. A person consenting under a *misconception of fact* cannot be said to consent within the meaning of the section. Such misconception may arise from fraud or a misrepresentation of fact.[86]
32. An assault by one child on another, or even by a grown up person on another, which causes injury may still be regarded as so slight, having regard to the way and State of life of the parties, relation between them, situation in which the parties are placed, and other circumstances, in which harm is caused, that the victim ordinarily may not complain of the harm.[87]
33. You cannot claim the right of private defence if you, yourself committed an attack, nor can such a right be claimed by a person who deliberately joins in a riot and finds himself attacked and his life is in danger.[88]
34. Inflicting blows in retaliation will not amount to an exercise of the right of private defence.[89]
35. There is nothing in the section to show that the right of private defence of property stands on a better footing than the right of private defence of person.[90]
36. It is for the party pleading self defence to prove the circumstances giving rise to the exercise of the right of self defence and this right can not be said to be proved as soon as we reach the conclusion that to the relevant time there was no threat either to the person of the appellant or the person or property of his companions.[91]
37. Even if the accused does not plead self defence, it is open to the Court to consider such a plea if the same arises from the materials on record.[92]
38. If we merely count the injuries received on both sides it would go to show that the complainant's party were the aggressors.[93]
39. In a free fight, no right of private defence is available to either party and each individual is responsible for his own acts.[94]
40. When there is evidence that a person acted in the exercise of the right of private defence, the Court would not be justified in ignoring that evidence and convicting the accused merely because he had set up a defence of *alibi* and set forth a

plea different from the right of private defence.[95]

Criminal Justice Administration in India

India has the accusatorial system of criminal justice which is different from the inquisitorial model found in many countries of the world. Hence, in awarding a conviction, particularly in the accusatorial system, the courts are always concerned with the accused and his rights in law. In the Indian legal system, the whole burden of proving the case rests upon the prosecution and the accused is presumed to be innocent until his guilt is proved beyond any shadow of doubt. The following case-laws will illustrate well how the system works in India.

1. "A criminal trial is not like a fairy tale wherein one is free to give flight to one's imagination and phantasy. It concerns itself with the question as to whether the arraigned at the trial is guilty of the crime with which he is charged. Crime is an event in real life and is the product of interplay of different human emotions. In arriving at the conclusion about the guilt of the accused charged with the commission of a crime the Court has to judge the evidence by the yardstick of probabilities, its intrinsic worth and the animus of witnesses. Every case in the final analysis would have to depend upon its own facts.[96]
2. "The function of a court in a criminal trial is to find out whether the person arraigned before it as the accused is guilty of the offence with which he is charged. For this purpose, it scans the material on record to find whether there is any reliable and trustworthy evidence on the basis of which it is possible to find the conviction of the accused and hold that he is guilty of the offence with which he is charged.[97]
3. "The principles of natural justice require that no court shall give a finding whether on fact or law and particularly on facts without giving an opportunity to all the contesting parties.[98]
4. "In all civilized countries, criminal jurisprudence has firmly established the rule that an accused person should not be placed on trial for the same offence more than once except

in very exceptional circumstances".[99]

5. "In criminal cases, it is often difficult for courts of law to arrive at the real truth. The judicial process can only operate on the firm foundations of actual and credible evidence on record. Mere suspicion or suspicious circumstances cannot relieve the prosecution of its primary duty of proving its case against an accused person beyond reasonable doubt. Courts of justice cannot be swayed by sentiment or prejudice against a person accused of the very reprehensible crime of patricide. If the pieces of evidence on which the prosecution chooses to rest its case are so brittle that they crumble easily, the superstructure built on such insecure foundations also collapses".[100]
6. "There are two important factors in every criminal trial that weigh heavily in favour of an accused person. One is that the accused is entitled to the benefit of every reasonable doubt and the other, an off-shoot of the same principle, that when an accused person offers a reasonable explanation of his conduct, then eventhough, he cannot prove his assertions, they should ordinarily be accepted unless the circumstances indicate that they are false".[101]
7. "If two views are possible, the view which is favourable to the accused should be adopted. If reasonable doubt arises, the benefit of that cannot be withheld from the accused".[102]
8. "If the Court entertains reasonable doubt regarding the guilt of the accused, the accused must have the benefit of doubt".[103]
9. "Justice would fail not only by unjust conviction of the innocent but also by acquittal of the guilty for unjustified failure to produce available evidence".[104]
10. "Suspicion however strong cannot take the place of proof. Sometimes truth is stranger than fiction".[105]
11. "Considered as a whole, the prosecution story may be true; but between "may be true" and "must be true", there is inevitably a long distance to travel and the whole of this distance must be covered by legal, reliable and unimpeachable evidence".[106]

SUGGESTED READINGS

Beattie, R.H. *The Public Defender and Private Defense Attorneys,* Berkeley, California, University of California Bureau of Public Administration, July, 1935.

Borchard, Edwin M., *Convicting the Innocent,* New York, Garden City Publishing Company, 1932.

Brown, Esther Lucile., *Lawyers and the Promotion of Justice,* New York, Russel Sage Foundation, 1938.

Chadbourn, James Harmon., *Lynching and the Law,* Chappel Hill, University of North Carolina Press, 1933.

Coe, Charles Francis., *Law and the Profits,* Atlanta, Harrison Company, 1939.

Cohen, Julius Henry, *The Law-Business or Profession?* New York, Banks Law Publishing Company, 1919.

Cohn, Alfred and Chisholm, Joe., *Take the Witness,* New York, Garden City Publishing Company, 1934.

Egerton, Robert and Goodhart, A.L., *Legal Aid,* London, Oxford University Press, 1945.

Frank, Jerome, *If Men Were Angels,* New York, Harper & Brothers, 1942.

Frank, Jerome, *Courts on Trial,* New Jersey, Princeton University Press, 1949.

Gisnet, Morris, *A Lawyer Tells the Truth,* New York, Concord Press, 1931.

Glueck, Sheldon, *Crime and Justice,* Boston, Little Brown and Co., 1936.

Hays, Arthur Jerome, *Our Lawless Police,* New York, Viking Press, 1931.

Jackson, Percivale, *Look at the Law,* New York, E.P. Dutton Company, 1940.

Jessup, Henry Wymans, *A Study of Legal Ethics,* New York, G.A. Jennings Company, Inc. 1925.

Mannheim, Hermann, *Criminal Justice and Social Reconstruction,* London, Oxford University Press, 1946.

Mayo, Katherine, *Justice to All,* New York, G.P. Putnam's Sons, 1917.

Moly, Raymond, *Our Criminal Courts,* New York, G.P. Putnam's Sons, 1930.

Moly, Raymond, *Politics and Criminal Prosecution,* New York, G.P. Putnam's Sons, 1929.

Osborn, Albert S., *The Mind of the Juror,* Albany, Boyd Printing Company, 1937.

Reith, Charles, *British Police and the Democratic Ideal,* London, Oxford University Press, 1943.

Reynolds, Quentin, *Courtroom,* New York, Garden City Books, 1950.

Rodell, Fred, *Woe Unto You, Lawyers!,* New York, Harcourt Brace and Company, Inc.1939.

Stapleton, Laurence, *Justice and World Society,* Chapel Hill, University of North

Carolina Press, 1944.

Sutliffe, Robert Stewart, *Impressions of an Average Juryman*, New York, D. Appleton and Company, 1922.

Train, Arthur, *Courts and Criminals*, New York, Charles Scribner's Sons, 1926.

Train, Arthur, *The Prisoner at the Bar*, New York, Charles Scribner's Sons, 1922.

Turney, Raymond, *Court Room Psychology*, Los Angeles, Times Mirror Press, 1924.

Vadackumchery James, *Acquittals in Administration of Criminal Justice*, Ph. D. Thesis, Kerala University, 1983.

Waite, John Baker, *Criminal Law in Action*, New York, Sears Publishing Company, 1934.

Wilkin, Robert N., *Spirit of Legal Profession*, New Haven, Yale University Press, 1938.

REFERENCES

1. See J.W. Cecil Turner, *Russel on Crime*, Stevens & Sons Ltd., London, 1964.
2. Subs. by *The Indian Penal Code (Amendment) Act*, 1870 (27 of 1870), Section 2, for the original Section 40.
3. Subs. by *The Repealing and Amending Act*, 1930 (8 of 1930), Section 2 and Sch. 1 for "chapter".
4. Ins. by *The Indian Criminal Law (Amendment) Act*, 1913 (8 of 1913), Section 2.
5. Ins. by *The Indian Penal Code (Amendment) Act*, 1882 (8 of 1882), Section 1.
6. Ins. by *The Indian Criminal Law (Amendment) Act*, 1886 (10 of 1886), Section 21(1).
7. Dr. Sir Hari Singh Gour, *The Penal Law of India*, Revised Edn., Law Publishers, 1982. Also See Ganpatrao, I.L.R., 19 Bom. 105 and Ganesh Khanderao, I.L.R. 13 Bom. 506.
8. Dr. Sir Hari Singh Gour, *The Penal Law of India, op. cit*; see also *Patris Jurisprudence*, 3rd ed. in which Kocourek puts it (in relation to tort) as denoting the external manifestaion of the actor's will and as not including any of its results, not even the most direct, immediate and intended.
9. J.W. Cecil Turner, ed., *Kenny's Outlines of Criminal Law*, Cambridge University Press, 1962.
10. J.W. Cecil Turner, ed., *Kenny's Outlines of Criminal Law, op. cit.*
11. J.W. Cecil Turner, ed., *Kenny's Outlines of Criminal Law, op. cit.*

14. J.W. Cecil Turner, ed., *Kenny's Outlines of Criminal Law, op. cit.*
15. J.W. Cecil Turner, ed., *Kenny's Outlines of Criminal Law, op. cit.*
16. See Cecil Turner, ed., *Kenny's Outlines of Criminal Law, op. cit.*
17. Cecil Turner, ed., *Kenny's Outlines of Criminal Law, op. cit.*
18. Cecil Turner, ed., *Kenny's Outlines of Criminal Law, op. cit.*
19. Molu *vs.* State of Haryana, A.I.R. 1976 S.C. 2499, 1976 Cr. L.J. 1895.
20. Rajinder Kumar *vs.* State of Punjab, A.I.R. 1966 S.C. 1322.
21. Yeshwant *vs.* State of Maharashtra, 1972 Cr. L.J. 1254.
22. State of Uttar Pradesh *vs.* Hariprasad, A.I.R. 1974 S.C. 1740; 1794 Cr. L.J. 1274
23. Ediga Anamma *vs.* State of Andhra Pradesh, A.I.R. 1974 S.C. 799; 1974 Cr. L.J. 683.
24. Faquire *vs.* State of Uttar Pradesh, A.I.R. 1976 S.C. 915; Cr. L.J. 677.
25. Cecil Turner, ed., *Kenney's Outlines of Criminal Law, op. cit.*
26. Cecil Turner, ed., *Kenney's Outlines of Criminal Law, op. cit.*
27. State of Maharashtra *vs.* M.H. Geoge, A.I.R. 1965 S.C. 722.
28. See the discussion by Jerome Hall, *General Principles of Criminal Law* Bobbs-Merril, Indianapolis, 1947.
29. E.H. Sutherland and D.R. Cressey, *Priniciples of Criminology,* Times of India Press, Bombay, 1965.
30. Mobarik Ali Ahmed *vs.* State of Bombay, A.I.R., 1957 S.C. 857.
31. James Vadackumchery, *Provisions in The Indian Penal Code,* Police Research and Development, Qtr. 11, Bureau of Police Research and Development, New Delhi, 1980.
32. James Vadackumchery, *Provisions in The Indian Penal Code, op. cit.*
33. The Code of Criminal Procedure , 1973 also provides for :
    1. the differentiation of criminal courts and definces their respective functions and powers;
    2. the formulation of police duties in arresting offenders, dealing with absconders etc.
    3. the production of documents and investigation of criminal cases.
    4. security procedings towards keeping peace and good behaviour on conviction in certain cases dealing with persons disseminating seditious documentation, suspects and habitual offenders;
    5. the maintenance of public order and tranquility, preventing unlawful assemblies, public nuisance, disputes relating to immovable property and regulating the use of the civil and armed forces to disperse unlawful assemblies;
    6. the preventive role of police, chargesheeting, administraction of justice and irregular proceedings etc.
34. James Stephen, *The Indian Evidence Act,* 1872.

35. J.W. Cecil Turner, *Russel on Crime, op. cit.*
36. Dr. Sir Hari Singh Gour, *The Penal Law of India, op. cit.*
37. King *vs.* Tustipada Mandll A.I.R. 1951 Orissa 284; I.L.R. (1950) Cut., 75; 52 Cr. L.J. 837.
38. Cecil Turner, *Russel on Crime, op. cit.*
39. See also, Saltpetre Case (1606) 12 Co. Res. 12, 13; Dewey *vs.* White (1827) M&M 56; Mouse's Case (1609) 12 Co. Rep. 63; Cope *vs.* Sharpe (1912) 1KB, 496.
40. R.V. Tolson (1889) 23 Q.B.D. 168, 187, per Stephen J.
41. Section 82, I.P.C.
42. Section 83, I.P.C.
43. See Ba Ba Sein, A.I.R. 1938 Rang. 400; 40 Cr. L.J. 80; Emperor *vs.* Wali Mohammad, A.I.R. 1936 Sind 185; 165 I.C. 642; 38 Cr. L. J. 83; L. Uitam Chand *vs.* Emperor, I.L.R. (1846) Lah. 54; A.I.R. 1945 Lah 238 (FB).
44. Cecil Turner, ed., *Keney's Outlines of Criminal Law, op. cit.*
45. Kussim, 51 I.C. (Bom) 802; Contra Levwis, I.L.R. 38 Mad. 773.
46. Dr. Sir Hari Singh Gour, *The Penal Law of India, op. cit.*
47. Hale P.C. 32 (see 75 E.R. 31).
48. See Cecil Turner, ed., *Kenney's Outlines of Criminal Law, op. cit;* R.V. M'Naghten (1843) 10 Cl. and F. 200 (T.A.C.)
49. Read, Kalicharan *vs.* Emperor, A.I.R. 1948 Nag. 20(2) : 48 Cr. L.J. 377; Ashiruddin Ahmad *vs.* Emperor, A.I.R. 1949 Cal. 182: 50 Cr. L.J. 255; Puncha *vs.* Emperor, A.I.R. 1932 All. 233; Hemu *vs.* State, A.I.R. 1951 Sau 19: 52 Cr. L.J. 369: Kashiram *vs.* State, A.I.R. 1957 M.B. 1045 1957 Cr. L.J. 370; Chenna Basappa *vs.* State of Mysore, A.I.R. 1957 Mys. 68: 1657 Cr. L.J. 985; Nitai Naick *vs.* State, A.I.R. 1957 Orissa 168: 1957 Cr. L.J. 875.
50. Dig. of Cr. Law Art 224.
51. See also Sir Hari Singh Gour's The *Penal Law of Indian, op. cit.*
52. Sunders 8 C. & P. 265.
53. See also Sir Hari Singh Gour's Penal Law of India *op. cit.*
54. King *vs.* Tustipada Mandal A.I.R. 1951. Orissa 284: I.L.R. (1950) Cut. 75:52 Cr. L.J. 837.
55. Karim Ullha *vs.* Ghulam Rasul Sah A.I.R. 1936 Sind 153: 37 Cr. L.J. 1068: 165/IC 78(2).
56. King *vs.* Tustipada Mandal, *op. cit.*
57. Kussim 15 I.C. (Bom) 802. Contra Lewis I.L.R. 38 Mad. 773.
58. State Government of Madhya Pradesh *vs.* Maganbhai Dasaibhai A.I.R. 1954 Nag. 41: 1953 N.S.J. 514:55 Cr. L.J. 89.
59. Waryam Singh *vs.* Emperor A.I.R. 1926, Lah. 554; Bonda Kui *vs.* Emperor A.I.R. 1943 Pat. 64:43 Cr. L.J. 77.

60. Chiranji *vs.* State, A.I.R. 1952 Mag. 282 : I.L.R. (1952) Mag. 348 :1952 Cr. C.J. 1212 : 1952 N.L.J. 350.
61. King *vs.* Tustipada Mandal, *op. cit.*
62. Chaman Lal *vs.* Emperor, A.I.R. 1940, Lah. 210:I.L.R. (1940) Law. 521
63. Latifkhan, I.L.R. 20. Bom. 394; Charan Das Narain Singh *vs.* State, A.I.R. 1950 E.P. 321:52 P.L.R. 331:5 D.L.R. (Simla) 286.
64. Sailajanand Pande *vs.* Suresh Chandra Gupta, A.I.R. 1969, Pat. 194:1969 B.L.J.R. 1084.
65. Amaranath, I.L.R. 5. All. 318.
66. Section 78 I.P.C.
67. Janki Persad, I.L.R. 3. All 205; Abdul Gafur, I.L.R. 23. Cal 896; Satis Chandra *vs.* Jadunandan, I.L.R. 26 Cal. 748; Durga *vs.* Nabin, I.L.R. 25 Cal. 274; H. Collville *vs.* Kristo Kishore, I.L.R. 26 Cal. 746.
68. Ouseph Thomen *vs.* Joseph Antony, 1956, K.L.T. 370:1957 Cr. L.J. 166.
69. Mohan Singh Balwant Singh *vs.* State, A.I.R. 1965 Punj. 291.
70. State Government, Madhya Pradesh *vs.* Rangaswami, A.I.R. 1952 Nag. 268: I.L.R. (1952) Nag. 93 (1901) 3 Bom. L.R. 678.
71. Ismail *vs.* Emperor, A.I.R. 1947 Lah. 220.
72. Hans Raj *vs.* Emperor, 30 Cr. L.J. 478.
73. Papallugan Veera Reddi *vs.* State, A.I.R. 1955, Andh, W.R. 426 (D.B).
74. Arjun Reghu *vs.* State, A.I.R. 1956, Bom. 183:1956, Cr. L.J. 389.
75. Nga Tun Kaing, 11 Bur. L.T. 135.
76. Debyabhai Chhaganbhai Thakkar *vs.* State of Gujarat, A.I.R. 1964 S.C. 1956; Sarju Merandy *vs.* State of Bihar (1978) 26 B.L.J.R. 267.
77. Madhya Pradesh *vs.* Ahmadulla, A.I.R. 1961, S.C. 998.
78. V. Ambi *vs.* State of Kerala (1952) 2 Cr. L.J. 135.
79. Kalicharan *vs.* Emperor, A.I.R. 1948 Nag. 20(2). 48 Cr. L.J. 277; Ashiruddin Ahmad *vs.* Emperor, A.I.R. 1949 Cal. 182: 50 Cr. L.J. 255; Hemu *vs.* State. A.I.R. 1951, Sau. 19:52 Cr. L. 369; Puncha *vs.* Emperor. A.I.R. 1932 All 233 Kulandi Thevar *vs.* Emperor, A.I.R. 1950 M.W.N. Cr. 95 : A.I.R. 1950 Mad. 592.
80. Bhalaka A. Ram, I.L.R. 20 Cal. 493.
81. Samman Singh Thakar Singh *vs.* Emperor. A.I.R. 1941 Lah. 454:198 I.C 252:453 P.L.R. 698.
82. Sheru *vs.* Emperor, A.I.R. 1926 Lah. 232; Muthu Goundan, 1931 M.W.N. 113.
83. Nga Chit *vs.* King, A.I.R. 1937. Rang. 467:172, I.C. 197:39 Cr. L.J. 117.
84. Sukaroo Kabiraj *vs.* Empress, I.L.R. 14 Cal. 566.
85. Parshottam Mahadev Patharphod *vs.* State, A.I.R. 1963 Bom. 74:64 Bom. L.R. 788, 1963, M.L.J. 157:1962 Nag. L.J. 529.
86. Jaladu, I.L.R. 36 Mad. 453; Soma, (1916) P.R. (Cr.) 17.

87. Mrs. Veeda Meneres *vs.* Yusuf Khan Haji, Ibrahim Khan, A.I.R. 1966 S.C. 1773.
88. Z.D. Samuel *vs.* Emperor, A.I.R. 1937, Pesh. 23.
89. Harbuns Singh *vs.* Emperor, A.I.R. 1947 Lah. 37:47 Cr. L.J. 358:223 I.C. 99.
90. Barisa Mudi *vs.* State, A.I.R. 1959. Pat. 22; 1957 B.L.J. 756:1959 Cr. L.J. 71.
91. Jai Dev *vs.* State of Punjab, A.I.R. 1963, S.C. 612; 1963 (i) Cr. L.J. 495.
92. State of Gujarat *vs.* Bai Fatima, A.I.R. 1975 S.C. 1978; 1975 Cr. L.J. 1079.
93. Tekchand *vs.* State of Haryana, A.I.R. 1972 S.C. 228; 1972, Cr. L.J. 51.
94. Viswas *vs.* State of Maharashtra. A.I.R. 1978, S.C. 414; K.N. Virji *vs.* State of Gujarat, A.I.R. 1970, S.C. 219; 1970 Cr. L.J. 363.
95. Gotti Pulla *vs.* Andhra Pradesh State, A.I.R. 1970, S.C. 1079; 1970, Cr. L.J. 1004.
96. Punjab *vs.* Jagir Singh, A.I.R. 1973 S.C. 2407; 1973 Cr. L.J. 1589.
97. Harichand Singh *vs.* State of Haryana, A.I.R. 1947 S.C. 344;1974 Cr. L.J. 366.
98. M. Narayanan *vs.* State of Kerala, A.I.R. 1963 S.C. 1116;1963(2) Cr. L.J. 186.
99. Abinash Chandra *vs.* Bimal Krishna, A.I.R. 1963 S.C. 316; 1963 (1) Cr. L. J. 261.
100. Datar Singh *vs.* Punjab, A.I.R. 1974 S.C. 1193; 1974 Cr. L.J. 908.
101. Aher Raja Khima *vs.* State of Sau. A.I.R. 1956 S.C. 217; 1956 Cr. L.J. 421.
102. Kaliram *vs.* State of Himachal Pradesh, A.I.R. 1973, S.C. 2773; 1974 Cr. L.J. 1.
103. Himachal Pradesh *vs.* Om Prakash, A.I.R. 1972 S.C. 975; 1972 Cr. L.J. 606.
104. Nageshwar *vs.* Maharashtra A.I.R. 1973 S.C. 165; 1973 Cr. L.J. 235.
105. Union of India *vs.* M/s. Chatur Bai, 1976, U.J. (S.C.) 120. Sarwan Singh *vs.* State of Punjab, A.I.R. 1957, Sarwan Singh *vs.* State of Punjab, *op. cit.*
106. Sarwansingh *vs.* State of Punjab, A.I.R. 1957, S.C. 637; 1957 Cr. L.J. 1014; Nachhet Singh *vs.* Punjab, A.I.R. 1976 S.C. 951; 1976 Cr. L.J. 691.

2

INVESTIGATION OF CRIME

The word investigation is derived from Latin *investigare* which means "to trace out or to search into"[1] i.e., to probe into for finding out the truth. Hence in criminal cases the duty of the investigator is not merely to bolster up a prosecution case with such evidence as may enable the Court to record a conviction but to bring out the real unvarnished truth.[2] Richard H. Ward says "The primary function of the criminal investigator is to gather information, determine the validity of the information, identify and locate the perpetrator of the crime and provide evidence of his guilt for a Court of Law. Inherent in this function is the responsibility to protect the innocent".[3] He continues: "The means by which the investigator carries out this function may be classified into two ways: *internal* and *external*. *Internal* r efers to the process of logic, expertise, intuition, experience and knowledge that he brings to the investigation. *External* refers to the tools, scientific aids, additional personal and other resources that he brings to bear on the investigation".[4]

Parts of Investigation

Investigation consists of a number of laborious, intelligent and painstaking processes. They are shown below.

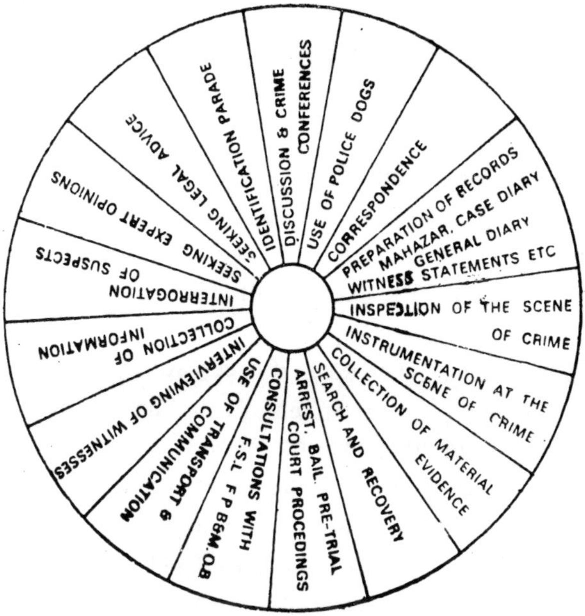

Fig. 2.1 : Parts of Crime Investigation

Steps in Investigation

1. Preparation of First Information Report (F.I.R.); completion of legal formalities prior to inspection of the scene of crime.
2. Varifying and ensuring all of the items in the Investigating Officer's Kit.
3. Selection of intelligent and work-knowing assistants.
4. Noting down the time of departure, the conditions of climate and the distance from the Station House to the scene of crime.
5. Guarding of the scene of crime.
6. Taking down the names and addresses of persons likely to give evidence relating to crime/criminals.
7. Arresting the suspect and providing first-aid to the victims, if necessary.

8. Taking of photographs.
9. Sketching the scene of crime.
10. Inspection of the scene of crime.
11. Collection of material evidence.
12. Use of scientific aids at the scene of crime.
13. Scientific packing, labelling and transportation of material evidence for expert opinion.
14. Calling of scientific experts to the scene of crime, if that is necessary
15. Requisitioning police dogs, if necessary.
16. Taking into custody of material evidence; preparing of mahazars and other records.
17. Interrogation of suspects/the accused persons.
18. Interviewing of witnesses, informers, complainants, etc.
19. Search and seizure of items connected with the crime and recovery in consequence of confessional statements.
20. Arresting the suspects or the accused persons and granting of bail in bailable offences, detention and pre-trial proceedings.
21. Writing of the general diary, case-diary, other official forms, statements of witnesses/suspects and correspondence.
22. Use of transport and other media of communication for the purpose of investigation.
23. Beat, patrol, enquiries and collection of information and criminal intelligence.
24. Seeking opinion of legal experts.
25. Discussion with scientific experts.
26. Conducting of identification parade.
27. Consultation with superior officers.
28. Contacting Finger-Print Bureau, *Modus Operandi* Bureau or other Expert Institutions.
29. Reconstruction of the incident.
30. Preparation of the case for court trial etc., etc.

The chapters that follow deal with all these aspects in detail. But in short, it can be said that police investigation means and includes all the steps which a police officer takes to probe into for finding out the *truth* regarding the crime and its criminals.

Investigation of Crime: Case-Laws

1. "Prosecution had nothing to gain by falsely showing the recovery of the brass fired catridge cases, for it was found in the forensic science laboratory that they had been fired from D's rifle which was recovered only in January. It was not possible for the prosecution to plant them at the scene of occurrence in December, when it had no reason to think that he would be arrested some 10 days later with the rifle from which those catridges had been fired".[5]
2. "It is necessary for the accused to throw a reasonable doubt that the prosecution evidence is such that it must have been manipulated or shaped by reason of the irregularity in the matter of investigation, that he was prevented by reason of such irregularity from putting forward his defence or adducing evidence in support thereof. There must be a sufficient nexus either established or probabilized between the conviction and the irregularity in the investigation".[6]
3. "While the benefit of defective investigation cannot go to the prosecution, but if, on a proper evaluation of the various facts and circumstances, it transpires that the apparent inconsistencies in the prosecution case are solely the result of remisses on the part of the investigating officer and not of any improvement on the part of the prosecution witnesses, there would be no justification for discarding the accusation"[7].
4. "There was inordinate delay in sending catridges, rifle etc. to the expert. The accused was interrogated after a lapse of a week. The memo relating to the recovery of empty catridges was not attested by independent witnesses. This throws doubt on the bonafides of the investigation"[8].
5. "Accused cannot be convicted on the ground that the investigation had been utterly perfunctory".[9]

6. "It is a novel proposition that if an I.O. conducts a search, his evidence cannot be relied on unless it is corroborated".[10]
7. "The Cr. P.C. in laying down the omissions or irregularities which either violate the proceeding or not does not anywhere specifically says that a mistake committed by an I.O. during the course of the investigation can be said to be an illegality or irregularity. Investigation is certainly not an inquiry or trial before the Court and the fact that there is no specific provision either way in Chapter XLV with respect to omissions or mistakes committed during the course of investigation except with regard to the holding of an inquest is a sufficient indication that the legislature did not contemplate any irregularity in investigation as of sufficient importance to vitiate the inquiry or trial. Hence the failure to comply with rule 109 U.P. Police Regulations relating to submission of police case diary, cannot in any way interfere with legality of a trial"[11].

Qualities of Investigating Officers

The personality traits and desirable qualities of an investigator often affect the nature and quality of crime investigation. Section 23, Police Act, 1861 reads: "It shall be the duty of every police officer...to detect and bring offenders to justice and to apprehend all persons whom he is legally authorised to apprehend and for whose apprehension sufficient grounds exist". This is not an easy task. The investgating officer should have some basic and inherent qualities to achieve the aim. If he does not possess such qualities, he should try to acquire such qualities for administering criminal justice. Of all the qualities necessary in a crime investigator, character and honesty are the most important ones. Remember that reputation is what other people may say about a man and character is what a man has inherently in himself. Ours is a welfare State where human rights and civil liberties are highly respected. Therefore every investigator must try to develop his character and a sense of righteousness in himself. A crime investigator has to work among criminals and underworld characters of all descriptions —thieves, murderers, gamblers, prostitutes, pimps, smugglers, hoarders, racketeers etc. Many of the qualities which a crime investigator should possess are the logical consequences of his character and honesty. The qualities which a police officer should try to acquire are contained in the world – POLICE — P-for politeness; O-for obedience; L-for loyality; I-for intelligence; C-for courage; and E-for efficiency. Added to these general qualities which every police officer should have, the crime investigator must especially try to acquire qualities shown in Fig. 2.2.

These qualities are important. But what they mean and how they help in crime investigation are not treated in this book as they do not fall within the scope of this book. All courts in India including the Supreme Court have commented over and again about the nature and importance of these qualities among investigating officers. Honourable Mr. Justice Mulla of the Allahabad High Court in a case where a sub-inspector of police had fabricated some evidence once observed : "Criminal cases which are placed before the courts are in a large measure frame-ups and they are supported by fabricated evidence and extorting confessions through

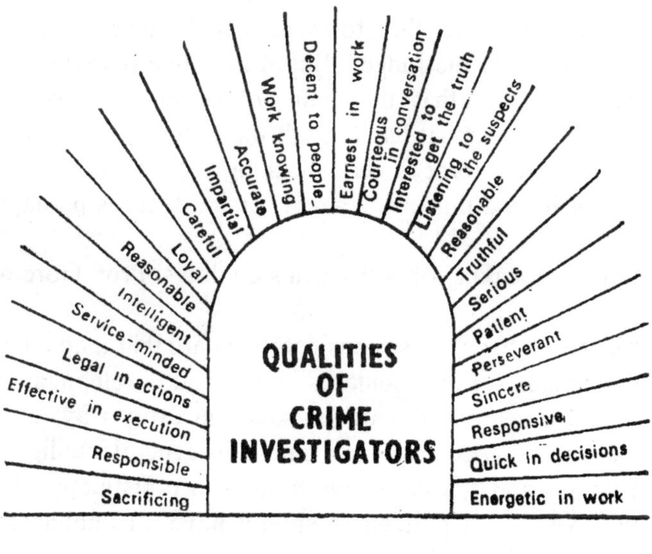

Fig. 2.2 : Quality of crime Investigation

third degree methods and by disregarding the prohibitions contained in the Constitution of India to safeguard the rights of citizens". He observed further : "there is not a single lawless group in the whole of the country whose record of crime comes anywhere near the record of the organized unit which is known as Indian Police Force. If the police force is manned by officers like Mohammed Naim, then it is better we tear up our Constitution, forget all about democracy and the rights of citizens and change the meaning of law and other terms not only in our penal enactments but also in our dictionaries." Ofcourse, these were very sweeping remarks which in a way stigmatised the entire police force in the country and therefore were challenged by the State of Uttar Pradesh. The Supreme Court in deciding the appeal preferred by the State for expunction of these remarks said "the remarks made by the learned Judge in respect of the entire police force of the State were not justified on the facts of the case. To characterize the whole police force of the State as lawless group is bad enough, to say that its record of crime is the highest in the State is worse and coming as it does from a Judge of the High Court is sure to bring the whole administration of law and order into disrepute. Hence we direct that the aforesaid remarks do stand expunged from the order of the Judge". But at the same time the Supreme Court held the view that "the conduct of the sub-inspector deserved the highest condemnation. Though the general condemnation of the entire police force is very shocking yet a close scrutiny will revel that behind this exaggerated version there is perhaps a lot of truth"[12]

While speaking of policemen's qualities, Prof: Gore writes:

> "Stated in brief, these considerations are that a policeman must reach certain standards of physical development and have a constitution which is sound in every way; a man cannot be a good policeman unless his general intelligence, memory and powers of observation are distinctly above the average; a policeman should have an unblemished character, be human and courteous, and should possess a

combination of moral, mental and physical qualities not ordinarily required in other employments; the burden of individual initiative, discretion and responsibility placed upon a policeman in all sorts of contingencies is much greater than that of any other public servant of subordinate rank; the police have a special obligation to the public as the duly constituted guardians of law and order and so hold a position of trust which it is important they should be able to maintain; the nature of their employment subjects them to certain social disabilities and requires them to maintain a standard of personal conduct which imposes upon them certain restrictions which do not exist in ordinary employments and hardly apply in the same degree even in the case of other public servants; they are liable to be called for duty at any time and are therefore restricted in their choice of residence; they are exposed to special temptations which are obvious and any lapse on their part has to be dealt with severely; and finally, their calling exposes them to special dangers"[13]

The Inspectors General of Police, as early as in 1960, adopted a set of principles for police conduct. They said: "The police are also citizens with the only difference that they are employed on a whole-time basis to perform duties which are normally incumbent on every citizens, which means that the police must not think of themselves as a body apart from the public; secondly, that the efficient performance of police duties is dependent on the ready co-operation of the people which will not be forthcoming unless they conduct themselves so as to gain the respect and confidence of the people and try, as far as possible to deal with situations without the use of force; and thirdly that they are sympathetic, considerate and mindul of the welfare of all sections of the people and always ready to offer individual service, friendships and assistance to people in need without regard to their social standing".[14]

QUALITIES OF A GOOD CRIME–INVESTIGATOR

1. Iron constitution and sharp intelligence.
2. Preseverance, zeal, tact and application of knowledge.
3. A strong common sense with ready wit.
4. Agreeable manners with firmness in dealings.
5. Good power of observation, analysis and deduction and an eye for details.
6. Be a good judge of human psychology.
7. A good basic education with a fair knowledge about elementary principles and application of science and technology.
8. Proficiency in writing reports.
9. Sincerity, honesty and integrity.
10. Indomiable will and determination to achieve the desired object.
11. He must have informers and sources from among the criminals of the area and should utilize them frequently for detecting the crime.*

In a study conducted by the author, it has been found that there were a number of instances in which public allegation against police were made about *informal arrests* of innocent persons or person suspected to have been involved in the commission of an offence. 41.73 per cent of the police officers interviewed for the purpose of the study stated that the police make *informal arrests* "at times". According to the Constitution of India and by virtue of section 57, Code of Criminal Procedure, 1973, a person arrested by police can be kept only for 24 hours in police custody and thereafter the police are to produce the arrested persons before the nearest Magistrate. *Informal arrests* enable the police to detain the arrested beyond 24 hours without producing him before the Magistrate. The most interesting and revealing aspects of *informal arrest* are brought out in the same study. Out of 56.30 per cent of the police officers who responded to the question: *"In cases a suspect is informally arrested, what do the police normally do with him"?,* 78.32 per cent stated that those who were informally arrested were kept in police custody until a confession was obtained from them. Of course, the police here may be morally convinced of the involvement of the arrested in the commission

* See *Crime Investigation:* Directorate of Police Training, B.P.R.& D., Ministry of Home Affairs, Government of India.

of offence and that may be the reason why the arrested person is detained till the confession is obtained. Nevertheless, however sublime the objectives of the police action may be, it can not be gainsaid that the law enforcement officers are doing a right thing here.

Organization of Crime Investigation

The Director General of Police has, for the purpose of investigation work, two different set-ups —i.e., investigation by officers who have territorial jurisdiction and the same by those who have only functional jurisdiction. Those in the territorial jurisdiction include Inspector General of Police (Law and Order), Deputy Inspector General of Police (Ranges) and officers under them —namely, the Superintendents of Police (Districts), Sub-Divisional, Circle and Station House Officers. The Superintendents of Police in the districts have under their control a Crime Detachment Unit, besides the local police at the police stations, to carry out the investigation work. A Specialised Unit called Crime Investigation Branch, C.I.D. functions under another Inspector General of Police (Crimes).

According to the Police Standing Orders,* it is the duty of the Deputy Inspectors General of Police (Ranges) to superintendent carefully the prevention, the registration, investigation and detection of crimes occurring in their jurisdiction. They, on receipt of grave crime reports, invariably call for progress reports and prescribe the interval at which the reports are to be sent to them. Superintendents of Police (Districts) supervise investigation and detection of crimes in their respective districts and for this purpose they have to visit the scenes of really serious offences where organized crime is indicated or organised gangs are at work, as well as of offences which affect markedly the general peace and quite of districts. They also supersive investigation of crimes of a sensational nature or which greatly agitate the public mind or in which prominent persons are politically or otherwise involved.

---

* Police Standing Orders in Kerala State.

The Sub-Divisional Officers in charge of Sub-Divisions are also responsible for all crime-work in their charge. They visit the scenes of all grave crimes and camp at the spot and supervise the investigation till it is concluded. However if a case comes within the category of a grave crime merely for technical reasons or if a murder is followed by the accused committing suicide or in a case already charged under sections 325 or 326, I.P.C. and the injured dies later and the charge is modified into murder or culpable homicide, personal supervision is a waste of an officer's time and need not necessarily be done. They visit the scenes of crime and inquire personally into serious occurrences endangering life and property such as train or boat disasters or fires in respect of which the commission of a cognizable crime reported or suspected and which involve heavy loss of life and property. A Sub-Divisional Officer is supposed to, after reaching the scene of crime, inspect it and examine all witnesses in the presence of the Sub-Inspector and the Inspector. He will, then along with the Sub-Inspector and the Inspector, study the case thoroughly and discuss the evidence available and further evidence to be collected and sees that the case diaries are written properly, promptly and correctly under his supervision. The Sub-Divisional Officer has to remain, as a rule, in the village with the Inspector till the investigation is practically complete. In cases where definite clues are not forthcoming, the Sub-Divisional Officer and the Inspector camp in the village of occurrence till the case is detected or till after long and strenuous efforts it is decided for want of clues to leave further investigation to local officers.

A circle Inspector, as per rule, engages himself entirely in crime investigation work by supervising and co-ordinating the work of different police stations in his jurisdiction. On the occurrence of a grave crime, the Circle Inspector proceeds to the spot without delay and takes up investigation himself. He investigates personally cases referred to him by the Superintendent of Police or Sub-Divisional Officer. He writes case diaries in all cases investigated by him. In addition, a Circle Inspector visits the scenes of the following crimes and supervises the investigation of (i) any disturbance, riot or affray of a serious nature, (ii) assault on police officers, (iii) cases of suspicious deaths, (iv) escape of prisoners from lawful police custody, (v) church thefts and temple thefts. A Circle Inspector assists the Crime Investigation Branch, C.I.D., in conducting an investigation in his jurisdication.[15]

According to Kerala Police Manual, the following cases are classified as grave crimes —i.e., (a) Dacoity, (b) Highway robbery, (c) Robbery of over Rs. 500/-, (d) Murder, (e) Culpable homicide not amounting to murder and attempt to murder, (f) House-breaking and theft of over Rs. 2,500/-, (g) Theft of over Rs. 2,000/-, (h) Serious motor accidents involving loss of many human lives, (i) Offences under section 126 of the Indian Railway Act, (j) Railway accidents involving loss of human lives, actual sabotage or serious accidents, (k) Big fires in which arson is suspected, (l) Cognizable offences registered against policemen not on leave.

Except when the information is given against a person by name and the case is not of a serious nature, the Station House Officer under sub-section (i) of section 156 of the Code of Criminal Procedure, 1973, always proceeds to the scene and makes the investigation of the case.

Crime Investigation by District Crime Detachment Unit

At present in Kerala, most of the grave crimes like murder, house-breaking and theft of above Rs. 5,000 etc., are investigated by Crime Detachment Unit under the control of the District Superintendent of Police. Any case in which the Superintendent of Police is of opinion that it should be investigated by Crime Detachment Unit, it can also be transferred to it. In such instances, an officer of the Crime Detachment Unit gets the powers of a Station House Officer. In case, a crime is investigated by the Crime Detachment Unit, the officers of the Local Police give necessary assistance. The rationale behind investigation of grave crimes by the Crime Detachment Unit may be:

(i) The local police officers are mainly concerned with law and order problems and as such, they may not get sufficient time to give the best of their personal attention to the investigation of grave crimes requiring systematic and scientific investigation.

(ii) The officers of the Crime Detachment Unit, as a rule, are presumed to be specialists in investigation work. Any anti-social force that might operate on local police to misguide the investigation or to exert undue influence can also be minimised if Crime Detachment Unit takes up the investigation.

Investigation by Crime Investigation Branch (CID)

Every State has a Crime Investigation Branch, C.I.D. directly under the control and supervision of an Inspector General of Police (Crimes). Under him, there is Deputy Inspector-General of Police and there are Superintendent of Police, Deputy Superintendents of Police, Detective Inspectors, Detective Sub-Inspectors and other ranks in police department. As per rule 698 of the Kerala Police Manual, this Branch controls:

1. Crime-Investigation Staff.
2. Crime Intelligence Bureau.
3. Finger Print Bureau.
4. Photographic Unit.
5. Forensic Science Laboratory.
6. Police Research Cell etc.

The Crime Investigation Branch, C.I.D. assists the District Police either by: (i) taking up the entire investigation of a case or, (ii) placing of one its officers at the disposal of the Superintendent of Police (District) when such a step is found necessary for investigation of a particular case.

All officers of and above the rank of Inspectors in the Crime Investigation Branch, C.I.D. (in Kerala) have the powers of an Officer-in-Charge of a Police Station under the Code of Criminal Procedure, 1973.[16]

Rule 703 of the Kerala Police Manual lays down the classes of offences which are investigated by Crime Investigation Branch, C.I.D. They are: (i) Note forgery cases, (2) cases of counterfeit coining when the counterfeits are struck from dyes and other cognate offences in respect of coining by dyes, (3) cases of professional poisoning, (4) theft of government arms and ammunition and illicit trade in arms, (5) important cases in which foreigners are concerned (including cases of international criminals and traffic in women by foreigners), (6) cases of dacoity, robbery and house-breaking of peculiar nature which indicate the work of an adept gang not particularly noticed or accounted for by the local police, (7) cases of fraud, theft or cheating of a peculiar nature which affect more than one district, (8) cases of such a nature, as in the opinion of the Inspector General, Deputy Inspector General or district authorities call for the services of Crime Investigation Branch, C.I.D., (9) important thefts of currency notes or important defalcations of public money, (10) cases of smuggling of opium, cocaine and other narcotics, (11) important conspiracy cases whose ramifications extend to several districts, (12) cases of bringing fraudulent civil suits, (13) gang cases, (14) pornography, (15) professional kidnapping, (16) cases of suspicions deaths when investigation by Crime Investigation Branch, C.I.D. is considered necessary, (17) any serious crime which appears to have a political motive including all offences connected with arms and explosives which are suspected to be of a political nature, (18) any other crimes which may be brought into the category by an order of the Inspector General of Police or the Deputy Inspector General of Police (Crime Investigation Branch C.I.D.) etc.

The Superintendents of Police of the District give the officers of Crime Investigation Branch, C.I.D., every facility for conducting investigation in their districts and make available for their assistance the local knowledge of the District Police.

Police Prosecutor and Judiciary in Crime Investigation

No doubt, the police, prosecutor and judiciary are the sub-systems in criminal justice administration. The investigator must recognize the fact that it is simply impossible for any sub-system to work independently during the investigation of a crime. Hence there should be coordination and co-operation among various agencies of criminal justice administration. For instance, in a criminal trial, it is difficult for the Court of Law to arrive at the real truth unless the police and prosecutor function properly and sincerely. In this context, K. Krishnamurthi writes:

(i) "The police have the right to decide whether and when to start investigation in respect of a cognizable offence and the courts have no power to order the police not to investigate or to say, quash or interfere in any manner with the investigation by police. There cannot be a court order for the stay or stoppage of arrest or search or investigation by police.

(ii) Every step in investigation like spot inspection, search, arrest etc. is in the discretion of the police. The power of the police to arrest, search and seize property during investigation cannot be successfully challenged in a Court Law.

(iii) Examining witnesses, any number of them, recording of their statements, citing them as witnesses for the prosecution, all are in the sole discretion of the police.

(iv) The police have the right to drop proceedings at any stage if they feel there is no sufficient evidence to proceed. The police could refuse to investigate a cognizable offence in which they feel it is futile to investigate because of delay in giving information or other cases".[17]

The Police carry out the investigative functions and in so doing they have to perform principally five different tasks.[18] They are:

(i) *Taking a decision that a crime has been committed:* Crimes in India are defined in the Indian Penal Code or in the special and local laws. All human conducts, however immoral or anti-social in nature cannot become crimes unless they are defined as offences in the penal statutes. After deciding upon the commission of a crime, the police officer must decide whether or not there has been a violation within his jurisdictions. Followed by this is the establishment of the *corpus delicti*:— Body of the Crime.

(ii) *Identifying the offender:* The concept of "Identify" means individualizing some person as the culprit and not necessarily ascertaining the offender's true name.

(iii) *Locating and apprehension of the accused:* The arrest of the suspect is very important in criminal prosecutions.

(iv) *Presenting evidence of guilt:* The investigating officer has to collect evidence against the offender to prove the crime and such evidence must be legally admissible ones and they should be of such a nature that the crime can be proved beyond any shadow of doubt.

(v) *Recovering property involved in criminal cases:* This includes both stolen property and contrabands. Any object which is not lawfully possessed by a person is known as contrabands.

The tasks discussed above are not mutually exclusive. At the beginning of a criminal investigation, the perpetrator of the crime could be theoretically any one. But, as investigation proceeds – i.e., as witnesses are interviewed, physical evidence collected and analysed, and other investigative leads pursued the number of potential suspects is reduced by eliminating non-suspects until the focus is upon a single individual or group of individuals. Jerry L. Dowling views that process of investigation in terms of mathematical set theory.

According to Jerry L. Dowling, Universal Set includes all persons who are considered as initially the potential suspects. But after a workable physical description, persons who cannot be filled in the description are eliminated. Then we get the un-named set. Physical descriptions coupled with other investigation data further reduces the set of suspects to one or more identifiable individuals. This is called Identifiable Set. Finally, by eliminating those suspects who additional investigation reveals are not the offenders or by proving a person to be the offender, a single suspect is left. This is named as the Unique Set by him.[19]

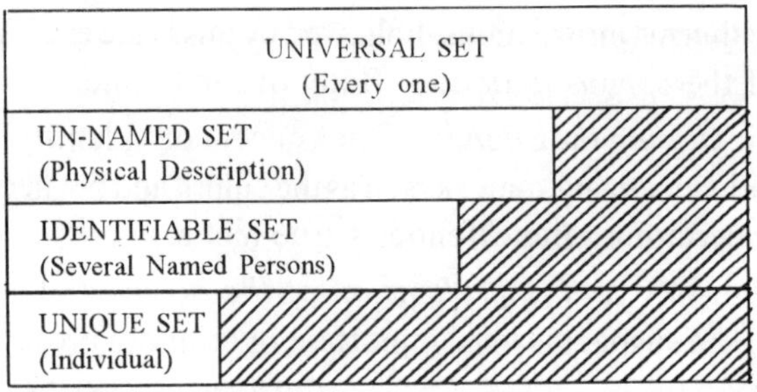

From Jerry L. Dowling *Criminal Investigation* Harcourt Brace Jovanovich Inc., New York, 1979

Fig. 2.3 : Universal Set

All these are things which the police may do without the help of the prosecutor. At the same time, the police will have to consult the prosecutors in many instances as the co-operation between the police and prosecutors is essential for any successful work during police investigation. The Law Commission of India has suggested: "It will be better to get legal assistance whenever necessary even at the stage of investigation. Many of the investigating officers are not law graduates nor do they possess sufficient knowledge of law and procedure. Some of the police officers are even unable to appreciate the significance or importance of the prosecution case".[20] In one of his research studies, the author observed that an attitude of indifference prevails in the two agencies– police and prosecutors. A good many among the members in legal profession think that non-cooperation is what one specially notices between the officers in the two departments. Proper liaison between the two departments becomes necessary and inevitable even during the period of investigation. It should continue at the time of trial or at any stage when mutual help is necessary for the effective prosecution of criminal cases. But, personality clashes between the officers in the two sub-systems and the consequent impact of such clashes find a way to the neglect by the prosecuting staff to the enquiries of police to them during and after the investigation of crime. Some of the prosecutors are simply reluctant to give proper legal advice to police. This sort of interdepartmental or inter-personal hostilities, clashes, differences and attitudes may spoil the future of any case. Realizing the facts, the police officers should try their best to get the maximum co-operation from their prosecuting brotheren in criminal cases".[21] Again, it should be remembered that a judicial system that is very much biased in favour of the accused and which believes in the innocence of the culprits cannot be suspicious of the investigating machinery. Often the judges may be helpless in such instances. Remember that any human organization may have its limits and limitations, merits and demerits. Hence, if the courts do not disbelieve the police in toto, atleast a good number of the judicial functionaries may be suspicious of police actions in criminal cases. Taking all these into consideration, the police have to move in such a manner that the judiciary gets more and more confidence in police work during criminal investigation.[22]

Qualities of an Investigating Officer — Case Laws

1. "The question of delay in examining a witness during the investigation is material only if it is indicative and suggestive of some unfair practice by the investigating agency for the purpose of introducing a got up witness falsely support the prosecution case. The investigating officer should be asked specifically about the delay and the reasons therefor."[23]
2. "The witness for no justifiable reasons was not examined for nearly 10 days."[24]
3. "The prosecution witness did not narrate what he said to the persons who had gathered. The other was not examined by the police, though he had accompanied the informant to the police station."[25]
4. "The mere fact that they are police officers is not enough to discard their evidence."[26]
5. "Today trust begets trust and the higher officers of the Indian police, especially in the Special Police Establishment, deserve better credence."[27]
6. "The panch witnesses had appeared as witnesses for the police for the last 15 years. Their statements were so similar that their whole evidence looks tutored and unconvincing."[28]

7. "Investigating officers are naturally interested in the success of the investigation and the practice of the investigating officer himself recording a dying declaration during the course of investigation ought not to be encouraged."[29]
8. "The very facts that she was questioned at the odd our of mid-night made it obvious that compulsion was being used on her to disclose the names. The police was acting against law in keeping the child confined in the police station. As the mother could not have supported the prosecution case, so the unconvincing excuse was put forward that she disappeared on the day fixed for her evidence, even though she was staying at the same place as her daughter and was looking after her during the trial of the case."[30]
9. "The evidence of a witness was not relied, when the police in contravention of section 162 Cr. P.C. asked him to write his statement."[31]

SUGGESTED READINGS

Beveridge, W.I.B., *The Art of Scientific Investigation,* Random House, New York, 1957.

Eiseman, James S., *Elements of Investigation Techniques,* McKnight and McKnight, Bloomington, 1949.

Else, Walter Martyn, *The Detection of Crime,* London Publishers at the Office of the Police Journal, 1934.

Gross, Hans and Adof Gustav, *Criminal Investigation,* Sweet and Maxwell, London, 1924.

International Association of Chiefs of Police, *Criminal Investigation,* Library Congress, 1968.

Kirk, P.L., *Crime Investigation,* Interscience Publishers, New York, 1953.

Leonard, V.A. *Criminal Investigation and Identification,* Charles C. Thomas, Springfield, 1971.

Morland, Niger, (ed.) *Crime and Detection,* Tallis Press, Oxford, 1966.

O'Hara, Charles, *Fundamentals of Criminal Investigation,* Charles C. Thomas, Springfield, 1956.

Parker, Brian, and Joseph Peterson, and Vonnio Gurgin *The Role of Criminalistics in the World of the Future,* Stanford Research Institute, Menlo Park, Calif, July, 1972.

Richardson, James R., *Scientific Evidence for Police Officers,* W.H. Anderson, Cincinnati, Ohio, 1963.

Soderman, Harry, *Modern Criminal Investigation,* Funk and Wagnails, New York, 1972.

Svensson, Arne, *Crime Detection: Modern Methods of Criminal Investigation,* American Elsevier, New York, 1965.

Thorwald, Jurgen, *Crime and Science: The New Frontier in Criminology.* Harcourt, Brace and World, New York, 1967.

Western, Paul B. and Kenneth M. Wells, *Criminal Evidence for Police,* Prentice Hall, Eaglewood Cliffs, N.J. 1971.

Willmer, M.A.P., *Crime and Information Theory,* University Press, Edinburg, 1970.

REFERENCES

1. *Webster's New Twentieth Century Dictionary,* William Collions and World Publishing Co., 1975.
2. Jamuna *vs.* Bihar, A.I.R., 1974 S.C. 1822; 1974 Cr. L.J. 890.
3. Richard H. Ward, *Introduction to Criminal Investigation,* Addison Wesley Publishing Company, London, 1975.
4. Richard H. Ward, *Introduction to Criminal Investigation, op. cit.*
5. Kartar Singh *vs.* State of Punjab, 1977 Cr. L.J. 214; A.I.R. 1977 S.C. 349.
6. State of Uttar Pradesh *vs.* Bhagwant Kishore, A.I.R. 1964 S.C. 221; 1964 (i) Cr. L.J. 140; H. N. Rishbad *vs.* State of Delhi; A.I.R. 1955 S.C. 196; 1955 Cr. L.J. 526; Durgadas *vs.* State Himachal Pradesh, A.I.R. 1973 S.C. 1379; 1973 Cr. L.J. 1138.
7. Chandrakant *vs.* State of Maharashtra, A.I.R. 1974, 220; 1974 Cr. L.J. 309.
8. Santu Singh *vs.* State of Punjab, A.I.R. 1956 S.C. 526.
9. Nageshwar *vs.* Maharashtra State, A.I.R. 1973 S.C. 165:1973 Cr. L.J. 235.
10. G.L. Gupta *vs.* Asst. Collector of Customs, A.I.R. 1971 S.C. 28:1971 Cr. L.J. 1.
11. See Niranjan Singh *vs.* State of Uttar Pradesh, 1957 Cr. L.J. 294; A.I.R. 1957 S.C. 142.
12. Quoted from O.P. Tandon, *Concoction of Evidence and Its Effect,* (memeo) Central Police Academy, Advanced Course, Abu.

13. *Central Committee on Police Training,* Government of India, New Delhi, 1973.
    (i) See *Central Committee on Polilce Training, op. cit.*
    (ii) James Vadackumchery, *Acquittals in Administration of Criminal Justice,* Ph.D Thesis, Kerala University, 1983.
15. The duties of police officers enumerated above are taken from *Kerala Police Manual,* Vol. II, Government Press, Trivandrum, 1970.
16. See Rule 700(3) of the *Kerala Police Manual* 1971, Vol. III, Government Presses, Trivandrum and also, Government notification No. H2-54642/28 Home (A) dated 14-8-1958.
17. K. Krishnamurthi, *Police Diaries, Statements, Reports, Investigations and Arrests, etc.* Law Book Co., Allahabad, 1973.
18. See Jerry L. Dowling, *Criminal Incestigation,* Harcourt Brace Javanovick Inc., New York, 1979.
19. Jerry L. Dowling, *Criminal Investigation, op. cit.*
20. The Law Commission of India, XIV Report, Vol. II, p. 742.
21. James Vadackumchery, *Acquittals in Administration of Criminal Justice, op. cit.*
22. James Vadackumchery, *Acquittals in Administration of Criminal Justice, op. cit.*
23. Ranbir *vs.* State of Punjab, A.I.R. 1973, S.C. 1409; 1973 Cr. L.J. 1120.
24. Balakrishna *vs.* State of Orissa, 1971 Cr. L.J. 670.
25. Hansa Singh *vs.* State of Punjab, A.I.R. 1977 S.C. 1801; 1977 Cr. L.J. 1448.
26. Nathu Singh *vs.* State of Madhya Pradesh A.I.R. 1973, S.C. 2783; 1974 Cr. L.J. 11.
27. Soma Prakash *vs.* Delhi, A.I.R. S.C. 989; 1974 Cr. L.J. 784.
28. Hazara Singh *vs.* State of Punjab, 1971 (i) S.C.C. 529; (1971) 3 S.C.R. 674.
29. Munna Raja *vs.* State Madhya Pradesh, A.I.R. 1976 S.C. 2199; 1976 Cr. L.J. 1781.
30. Bihar State *vs.* S. Kapil Singh, A.I.R. 1969 S.C. 53; 1969 Cr. L.J. 279.
31. Kanu Ambu Vish *vs.* State of Maharashtra, 1971 (i) S.C.C. 503.

3

FIRST INFORMATION REPORT

F.I.R. is not defined in the Code of Criminal Procedure, 1973. Nervertheless, section 154 Cr. P.C., 1973 reads: "Every information relating to the commission of a cognizable offence, if given orally to an Officer-in-Charge of a police station, shall be reduced into writing by him or under his direction, and be read over to the informant; and every such information, whether given in writing or reduced to writing as aforesaid shall be signed by the person giving it, and the substance thereof shall be entered in a book to be kept by such officer in such form as the State Government may prescribe in this behalf".

The book mentioned in the section wherein the substance of the report is entered is called 'General Diary' or 'Daily Diary'. Besides the General Diary, there is the First Information Book or the F.I.R. Register kept in every police station. "The conditions as to the writing under section 154 Cr. P.C. are merely procedural. If it is an information relating to the commission of a cognizable offence, it falls under section 154 and becomes admissible in evidence".[1]

This means that the criminal law can be set into motion not only by filing a complaint before a competent Magistrate, but also by laying an information to the police. In the former case, a complaint is preferred under section 190 Cr. P.C. and in the latter case an information is lodged to the police under section 154

Criminal Procedure Code. There is a big difference between First Information and First Information Report. First Information means as information received by police about the commission of a cognizable offence and it becomes an F.I.R. only when it is recorded in the F.I.R. register under section 154 Cr. P.C. The Station House Officer can '*suo-motu*' record in information in the F.I.R. register in which case he is deemed to be the informant.

The Information Report acts as the basis for investigation. Therefore, it should be accurate, precise and concise and above all complete. The following information in an F.I.R. is essential and should be included.

1. Date and time of report — This means the date and the time of the receipt of the information.
2. Date and time of the occurrence of the crime — This should be accurate. If the exact time is uncertain, indicate the parameters – viz., between 9 p.m and 12.30 a.m.
3. Place of occurrence, distance and direction from police station — The information regarding the place of occurrence should be specific and precise. The distance from the police station can be approximate.
4. Date of despatch from police station — This is very essential. Otherwise the delay in despatching the report will be viewed with suspicion.
5. Full name, address and residence of the informant or complainant — The permanent and temporary addresses must be obtained.
6. Name and residence of the accused/suspects — If the accused can be named and address can be furnished it will prove to be a valuable information for investigation and later in the Court of Law.
7. Brief description of offence with section of law and of property carried off, if any — The more serious violation should be written first if there is more than one crime involved. It should be remembered to list

		the I.P.C. citation where applicable. A brief and concise narrative will be enough.
8. Steps taken regarding investigation and explanations of delay in recording information	—	As a rule, the inspection of the scene of crime is the first thing to do after despatching the report to the authorities concerned. Delay in recording the information has been severely criticized by the Supreme Court in several cases.

The First Information Report must be read over to the informant and must be authenticated by the signature/thumb impression of the informant and attested by the signature of the officer recording it. The signature/thumb impression of the informant should be affixed at the foot of the information.

Questioning the First Informant

Research studies show that some informants give an exaggerated or over-exaggerated version of the incident when they lay information to the police. This is really bad and often may prove to be harmful for the prosecution at a later stage.[2] Hence a thorough questioning of the informant becomes all the more necessary before recording the F.I.R. Why do the people give exaggerated or over-exaggerated version? Many investigating officers think that the people do so to make the offence appear to be more serious than what it really is or to make a non-cognizable offence to appear as a congizable one.[3] Under sections 182 and 211 I.P.C. 1860, a person who gives a false F.I.R. is liable to be prosecuted. But, more often than not, the first informants are not lodging a false F.I.R., but they merely exaggerate or over-exaggerate an incident to get serious attention from the police. The investigating officers must know the methods of questioning the informants to elicit a precise, accurate and complete narration of the facts of the case.

QUESTIONS TO BE ANSWERED BY THE STATION HOUSE OFFICER

FIRST INFORMATION REPORT

(See Section 154 Cr. P.C. 1973)

1. Does this information relate to the commission of a cognizable offence? If so what is/are the offence/s.

2. Who is the informant? What is his name and address? Temporary and permanent addresses?

3. Who are the suspects? Their names and addresses? The reasons for suspicion?

   Can it be a true suspicion?

4. What is to be recorded in the General Diary?

5. How should the information be recorded in the F.I.R. register? What is the time of the occurrence of crime? Is it accurate or approximate? What is the time of the receipt of the information? Is the information delayed? If so what is the reason for it? What is the motive of the informant in filing the information?

6. How to question the informant?

How to Question?

The following questions should be asked to the first informant before the investigating officer starts preparing the F.I.R. One and the same question should be asked several times to check the validity of the responses and to ensure certainty. The questions put under are not exhaustive. The informants, sometimes, can not answer all the questions asked by the investigating officer. Does not matter and if it is the case it should not irritate the investigator also. The questioning procedure is as under –

WHAT
— is the reason for the commission of the offence?
— is the name of the suspect/s in the crime?
— is the temporary/permanent addresses of the suspect/s ?
— is the profession/occupation of the suspects?
— is the relationship of the victim to the suspect/s?
— is the value of the articles stolen?
— is the method of committing the offence?
— is the reputation of the suspect/s?

WHO
— else be involved in the commission of the crime?
— has informed the crime? and the reasons for it?
— has visited the scene of crime after the commission of the offence?
— has seen the culprits?
— were present at the scene of crime before, during or after the commission of the crime? If they have not seen the commission of the crime, why?
— gave the provocation first? And the reason for the same?
— was contacted by the informant after the crime has taken place? And why?
— was behind the actual commission of the crime? Any abettors etc.?
— is to blame? – the culprit or the victim?

— is the informant? temporary and permanent addresses?

WHY — did the crime occur?

— did the culprit commit the crime in the manner narrated?

— did the culprit chose the particular spot, person, property etc. as the target of his attack?

— was the victim/witness(es) unable to identify the culprits?

— does the informant prefer the information to the police?

— cann't the victim prevent the commission of crime if he could at the time of commission of offence?

— was the victim not taking precautions for safeguarding himself/his property?

— was the information delayed for reporting to police?

— did the perpetrator use the particular tools or weapons?

— did the perpetrator use the particular means of entry?

— did the perpetrator injure the victim?

WHOSE — property is stolen?

— brain is behind the commission of the offence?

— provocation was there for the commission of the offence?

— injury is serious —the victim's or offenders?

— name could be suggested as the possible offender?

WHERE — is the place of occurrence?

— is the suspect/s now? Where can he/they be located?

— is the property? Where can they be found out?

— is victim now? Why?

— did the perpetrator obtain tools and weapons from?

— was the perpetrator last seen?

— were the witnesses at the time of committing the offence?

— are the witnesses now?

— were the informants at the time of committing the offence?

— can the tools and weapons of offence be located?

WHEN — did the crime occur?

— did the informant come to know of the incident? Why? If delay in lodging the information is seen, why? Was the suspect seen in the vicinity of the scene of crime by witnesses?

— did the suspect leave the scene of crime?

— did the victim arrive at the scene?

— was the victim last seen alive and by whom?

— did the witnesses see the incident? did the witnesses arrive and leave the scene?

— did the victim leave or was removed from the scene?

— was the offence discovered?

WHICH — is the manner in which the crime has been committed? are the pieces of evidence likely to be seen at the scene of crime?

— are the pieces of evidence likely to have been destroyed?

— are the methods likely to be adopted by the culprit to conceal the crime? evidence?

HOW — did the crime occur?

— did the criminal approach the victim/the scene to commit the offence?

— did the criminal escape the scene of crime/ occurrence after the commission of the crime?

— difficult or easy was it for the culprit to commit the crime?

— best can the crime be proved in the Court of Law?

— much is the loss? how is the loss estimated?

— much is the gain to the culprit? how is the gain estimated?

— far is the scene of crime/occurrence from the police station?

— did the witnesses happen to be on the scene?

— did the perpetrator obtain the tools and weapons used?

First Information Report — Case Law

1. "A confessional statement which was made by the accused to the police and which formed the basis of the F.I.R, was not admissible in evidence as the same was hit by section 25 of the Evidence Act."[4]
2. "The object of insisting upon prompt lodging of the report to the police in respect of commission of an offence is to obtain early information regarding the circumstances in which the crime was committed, the names of the actual culprits and the part played by them as well as the names of the eye-witnesses present at the scene of occurrence. Delay in lodging the F.I.R. quite often results in embellishment which is a creature of afterthought. It is therefore essential that the delay in lodging the report should be satisfactorily explained."[5]
3. "Several F.I.Rs. are recorded on plain pieces of paper and then transcribed into the First Information Register. Infact, if a written report is brought it is verbatim copied into the F.I.R. register."[6]
4. It is not necessary that an elaborate account of everything to mention every minute details in the F.I.R. Details could not be given as the informant was in state of mental agony. However, all the necessary information such as the names of assailants, the motive and how the incident had taken place has been stated in the F.I.R."[7]
5. "When the first information was received in this case no sub-inspector was present in the police station. The head constable was the officer-in-charge of the station at that time. Hence the law permitted him to investigate the case."[8]

6. "The telephonic message recorded in the daily diary of the police station was a cryptic and anonymous oral message, which did not in terms clearly specify a cognizable offence, can not be treated as F.I.R. The mere fact that the information was the first in point of time could not by itself clothe it with the character of F.I.R."[9]
7. "Now this information was apparently based on the talk in the village and Talavari himself was not an eye-witness to the occurrence. It was clearly open to the authorities concerned to take action on this information if they chose, but it was equally open to them to wait for more authentic or reliable information for taking appropriate action treating the earlier information as based on mere village gossip."[10]
8. "Section 154 does not require that the report must be given by a person who has personal knowledge of the incident. It only speaks of an information relating to the commission of a cognizable offence given to an Officer-in-Charge of a Police Station."[11]
9. "The F.I.R. was made not by one of the persons immediately concerned but by a person who had the information from another. In these cases sometimes a fact gets omitted which should have been mentioned."[12]

Who can Record an F.I.R.?

Section 154 Cr. P.C. and the decided cases suggest that only an Officer-in-Charge of a Police Station can record a F.I.R. The Station House Officer as defined in Section 2 (0) Cr. P.C. 1973 does not include a constable. However, if a constable received a duly signed report concerning the commission of a cognizable offence, he must record in the General Diary and should immediately convey the message to the Station House Officer wherever he is. If this is not possible, the first informant can be directed to the Station House Officer with a note about the case. If the case refers to a serious or grave crime, the constable should communicate immediately the information to the Circle Inspector and also should initiate steps to guard the scene of crime and if possible should apprehend the accused without delay.

Suo Motu F.I.Rs.

If the rumour about the commission of a cognizable offence is a vague one, the Station House Officer should not make a F.I.R. He can very well record the rumour in the General Diary and in case reliable and sufficient information is collected about the commission of the offence, he should record a F.I.R. If a telegraphic message is received, the Station House Officer can register a F.I.R. if feels that immediate action is warranted. In such cases *suo motu* F.I.R. should be prepared. On the other hand, if a telephonic message comes to the Station House Officer, the informant should be asked to lodge the information in person. If the informant is not prepared , a F.I.R. can be registered *suo motu*. In that case an entry in the General Diary is very essential.

Despatch of the F.I.R.

Under section 157 Cr. P.C., 1973 the original copy of the F.I.R. is to be sent without delay to the Magistrate having jurisdiction. Another copy should be sent to the Circle Inspector who forwards it to the Sub-Divisional Officer. One copy is kept in the police station for future reference. In some States in India F.I.Rs. of grave crimes are sent to the Circle Inspectors and Sub-Divisional Officers and if the offence is particularly serious, then to the Superintendent of Police as well.

A copy of the F.I.R. should be forthwith given to the informant in all cases.

Despatch of the F.I.R.—Case Laws

1. "As there is no evidence to show that F.I.R. was sent to the Magistrate, it throws considerable doubt on the prosecution case".[13]
2. "The extra-ordinary delay in sending the F.I.R. to the Magistrate is a circumstance which provides a legitimate basis for

suspecting that the F.I.R. was recorded much later than the stated date and hour affording sufficient time to the prosecution to introduce improvements and embellishments and set up a distorted version of the occurrence".[14]

3. The time when it was sent to the Magistrate was not properly proved. F.I.R. must have been lodged much later than is stated by prosecution".[15]

Evidentiary Value of F.I.Rs.

The Indian Evidence Act, 1872 attaches great importance to the contents of a F.I.R. It is so because, the F.I.R. contains statements soon after the occurrence of a crime when memory is fresh and there is no time for fabrication or embellishment. It is the first information or report about the occurrence of a cognizable offence and therefore any subsequent improvements in the statements of witnesses regarding the occurrence can be checked up in the light of the F.I.R. particularly when they are made by the complainant himself.[16]

Importance of F.I.R. — Case Laws

1. F.I.R. is not a substantive evidence but can be used to corroborate or contradict the evidence of the informant given in court or to impeach his credit".[17]
2. "The F.I.R. was made very soon after the incident, and there is no justification for the argument that it discredits the statement of its maker".[18]
3. "The F.I.R. could by no means be utilized for contradicting or discrediting the other witnesses who obviously could not have any desire to spare the real culprit and to falsely implicate the appellant".[19]
4. "Omissions of important material fact in the F.I.R. shows the bonafides of the complainant who appears to be so mentally agitated that he did not remember to mention these facts in the F.I.R. which was lodged without delay."[20]

5. "Only because F.I.R. is not as full as it could be, there is no warrant that it should be ignored. It can be used as provided under section 145 E. Act."[21]
6. "One defect in the evidence of P.W. is that in the F.I.R. he did not state that he was an eye-witness. In the evidence he claimed to have seen his mother being murdered. This part of the testimony is an improvement and rightly rejected."[22]
7. "The F.I.R. is not a confession. It is not a statement made to a police officer during the course of investigation. Section 25 E. Act and section 162 Cr. P.C. do not bar its admissibility. The report is an admission by accused of certain facts, which are admissible under section 21 E. Act."[23]
8. "In the F.I.R. it is not mentioned that the appellant had stabbed the deceased. The omission of such an important fact is relevant under section 11 of the E. Act in judging the veracity of the prosecution case."[24]
9. "The F.I.R. under section 154 Cr. P.C. is not a substantive piece of evidence. The absence of a first information report, therefore, by itself cannot destroy the prosecution case."[25]

Thus one sees that the F.I.R. is an important document and often it is the basis for the initiation of crime investigation. It, therefore, goes without saying that the officer-in-charge of a police station must take all care and caution to avoid additions, alterations etc. in the F.I.R. No doubt, in unavoidable circumstances, additions can be made. In any case, subsequent writings must invariably be initialled and corrections, if any, must be made before the F.I.R. has been signed by the informant.

Informant's Interview Guide

In case, the informant does not know the offender by name, still he will be able to identify the culprit by description. In such cases, it will be good if the police officer asks him to furnish details on the following items.

INFORMANT'S INTERVIEW GUIDE – I
(in case of property)

1.	Number of items..................	2.	Kind of items..........................
3.	Material of the items...........	4.	Colour of the items.................
5.	Manufacture........................	6.	Model designation..................
7.	Cost..................................	8.	Weight..................................
9.	Any speciality....................	10.	Manufacturing defects............. (if any)
11.	Resale value........................	12.	Any other information...........

INFORMANT'S INTERVIEW GUIDE – II
(in case the offender is not known by name)

1.	Sex....................................	2.	Approximate age....................
3.	Height................................	4.	Weight ....
5.	Hair (colour)........................	6.	Combing (hair) speciality ....
7.	Eyes....................................	8.	Nose....................................
9.	Mustache............................	10.	Teeth..................................
11.	Complexion.........................	12.	Build...................................
13.	Posture...............................	14.	Manner of walk....................
15.	Scars...................................	16.	Voice..................................
17.	Eye-glasses.........................	18.	Dress..................................
19.	Caste (if it can identifiable)..		
20.	Disguise..............................	21.	Language.............................
22.	Any statements made...........	23.	Tattoos...............................
24.	Means of arrival..................	25.	Means of escape..................
26.	If a vehicle is used, description of the vehicle...............................		

SUGGESTED READINGS

The full text of the following judgements of the courts may be seen.

1. F.I.R. is not a Substantive Evidence

a) State of Bombay *vs.* Rusy Mistry, A.I.R. 1960 S.C. 391.

b) A. Nagesha *vs.* State of Bihar, A.I.R. 1966 S.C. 119.
c) Nisar Ali *vs.* State of Uttar Pradesh, A.I.R. 1957 S.C. 366: 1957 Cr. L.J. 550.

2. F.I.R. Lodged by the Accused—Inadmissible

a) Nisar Ali *vs.* State of Uttar Pradesh, *op. cit.*
b) A. Nagesha *vs.* State of Bihar, *op cit.*
c) Faddi *vs.* State of Madhya Pradesh A.I.R. 1964. S.C. 1950.
d) K.H. Amulakh *vs.* State of Gujarat, A.I.R. 1972 S.C. 922: 1972 Cr. L.J. 626.

3. Delay in Lodging F.I.R. Effect

a) Thullia Kall *vs.* State, A.I.R. 1973 S.C. 501: 1972 Cr. L.J. 1296.
b) Pala Singh *vs.* State of Punjab, 1973, Cr. L.J. 59: A.I.R. 1972 S.C. 2679.
c) Ram Jag *vs.* Uttar Pradesh State, A.I.R. 1974 S.C. 606: 1974 Cr. L.J. 479.
e) Apren Joseph *vs.* State of Kerala, A.I.R. 1973 S.C.I.: 1973 Cr. L.J. 185.
f) Kartar Singh *vs.* State of Punjab, 1977 Cr. L.J. 214:A.I.R. 1977 S.C. 349.
g) Dargahi *vs.* State of Uttar Pradesh, A.I.R. 1973 S.C. 2695: 1973 Cr. L.J. 1828.
h) Sarwan Singh *vs.* State of Punjab, A.I.R. 1976 S.C. 2304: 1976 Cr. L.J. 1757.

4. Delay in Lodging the F.I.R. Explained

a) Jhamman *vs.* State of Uttar Pradesh, A.I.R. 1975 S.C. 1083: 1975 Cr. L.J. 926.
b) N.D. Dhayaguda *vs.* State of Maharastra, A.I.R. 1977 S.C. 381: 1977 Cr. L.J. 238.
c) Dalip Singh *vs.* State of Punjab, A.I.R. 1953 S.C. 364: 1953 Cr. L.J. 1465.
d) Dalbir Kaur *vs.* State of Punjab, 1977 Cr. L.J. 273: A.I.R. 1977 S.C. 472.
e) Lalai *vs.* State of Uttar Pradesh, A.I.R. 1974 S.C. 2118: 1974 Cr. L.J. 1393.

5. Delay in Lodging or Sending F.I.R. Promptly not Explained

a) Birsingh *vs.* State of Uttar Pradesh, 1977 U.J. (S.C.) 148.
b) Ishwar Singh *vs.* State of Uttar Pradesh, A.I.R. 1976 S.C. 2423: 1976 Cr. L.J. 1883.
c) Datar Singh *vs.* State of Punjab, 1974 Cr. L.J. 908: A.I.R. 1974 S.C. 1193.

6. Evidentiary Value of F.I.R.

a) Dharma *vs.* Maharashtra, A.I.R. 1973 S.C. 476: 1973 Cr. L.J. 680.
b) Narpal Singh *vs.* State of Haryana, 1977 Cr. L.J. 642.
c) Soma Bhai *vs.* State of Gujarat A.I.R. 1975 S.C. 1453: 1975 Cr. L.J. 1201.
d) State of Uttar Pradesh *vs.* Lalla Singh, A.I.R. 1978 S.C. 368.
e) Tara Chand *vs.* State of Haryana, 1971 Cr. L.J. 1411: A.I.R. 1971 S.C. 1891.
f) Abdul Gani *vs.* State of Madhya Pradesh, A.I.R. 1954 S.C. 31: 1954 Cr. L.J. 323.

7. F.I.R. Need not be an Encyclopaedia

a) N.M. Naik *vs.* State of Maharashtra, A.I.R. 1971 S.C. 1656.
b) Ram Lakhan *vs.* State of Uttar Pradesh, 1977 Cr. L.J. 1566: A.I.R. 1977 S.C. 1936.
c) Bhopat Singh *vs.* State of Maharashtra, 1973 Cr. L.J. 343: A.I.R. 1973 S.C. 446.
d) P. Narayana *vs.* State of Andhra Pradesh, A.I.R. 1975 S.C. 1252: 1975 Cr. L.J. 1062.

8. Omissions in F.I.R. —Effect

a) Chandmal *vs.* State of Rajasthan, A.I.R. 1976 S.C. 917: 1976 Cr. L.J. 679.
b) R. K. Pande *vs.* State of Madhya Pradesh, A.I.R. 1975 S.C. 1026: 1975 Cr. L.J. 870.
c) Hallu *vs.* State of Madhya Pradesh, A.I.R. 1974 S.C. 1936: 1974 Cr. L.J. 1385.
d) R. P. Sharma *vs.* Bihar, A.I.R. 1970 S.C. 326: 1970 Cr. L.J. 496.
e) Brij Mohan *vs.* Priya Brat, A.I.R. 1965 S.C. 282.
f) Mitter Sen *vs.* State of Uttar Pradesh, A.I.R. 1976 S.C. 1156: 1976 Cr. L.J. 857.
g) Bhat Singh *vs.* State of Uttar Pradesh, 1972 Cr. L.J. 1704.
h) Jagdip Singh *vs.* State of Haryana, A.I.R. 1974 S.C. 1978: 1974 Cr. L.J. 1378.
i) Ashok Kumar *vs.* Delhi Administration, 1977 Cr. L.J. 814.
j) Bhagirath Singh *vs.* State of Bihar, 1976 Cr. L.J. 685: A.I.R. 1976 S.C. 92.

REFERENCES

1. Mani Mohan Ghosh *vs.* Emperor, A.I.R. 1931, Cal. 745.

2. James Vadackumchery, *Acquittals in Administration of Criminal Justice* Ph.D. dissertation, Kerala University, 1983.
3. James Vadackumchery, *Acquittals in Administration of Criminal Justice, op.cit.*
4. Nisar Ali *vs.* State of Uttar Pradesh, A.I.R. 1957, S.C. 366: 1957 Cr. L.J. 550; A Nagesa *vs.* State of Bihar, A.I.R. 1966 S.C. 119: 1966 Cr. L.J. 100; Faddi *vs.* State of Madhya Pradesh A.I.R. 1964 S.C. 1850: 1964 (2) Cr. L.J. 144; K.H. Amulkh *vs.* State of Gujarat, A.I.R. 1972 S.C. 922: 1972 Cr. L.J. 626.
5. Thulia Kall *vs.* State, A.I.R. 1973 S.C. 501: 1972 Cr. L.J. 1296.
6. N.M. Naik *vs.* Maharashtra, A.I.R. 1971, S.C. 1656.
7. P. Narayana *vs.* State of Andhra Pradesh, A.I.R. 1975 S.C. 1252: 1975 Cr. L.J. 1062.
8. Pati Ram *vs.* State of Uttar Pradesh, 1970(3) S.C.C. 703.
9. Tapindar Singh *vs.* Punjab, A.I.R. 1970 S.C. 1566: 1970 Cr. L.J. 1415.
10. Duranpande *vs.* State of Tamil Nadu, 1973 Cr. L.J. 602.
11. Hallu *vs.* Madhya Pradesh State, A.I.R. 1974 S.C. 1936:1974 Cr. L.J. 1385.
12. State of Rajasthan *vs.* Kartar Singh, A.I.R. 1970 S.C. 1305: 1970 Cr. L.J. 1144.
13. Birsingh *vs.* State of Uttar Pradesh, 1977 U.J (S.C.) 148.
14. Ishwar Singh *vs.* State of Uttar Pradesh, A.I.R. 1976 S.C. 2423:1976 Cr. L.J. 1983.
15. Datar Singh *vs.* State of Punjab, 1974 Cr. L.J. 908: A.I.R. 1974 S.C. 1193.
16. 1952 Cr. L.J. 1957.
17. State of Bombay *vs.* Rusy Mistry, A.I.R. 1960 S.C. 391; A. Nagesha *vs.* State of Bihar, A.I.R. 1966 S.C. 119: 1966 Cr. L.J. 100; Nizar Ali *vs.* State of Uttar Pradesh, A.I.R. 1957 S.C. 366: 1957 Cr. L.J. 550.
18. Kartar Singh *vs.* State of Punjab, 1977 Cr. L.J. 214: A.I.R. 1977 S.C. 349.
19. Dharama *vs.* Maharashtra, A.I.R. 1973 S.C. 476: 1973 Cr. L.J. 680.
20. Soma Bhai *vs.* State of Gujarat, A.I.R 1975 S.C. 1453: 1975 Cr. L.J. 1201.
21. Abdul Gani *vs.* State of Madhya Pradesh, A.I.R. 1954 S.C. 31: 1954 Cr. L.J. 323.
22. State of Uttar Pradesh *vs.* Lalla Singh, A.I.R. 1978 S.C. 368.
23. Faddi *vs.* State of Madhya Pradesh, A.I.R. 1964 S.C. 1950.
24. R.K. Pande *vs.* State of Madhya Pradesh, A.I.R. 1975 S.C. 1026: 1975 Cr. L.J. 870.
25. Jagesh B. Rao *vs.* Government of the Union Territory of Goa, Daman and Diu, 1976 Cr. L.J. 132.

4

SCENE OF CRIME
Protection, Photographs and Sketches

Crime Scene: What is It?

In H.N. Rushbud *vs.* State of Delhi, the Supreme Court observed: "Under the Code, investigation consists generally of the following steps: (1) proceeding to the spot, (2) ascertainment of the facts and circumstances of the case, (3) discovery and arrest of the suspected offender, (4) collection of evidence relating to the commission of the offence which may consist of (a) the examination of various persons (including the accused); (b) the search of places and seizure of things, (5) formation of the opinion as to whether on the material collected, there is a case to place the accused before the Magistrate for trial and if so, taking the necessary steps for the same by filing a charge-sheet under section 173".[1]

Section 156, Code of Criminal Procedure, 1973 empowers an officer-in-charge of a police station to investigate any cognizable offence. Section 157 of the same Code provides that "if from the information received or otherwise, an officer-in-charge of a police station has reason to suspect the commission of a cognizable offence, he shall proceed to the spot to investigate the fact and circumstances of the case and to take measures for the discovery and arrest of the offenders. But the impressions gathered or the circumstances ascertained by a police officer at the scene of crime are not required to be recorded in the General Diary maintained in the station house. Such things are not relevant facts under section 35 of the Indian Evidence Act, 1872. However, these facts can appropriately be mentioned in the case diary under section 172 of the Criminal Procedure Code, 1973.

After the registering of the F.I.R., the investigating officer along with two of his assistants and the photographer goes to the scene of crime. The Investigating Officer's Kit should, in all cases, be carried to the scene of crime. He should check whether or not all items in the Investigator's Kit are available. Note down the time of departure, climatic conditions and the approximate distance from the station to the scene of crime.

A crime scene, in the current understanding, means the location where the offence took place. It may be a room, a cellar or a roof. It may as well be a road or a road side, an open field, a jungle, a hill, a mountain, a stream or a river. Again it may be a vehicle, a train, a boat or an aeroplane. Every scene of crime presents unique and special aspects for which techniques of inspection may have to be modified by the crime investigator.

Usually crime scene involves one place. But there may be cases of forgery, kidnapping, rape etc. where more than one location may be seen as the crime scenes. Therefore, in such cases the scene of crime is defined as the place or places where material evidence to prove a crime can be located. Inspection of the scene of crime is done principally for collecting physical/material evidence and therefore a definition basing on material evidence seems to be better than any other definition.

Illustration

1. A murder was committed at the spot X, the dead body is thrown at Y, the knife with which the murder was committed is hidden at Z. For the purpose of inspection X,Y and Z are considered as the scenes of crime.
2. Illicit liquor is manufactured at A, stored at B, and sold at C. Here A, B and C are scenes of crime.For the investigating

officer can collect pieces of material evidence from A,B and C.

There may be cases in which crime scenes are not at all found. In such instances, no physical evidence will be found out if at all an inspection is conducted. Such scenes of crime are known as scenes of occurrence i.e., a place where the crime has occurred, but no physical evidence available.

Illustration

A forges a cheque in the compartment of a train. He mails the same at B. Here it is futile to conduct an inspection of the cabin of the train. There is only scenes of occurrence here as no physical evidence is available in the cabin.

Crime Scene – Protection

Protection of the physical evidence at the scene of crime being one of the most important functions of the investigating officer during inspection, every police officer must know how best he can protect the crime scene. Sometimes, it becomes necessary to depute a constable to a scene of crime if the officer-in-charge of the police station cannot immediately proceed to the crime scene. In such occasions, it is very necessary to instruct the constable how best he should protect the scene until the arrival of the officer-in-charge of the police station.

Locating the Scene of Crime

The scene of crime is located in any one or more of the following ways:

1. Accounts of the first informant or eye-witnesses.
2. *Corpus delecti.*
3. Marks of struggle.
4. Presence of material evidence.
5. Traces carried over from the scene.

Once the crime scene is located and it is seen that the scene is not guarded by some civic-minded person/s, the investigating officer or the constable deputed by the investigator must isolate the scene by either making a round mark on the crime scene or roping it off. If a team is investigating, then post a uniformed constable there with instructions to guard it.

If on examination any signs of life is found on the injured victim/s, medical help should immediately be called for. If this is not possible, the injured should then be transported to the nearest hospital. In so doing adequate caution should be taken not to disturb the crime scene and the evidence likely to be available there. Before removing the injured, the position of the victim at the scene of crime should be marked well in the scene itself. If the victim is dead, the scene should be left as it is without it being disturbed.

All unauthorized men, relatives and friends of the victim or the culprit, onlookers, photographers and pressmen should be excluded from the scene. They should be handled carefully, persuasively, yet firmly. The members of the public under no circumstances be permitted to discuss the case with the suspect and the witnesses should not be allowed to talk to the suspect.

If by some means or information, the suspect or the culprit is identified at the scene of crime, he should be detained then and there. No elaborate interrogation with him in public is advisable. It shall be done only after the inspection of the scene of crime is completed. The names and addresses of all witnesses to the incidence and bystanders who volunteer to give information regarding the commission of the offence should at once be collected. No attempt shall be made to interview them so as to collect more details about the crime and the criminal. This shall be postponed until the inspection is over.

Fellow policemen (including senior police officers) should realize that they are not to enter the scene of crime to satisfy their curiosity. They should understood that it is the investigating officer who should decide when, why and who should enter the scene. Again the officers assisting the investigating officer are not to start independent searches and enquiries. They should do only those things specifically asked to them by the investigating officer. Assistance of police officers, draftsman, experts and doctors should be requisitioned at the earliest, wherever, necessary. If possible and necessary, the superior police officers should be informed about the nature of crime and help required etc., through wireless, telephone or special messenger.

The investigating officer is not to discuss the case with suspects, complainants, victims, the witnesses, the onlookers and pressmen at the scene of crime. At the same time, he has to invariably keep his eyes and ears open to see and listen to any passing remarks and also he should observe the behaviour of the persons around. He should not introduce any fresh materials like cigarette ends, cigarette ash, foot or foot wear marks or finger prints at the scene. The officer should not forget to record the arrival, the weather and other information in his note book. The officer is not expected to use the utensils, bathroom, wash basin, lavatory, towels etc., available at the scene of crime.

Bird's Eye-view of the Crime Scene

After guarding the scene of crime, expert investigators always like to have a *'Bird's Eye-View'* of the scene of crime. The purpose behind this is to get an overall picture of the scene of crime and to think deeply about the physical clues likely to be found at the scene of crime/on the victim etc. The *birds eye-view* is helpful to identify specific pieces of material evidence which are to be protected from being contaminated. *Contamination* means altering adding or destroying the material evidence in such a way as to affect the evidentiary value of such clues.

Thus the *bird's eye-view* refers to the investigating officer's look at the scene of crime to find out:

1. how the crime was committed;
2. the physical clues that are likely to be collected, packed and transported;
3. the experts to be contacted or called to the scene of offence;
4. what does and what does not form part of the subject matter under investigation;

INVESTIGATING OFFICER AT THE SCENE OF CRIME
(Points to Remember)

1. Was the scene of crime guarded when arrived?
2. If the scene of crime was not guarded, was the scene isolated? If so, by whom?
3. If the scene was isolated, how?
4. Were the time of departure from the station and the distance to the scene of crime, time of arrival at the scene of crime and the climatic conditions noted?
5. Is the victim to be examined for signs of life? If the victim has signs of life, what is to be done now?
6. Are the names and addresses of the witnesses and addresses of the bystanders who volunteer to give information regarding the incident noted? Who are the witnesses?
7. Are the suspects/culprits at the scene of crime detained? Who are they?
8. Did any unauthorized persons enter the scene of crime before the arrival? Who were they and for what purpose?
9. Are the public allowed to discuss the case with the suspect and the witnesses to the suspect? If so why?
10. Who are the police officers who assist you at the crime scene? Who were the police officers, if any, who visited the scene before? Do you make any requisition to police officers, draftsman, experts, doctors etc. and for what purpose? Do you inform your superior officers about the nature of the crime and the help required?
11. Do you discuss elaborately the case with suspects/complainants/victims/witnesses/onlookers/pressmen at the scene of crime? What was the matter discussed? And why did you discuss them?

5. what method of search to be employed for the collection of physical clues etc.

Physical Evidence – Protection

The investigator has to take the following precautions to see that the physical clues available at the scene of crime are not disturbed or contaminated. Such precautions include:

1. Taking careful stock of the situations, and acting methodologically and with care and caution. Isolate the scene of crime too much rather than too little.
2. Nothing at the scene of crime should be moved or in any way interferred with. If any physical clue is found to be likely to fade because of the atmospheric conditions, e.g., finger print on an article, then take them to a safe place. Be able to account for the position and condition of the article when it is so removed.

Usually the sub-inspector of police (crime-investigator) is accompanied by a head constable and one or two other constables. The investigating officer, on no account, shall permit the head constable or the constables to perform the task he is supposed to do. The head constable is only a help to the investigator. The investigator as said earlier, decides firmly when, why and who should enter the scene and under no circumstances should allow the head constable or constables to start independent searches and enquiries. The investigating officer should never leave the scene until the complete inspection is over. In case of emergency, he can send a constable or a civic-minded citizen for getting things done. The investigating officer should see to it that the doors, windows, stair-cases, lightings, routes of ingress or engress are preserved in their original condition till the examination is finalized. If police dogs are to be brought, he should take note of items which are to be smelled by the dogs for purpose of tracing. If the dogs do not reach in time, the items must be preserved. In such instances, see that the persperation is not transferred to the article.

Since the weather is likely to ruin the persperation left by the culprit, see that it is kept in a place where the atmospheric conditions do not affect them.

The investigator or the photographer has to photograph every item and its location fixed in the crime scene sketch. Do not move anything until the photograph and sketching are over. After deciding upon the plan of action at the scene of crime, the crime investigator can detail his assistants for specific duties in connection with the inspection of the crime scene and search for clues. The investigation officer now should brief his assistants about the specific tasks they should perform. He guides and supervises performance and coordinates the work of all his assistants.

Photographs and Sketches

'A picture is worth a thousand words' – and therefore every scene of crime should be photographed before sketch is drawn and the inspection is conducted. The photographs are important because:

1. *It Refreshes the Investigator's Memory*

An investigator gets the chance of visiting and inspecting the crime scene only once. Immediately after the inspection, he can very well recollect many things but as time elapses, he starts forgetting at least minute details at any scene of crime. His pre-occupation with other duties—like law and order, patrolling, petition enquiry, investigation of many other crimes —usually obliterates the vivid memory he has had at the initial stage. Together with the sketches and accurately written documents at the crime scene the photographs provide a permanent visual record of the entire things which were seen only once at the inspection of the crime scene.

2. *To Brief Newly Assigned Investigators*

It so happens that the investigators are transferred very often and more often than not, the same investigator cannot and does not complete the investigation which he has initiated already. The investigation reports and sketches, however elaborate they may be, cannot substitute photographs. Therefore to brief the newly assigned investigators about a crime scene, photographs are of immense utility. It happens sometimes that the cases are transferred to Crime Detachment Units or Crime-Investigation Branch (C.I.D.). In such cases no doubt the photographs are of invaluable assistance to the newly assigned officers.

3. *To Exhibit as an Evidence*

1. The law admits photographs as evidence. Instances are reported in which cases were thrown out merely because photographs were not produced. As an evidence in a Court of Law, Photographs can prove many things: viz., The photograph of the corpse can reveal how was the face of the deceased? showing fear? surprise? hatred? or contempt and also the position in which it was lying, post-mortem stains, etc. In suicidal cases it is very important to show the face of the dead.
2. The photographic camera sees farther than the human eye can and howsoever carefully the scene might have been observed and particulars noted down by the investigator, still somethings may escape human vision and observation. Photographs do preserve the perishable things for ever and are objective and always impartial. Perishable evidence like wounds, traces of resistance, scratches, swollen flesh, strangulation marks etc. on human body are imprinted and preserved well through photographs. Eye-witnesses may lie, but a photograph does not.
3. *Modus-operandi* (e.g., man-hole made or window bars removed), type—impressions, tool and skid marks, foot prints, finger prints, bullet holes, injuries on human body etc. cannot be sometimes picked up easily. Photographs are of immense aid in such cases.
4. Sometimes photographs taken at the scene of crime can be used for comparison purposes in the Forensic Science Laboratory.

5. The judges often do not visit or inspect the scene of crime. No doubt, the judges can visualize the details of crime-scenes if photographs are produced. Most of the prosecutors and investigating officers may find it extremely difficult to describe minutely a scene of crime and if at all they explain the details meticulously, it will be arduous for a judge to form a mental image or picture from the descriptions given by the prosecutor/investigator and to retain them for long. A few well chosen photographs taken from different angles can undoubtedly create the mental reconstruction of the scene by any judge hearing a case.

Crime Scene – Camera

A handy 35 m.m. camera is more than enough for most of the work at the scene of crime. If only a 35 m.m. camera is found to be not satisfactory, then one may need a studio camera. The 35 m.m. camera should have all the necessary accessories such as (i) wide angles lens; (ii) telephoto lens; (iii) close-up attachment; (iv) flash gun; (v) photo-flood lamps; (vi) exposure meter; and (vii) collapsible stand. Most of the police departments in India have Photography Units and well trained police photographers. Besides, the investigating officers are also trained in the use of camera. If police photographer is not easily available and if the investigating officer is quite ignorant of handling a camera, then a professional photographer can be called for. Remember that a photographer is an expert and he is examined later in the court of law. Hence the photographer should be a qualified person. Nevertheless, a professional photographer who has 25 years of experience in photography can be considered as an expert even without any academic qualifications.

As far as possible, the photographs should express the natural scene of crime as it appears to be. The use of wide angle lenses or unusual angles should as far as possible be avoided. The photographs need not exceed a size of 8" × 10".

Photographs at the Scene of Crime

Photographs at the scene of crime are of four types. They are (i) general photographs (over-all photographs); (ii) medium view photographs; (iii) close-up photographs; and (iv) very close-up photographs.

General View Photographs

This is also called the *Bird's Eye-View* photograph. It includes the photograph of the surrounding territory—in other words, it should show the scene of crime with respect to neighbourhood in which the crime was committed. The photographs are used to identify the locality in question and will help to orient the judge as to the surrounding terrain.

Medium View Photographs

They include those photographs taken within 10-20' of the object. They will show the specific object desired. It may be taken from the places of entrance or exit to the scene of crime and will be sufficient as to enable the judge to tie them in with the general view photographs.

Close-up Photographs

The close-up photographs should clearly show some particular item of interest. It can be a knife, a gun, a tool–mark on a window, a foot print on the exit or anything of special interest. They should generally be taken at distance of 4 – 6' and should include some identifiable object or article of evidence.

Very Close-up Photographs

These photographs are taken at a distance of one foot or less from the object as the case may be. It is to show the scratch marks, minute spurts of blood or other characteristics too small to be distinctly shown in the close-up photographs. A photograph taken in this way should include a rule or scale so that the final print may be accurately reproduced for comparison.

Sketching the Scene of Crime

Photographs are two dimensional pictures while a crime–scene sketch is three dimensional. As such, all the advantages of a three dimensional picture are possible for a crime–scene sketch. The sketch indicates the inter–distances between relevant objects and also it is devoid of superfluous detail which may be seen in a photograph.

Sketches are of two types – (i) *rough sketch* of the scene of crime, and (ii) sketching the *crime scene on scale.* The former is prepared by the investigating officer himself at the scene of crime and the latter may be prepared either by himself or by a draftsman under his personal supervision. The details in the rough sketch should be transferred to the sketch on scale. The following principles should be observed while sketching the scene of crime:

1. The sketch should be prepared at the scene of crime and never in the office or at residence of the investigating officer.
2. Distances should be measured exactly by the help of a scale or tape.
3. Directions should be made clear. For this purpose, mariner's compass should be used.
4. As stated by the Supreme Court in several decisions, superfluous materials should not be introduced into the sketches.
5. Symbols, letters or digits and legends can be used to avoid crowding.
6. Spots from where photographs are taken should be indicated in the sketch.

A rough sketching does not need elaborate equipments. A drawing board, a white sheet of paper, pencil, rubber eraser, measuring tape etc. are necessary for the purpose.

Richard H. Ward writes about the uses of sketches as: [2]

1. While crime scene sketches are most commonly used as visual aids in court room presentation, the investigator should be aware that they can be of assistance during the investigation. Combined with photographs, sketches may be used to analyse the scene or to determine the relative probability of various aspects concerning the scene.
2. Sketches might also be used to refresh the memory of the investigator or witnesses as well as to develop a clear understanding of the occurrence. For example, participants may be asked to indicate their positions and movements during the crime, as well as those of others. If a sketch is used the individuals can be asked to trace their actions on separate sketches. A comparative analysis of their sketches may then be used to develop inconsistencies that might not seem apparent in a verbal description.
3. In some crimes, the position of objects or items may be inconsistent with the statement of witnesses or may indicate a staged scene. Examples of this occur sometimes in apparent suicides. What may appear suicide may in fact be a murder. Thus the position of weapons, furniture or other items may be improbable and readily apparent in sketches. The distance of the chair from the deceased in a hanging may prove to be very important; in many such cases, this is not recorded because the investigator assumes that a suicide has taken place. However, later examination may reveal that murder is a possibility. In such cases, an adequate sketch can be an invaluable aid.
4. Body position may also prove important in homicide cases, the sketch being used to trace apparent movement or theoretical movement.
5. If a sketch has been prepared for use in court, the investigator should familarize himself with all its various

aspects. He should be familiar with the key or legend as well as various distances and other items that may be the subject of cross examination. In some instances, it may be advisable to prepare 'insets' or sketc hes of special aspects of the crime scene to clarify particular points.

6. Finally, the use of diagrammatic sketches illustrating position, movement or trajeitory can be prepared to clear up any misunderstanding that might result in the jurors' minds concerning a complex incident.

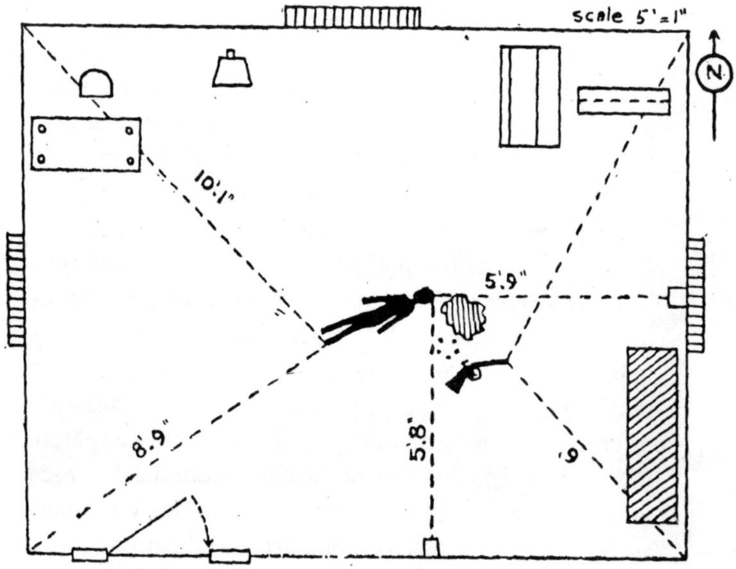

Fig. 4.1 : Sketching of a Scene of Crime

How to Prepare Sketches?

As stated earlier, sketches are of two types, viz., (i) rough sketches, and (ii) final or finished sketches on 'scale'.

Rough sketches are nothing but graphic notes prepared during the process of crime scene inspection. It is advisable to have three officers to share the work of rough sketching—here one can sketch, one can hold the end of the measuring tape and the third one can read out the measurements. The investigating officer should take the responsibility of sketching and others— i.e., the head constable and one of the constables should be asked to assist him as he directs them.

The investigating officer may have a smooth and plain paper (9" × 11") for drawing the sketch. Some firm support (a clipboard is enough) should be used for the paper to be fixed on it. A sharply cut pencil can be used for the sketching work because sometimes changes and corrections will have to be made. The officer, it must be borne in mind, should make all alterations to the sketch before he leaves the scene. He can use a ruler or other straight edge or drafting instruments for the purpose. Use only a steel tape measure (the advantage is that it does not stretch like a cloth or fabric tape) having 100 feet length. This can be usefully employed both for indoor and outdoor scenes of crime. For measuring short or very short distances or awkward places, a straight ruler can be used.

See that the same officer reads all distances measured with the tape. After announcement of the distances by the 'reading officer' the investigating officer (here the sketching officer) should loudly announce the measurements heard by him back so that accuracy is ensured before he writes the measurements on the sketch.

Sequence of Measurements

The following sequence should be followed to prepare the sketches. The officers first measure and record the position of all fixed objects within the scene of crime. This will include walls, windows, doors, built-in-appliances and furniture, hall ways and stair walls etc. in an indoor scene of crime. Paved streets and highways, telephone, or electricity poles, man-holes, parking meters, trees, building exteriors and bodies of water etc. will include in an outdoor scene of crime. When the measurement of permanent features or fixtures is over and is recorded, the remaining items of importance in an inspection are filled in, using the fixed points

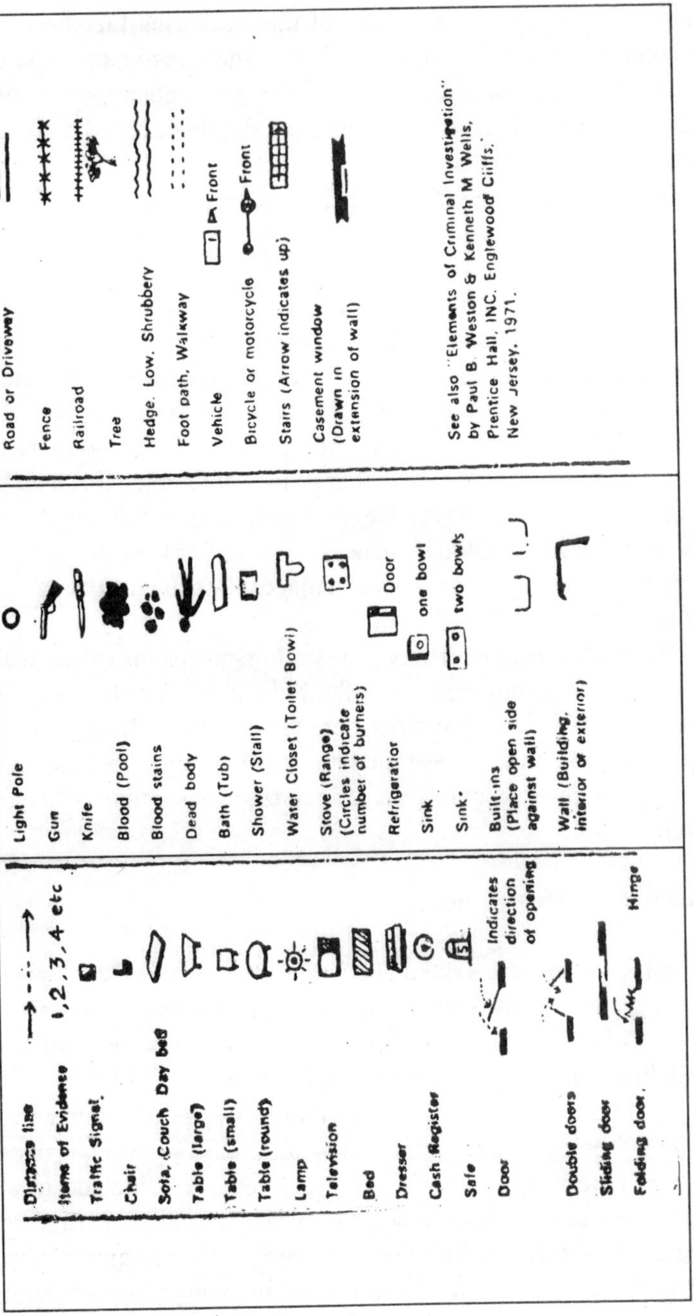

Fig. 4.2 : Graphic Symbols – Crime Scene Sketching

for reference in locating the movable articles. How to locate these movable items is discussed later in this chapter.

The rough sketch is not prepared on scale. But remember that it should as far as possible be relatively proportional. (For example a room 20' × 15' should have its long side about a third again as long as the short side). This will surely help the investigating officer to appreciate better the spatial relationships in a more or less realistic way.

The units of measurements should be uniform all throughout the crime scene sketch. Never use yards in measuring the outside dimensions of a room and then use feet and inches to measure the inside of the scene of crime. The investigating officer can use any convenient unit, preferably feet and inches. The sketch should contain the following information.

1. Title of the sketch..
2. Crime No.............and Section of law.............................
3. Police station...
4. Name of the officer making the sketch..............................
5. Names of the officers taking measurements/assisting.........
6. Date and time the sketch was started.................................
7. Indicate the direction of north..
8. Location identification...
9. Scale...
10. Legends identifying all items of evidence should be shown in the sketch. Items placed in the sketch are identified with a key letter or number. They are put at the bottom (side of the sheet) followed by a description of the item.

    In the court the defence may need original field-sketch prepared by the investigating officer. Hence care should be taken to see that the field-sketch prepared by the investigating officer is not mutilated, altered or destroyed.

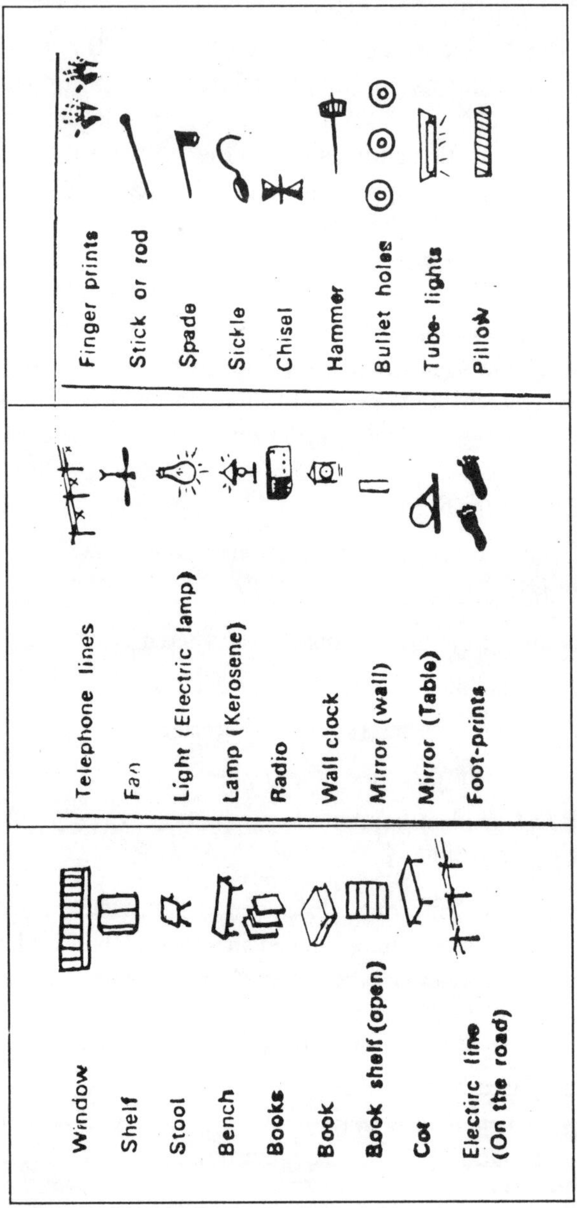

Fig. 4.3 : Graphic Symbols – Crime Scene Sketching

Final Sketches

Basing on the rough sketch, the final sketch is prepared. It is neat, precise, accurate and large with straight lines, square corners and uniform letterings. The investigating officer if he resorts to the services of a plan-drawer, or of a draftsman, his name should be written in the final sketch and invariably be attested by the investigating officer as to the correctness/truthfulness of the final sketch as accurately, precisely and truthfully representing the scene. This should be done only after meticulously comparing and checking the final sketch with the rough sketch.

The final sketch should be prepared to a certain scale— all distances should be precisely proportional and depict true spacial relationships. To scale means that if the scale is 5'= 1" then; 5 inches in the sketches will represent 25 feet at the scene of crime. And the size of the paper will decide the scale to be used. Use the largest scale possible so that the sketch will be clear and beautiful Graph papers no doubt greatly facilitate entering measurements. The finished sketch, when made ready, should be introduced into evidence.

Measurement Technique

The sketch should have measurements of distances between an item of interest or importance and some fixed points at the scene of crime. The measurements between two movable items at the scene serve no useful purpose and likewise is the case between an item of evidence and another easily movable point. Hence measure an item of evidence only from two permanent fixtures at the scene of crime (see Fig.4.4).

Perpendicular Distance Method

This method locates an item of evidence by measuring the distance to the material object along a line extending at right angles from a wall or other straight line. The perimeter of the crime scene can be taken for the purpose of measuring the distance. Measure

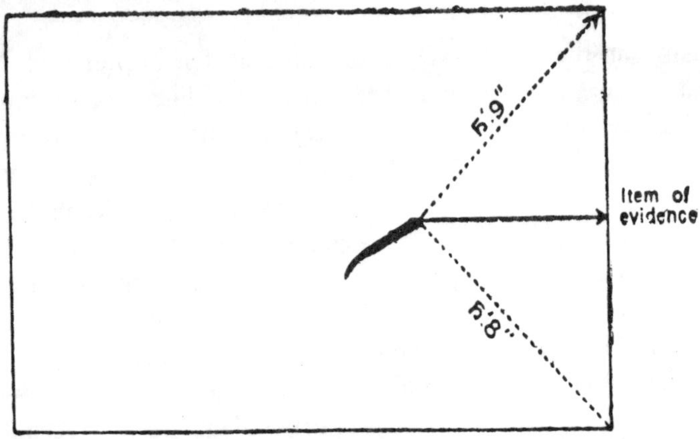

Fig. 4.4 : Measurements to the item of evidence are taken from two corners of the room

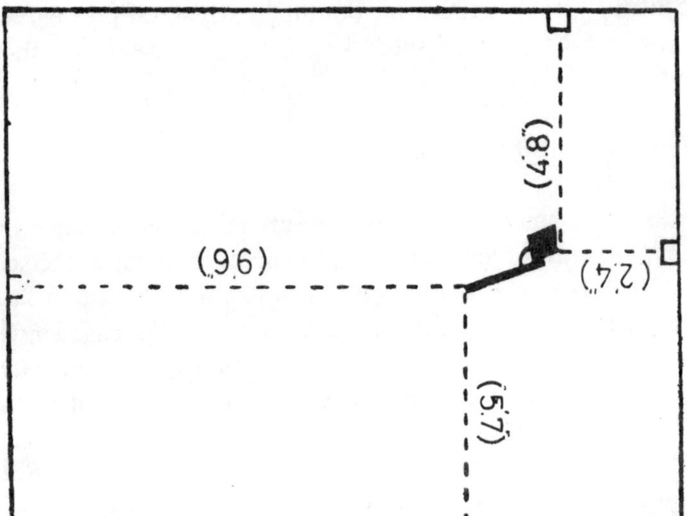

Fig. 4.5 : Showing perpendicular distance method of locating an item of evidence

the distance from two points to correctly locate any one point within the scene and in so doing measurements should be made from surfaces at right angles to each other.

In measuring distances remember that one point will be enough to locate the evidence within the sketch if the item is small. On the contrary, if the item has length, then (e.g., dead body, knife, sickle etc.,) take two points (see Fig. 4.5), to correctly locate the item. In Fig. 4.5 the both ends of a piece of evidence are located. Special mention should be made in the notes if an object could be placed on the floor with one or more sides facing up, about the side which was up when the item was found.

Base-Line Method

This method is employed usually in out door scenes of crime where one can find straight perimeter boundaries. Here, draw a straight line through the scene and consider it to be the base-line. All measurements can be taken from this base line. When base-line is drawn, the investigator must make special note of the location of both ends of the base-line for future references. One end of the base-line should be designated as the starting point. Each point within the sketch should be described by measuring two distances. The first is the distance along the base-line from the starting point to a point where another line perpendicular to the base-line would meet the item of interest. The second distance should be along the line perpendicular to the base-line, extending from the point to be located to the base-line itself.

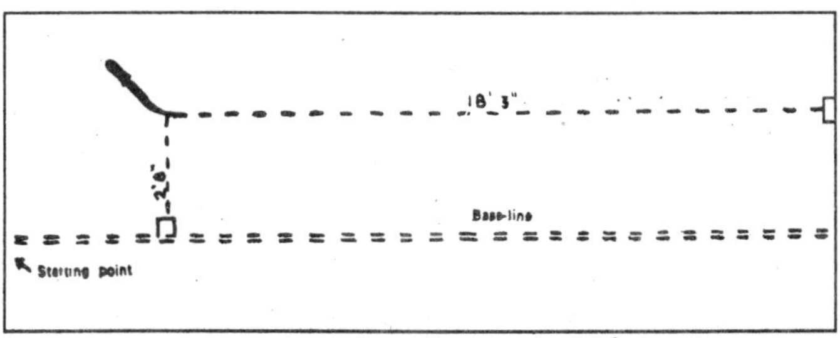

Fig. 4.6 : Base-line method of locating an item of evidence. If the item is large enough, take two points of the item to locate the evidence

Two Fixed Points Method

Many a time, determining right angles for each measurement will be difficult and time consuming. Therefore, it is better to take [illegible] two fixed points in the scene of crime. Here the investigator, while not bothering about the angles, has to see that the two points used as references are not too close ones to each other. In Fig. 4.4, the distances are taken from two corners of the room.

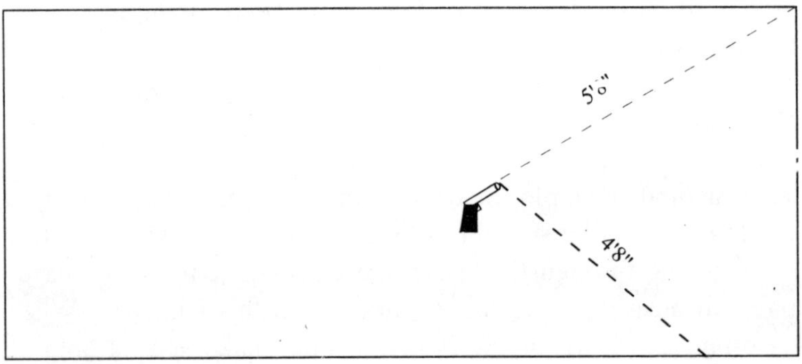

Fig. 4.7 : Incorrect use of two fixed points method for locating an item of evidence. Here, while the investigator has taken 'one fixed point' as the corner of the room, he has taken the other from a 'point' which is not clearly fixed.

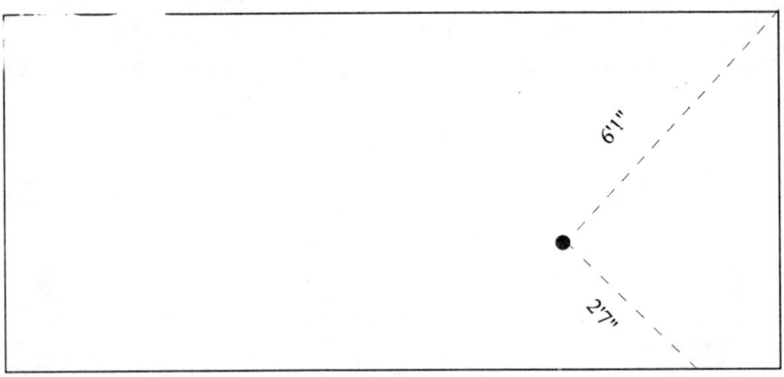

Fig. 4.8 : Here too one of the points is not clearly a fixed one.

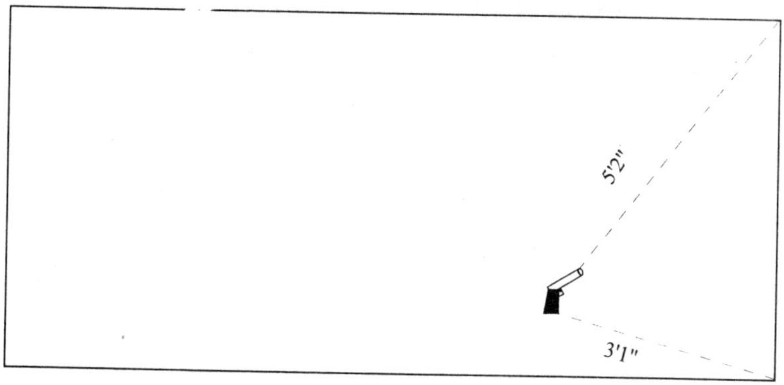

Fig. 4.9 : Since the item of evidence is a large one, the investigator should measure from two fixed points to one and the same point in the item of evidence.

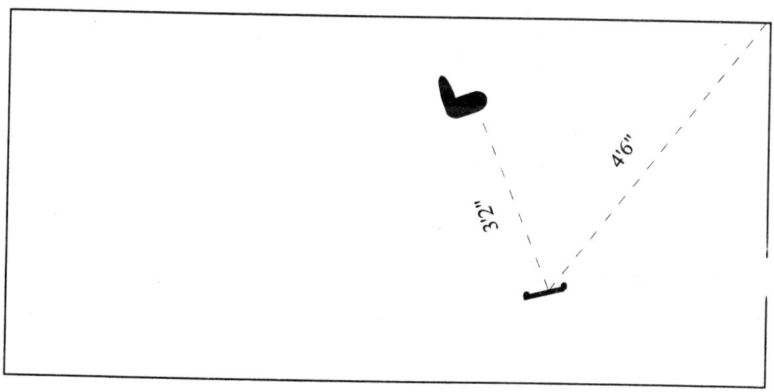

Fig. 4.10 : Incorrect use of two fixed points method of locating an item of evidence. Chair which is a movable item should not be taken as a fixed point to measure the distance.

CHECK LIST FOR CRIME SCENE SKETCH

1. Have you indicated the direction to the north?
2. Have you indicated the scale?
3. Have you used any legends? If so, have you given any numbers to them and have you indicated the items against the numbers? Have you given a brief description of the items against each one of them?
4. Have you marked the spots from where photographs were taken by A.B.C.D. etc.?
5. Have you exactly measured the distance of the evidence from corners? Or have you employed any other methods of measurements?
6. Have you written the title of the sketch?
7. Have you written crime number and section of law?
8. Have you written your name and the name of the draftsman if his services were used?
9. Have you attested the sketch if the services of the sketch drawer have been used?
10. Have you written the date and the time when the sketch was prepared?
11. Have you written the name of your assistants who helped you in measurements?
12. Any other information found to be relevant?

Procedure of Photographying and Sketching

After guarding and protecting the scene of crime and also taking a bird's eye-view and conducting a preliminary survey, the investigating officer can ask the photographer to take general view photographs. The investigating officer should tell him as to from which positions he should take the photographs. If the photographer can not transfer the entire scene with its background in the general view photograph in one film, the scene of crime may be divided into parts and he should take the general view photographs of the parts in such a way that when the photographs are put together, an over-all view of the scene of crime can be obtained. After taking the general view of the scene of crime, the photographer may be asked to retire from the scene until he is called for further services. The investigator should now prepare the rough sketch and then the photographer may be called to take the medium view photographs. The positions from where the photographs are taken should be clearly indicated in the sketch plan of the scene of crime. Care must be taken not to disturb the physical clues at the scene of crime when the medium size photographs are taken. Nothing should be altered until the inspection of the scene is made by the investigating officer. After taking the medium view photographs the photographer should be asked to retire from his works until he is again called for when the inspection of the scene of crime is done.

Sketching and Photographying of the Scene of Crime – Case Laws

1. "The sketch map would be admissible so far as it indicates all that the inspector saw himself at the spot, but any mark put on the sketch-map based on the statements made by witnesses to the inspector would be in admissible in view of the clear provisions of section 162 Cr. P.C. as it will be no more than a statement to the police during investigation."[3]
2. "The notes in question of the site plan were statements recorded by police officer in the course of investigation, and were hit by section 162 Cr. P.C. These notes could be used only for the purpose of contradicting the prosecution witness concerned in accordance with provisions of section 145 of the Evidence Act and for on other purpose."[4]

3. "The note on the site plan prepared by the investigating officer in according with the various situations pointed out to him by witnesses are statements recorded by the police officer in the course of investigation, and are hit by section 162".[5]
4. "It is a legal evidence, if the draftsman draws the plan after ascertaining from the witnesses where exactly the assailant and the victim stood etc., and the witnesses corroborate his statement in testimony."[6]
5. "The two negatives, i.e. one of the photo of the deceased and the other in respect of the skull found were then superimposed to determine the identity of the skull, the evidence is admissible under section 9 of the Evidence Act."[7]
6. "A sketch map of the scene of happening is an invaluable piece of evidence."[8]

SUGGESTED READINGS

Arther, Richard O, *"The Scientific Investigator"*, Charles C. Thomas, Springfield. Illinois, 1965.

Bailey, F. Lee & Rothblatt, Hery B. *"Investigation and Preparation of Criminal Cases: Federal and State"*, Lawyers Co-operative Publishing Company, Rochester, New York, 1970.

Bloch, Peter & James Bell, *"Managing Investigations: The Rochester System,* Urban Institute Police Foundation, 1975.

Bloch, Peter & Donald Weidman, *Managing Criminal Investigations"*, The Urban Institute, Washington D.C., 1975.

Deinstein, William, *"Techniques for the Crime Investigator"*, Charles C. Thomas, Springfield, Illinois, 1974.

Fricke, Charles W., *"Criminal Investigation"*, Revised by Le Roy M. Lolbrek, Legal Book Store, Los Angeles, 1962.

Gross, H., & R.L. Jackson, *Criminal Investigation"*, Sweet and Maxwell Ltd. London, 1962.

Inabau, Fred, & Andre A. Moenssens, & Louis R. Vitullo, *"Scientific Police Investigation"*, Chilton Book Company, Philadelphia, 1972.

International, Association of Chiefs of Police, *"Criminal Investigation"* I.A.C.P, Washington, D.C. 1971.

Jackson, Richard L. *"Criminal Investigation,"* Carswell Company, Toronto, Canada, 1962.

Jones, Leland, *"Scientific Investigation and Physical Evidence"*, Charles C. Thomas, Springfield, Illinois, 1959.

Kirk, Paul L. *"Crime Investigation,"* Interscience Publishers, Inc., New York, 1953.

Leibers, Arthur, *"The Investigators Hand Book"*, Arco Publishing Co., New York, 1972.

Mcintyre. Donald M., *et. el.* *"Detection of Crime,"* Little Brown and Co., Boston, 1967.

Paper, John P., *"Basic Criminal Investigation,"* California State Department of Education. Sacramento, California, 1956.

Paper, John P., *"Elements of Police Investigation,"* California Peace Officer's Training Series No. 25, California State Department of Education, Sacraments, California, 1964.

Rhodes, Henry T.F., *"Clues and Crime's: The Science of Criminal Investigation"* John Murray, London, 1963.

Richardson, James R., *"Scientific Evidence for Police Officers,"* W.H. Anderson, Co., Cincinnat:, 1963.

Samen, Charles, C., *"Major Crime Scene Investigation Basic Photography, Part II,"* Law and Order, September, 1971.

Samen, Charles, C., *"Major Crime Scene—Investigation – Sketching the Scene, Part III,"* Law and Order, October, 1971.

Svenarme, Arme, *"Technique of Crime Scene Investigation,"* American Elsevier Publishing Co., New York, 1965.

Venderbosch, Charles G., *"Criminal Investigation,"* I.A.C.P. Training Keys, Washington, D.C.V. 1968.

Weston, Paul B. and Kenneth Wells, *"Criminal Investigation: Basic Perspectives,"* Prentice-Hall, Engewood Cliffs, New Jersey, 1970.

REFERENCES

1. H.N. Rushbud *vs.* State of Delhi, A.I.R. 1955 S.C. 196: 1955 Cr. L.J. 526.
2. Rihard H. Ward, *Introduction to Criminal Investigation,* Addison Wesley Publishing Co., California, 1975.
3. Tori Singh *vs.* State of Uttar Pradesh, A.I.R. 1962 S.C. 399: 1962 (1) Cr. L.J. 469.
4. Jit Singh *vs.* State of Punjab, 1976 S.C. (Cr.) 341.
5. Jit Singh *vs.* State of Punjab, A.I.R. 1976 S.C. 1421: 1976 Cr. L.J. 1162.
6. Santa Singh *vs.* State of Punjab, A.I.R. 1956 S.C. 526.
7. Ram Lochan *vs.* State of West Bengal, A.I.R. 1963 S.C. 1074: 1963 (2) Cr. L.J. 170.
8. Ramlal *vs.* State, 1958 M.P. 380:1958 Cr. L.J. 1402: Drigpal Singh *vs.* State 1955 A.L.J. 112.

5

SCENE OF CRIME
Principles and Methods of Inspection

In the previous chapter, it has been brought out the need for taking of the photographs of the scene of crime by an expert photographer. Thus after taking only the general and medium view photographs, the investigating officer examines the various physical clues available at the scene of crime. When inspecting a scene of crime, the investigating officer should bear in mind certain general principles and methodology for inspection and search. This is important, otherwise the investigating officer may fail to achieve the desired objectives in inspection.

Locard's Principle of Exchange

The principle is that when things come into contact, there is always an exchange of material. The more the contact, the better is the exchange. In other words – contact exchanges traces.

Illustration

Locard's principle of exchange in a traffic accident scene can be illustrated as under.

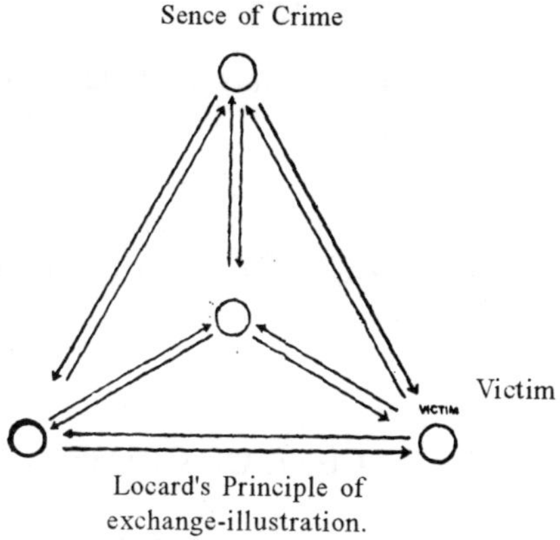

Fig. 5.1 : According to Locard's Principle, materials are exchanged among various articles or persons at the Scene of Crime

According to this principle when a criminal or his instruments come into contact with anybody/anything/any place, there is always an exchange of material, between the criminal/his instruments, and the person/thing/place as the case may be. In the above illustration traces are exchanged between the criminal (driver) and the victim; between the vehicle and the driver; between the victim and the vehicle; between the scene of crime and driver/vehicle/victim. This means that an investigating officer reaching at a scene of crime should seriously think over and over about the various persons/things/places that are likely to have come into contact and the traces that are likely to have been exchanged among them. To this end the investigating officer should have a thorough knowledge of the possible physical clues that are likely to have been exchanged among various items that have come into contact. The investigating officer should at the outset itself write down the traces he likes to look for at the scene of crime on every item that has come into contact with the criminal/his instruments. Dr. B. R. Sharma writes: "What are the places or objects with which the criminal and his tools actually came in contact? If the investigating officer is able to establish the points of contact, he is likely to reach to reap a rich harvest of physical clues."[1]

He says:

1. If a criminal enters the premises through a ventilator, he leaves his foot prints on the sill.
2. The burgler, who opens a safe by an explosive, leaves the area around and the clothes (including shoes) covered with insulating material as well as some exploded and unexploded explosive material.

QUESTIONS BY AN INVESTIGATING OFFICER AT THE SCENE OF CRIME

A. What are the traces likely to be exchanged between:

1. Criminal and the victim?
2. Criminal and the scene of crime?
3. Victim and the scene of crime?
4. Victim and the criminal?
5. Scene of crime and the criminal?
6. Scene of crime and the victim?

B. What are the traces likely to be exchanged between:

1. The tool and the criminal?
2. The tool and the victim?
3. The tool and the scene of crime?
4. The criminal and the tool?
5. The victim and the tool?
6. The tool and the scene of crime?

C. What else should be looked for? And why? And How?

Quatlet's Law of Individuality

The law is that nothing created by God or made by man is ever identical – In other words: *every object natural or man made has an individuality which is not duplicated in any other object.*

Identification is an important aspect in crime investigation.

The investigator has to identify the criminal, the victim, their associates, the tools used by them and their *modus operandi* etc. The principle – i.e., everything or everybody is individualistic in nature holds good for identification of persons, places and things. It is true that the grains of sand, seeds of plants, fabrics etc., may appear to be alike to the naked eye; but microscope examination can and will reveal that there exist formidable differences. Therefore whenever a physical clue is located, the investigating officer should ask to himself:

1. How is this crime committed and how does this particular physical clue become important in this case?
2. How is a particular weapon or instrument used to commit the offence?
3. How does the physical clue link the suspect to the scene of crime or vice versa. And how can the identity or the possible location of the culprit be established by this physical clue?
4. How best can this clue be used to form circumstantial evidence. And what are the motives behind the commission of this crime?

Law of Progressive Change

The law reads: *'Every thing' changes with the passage of time and the rate of change varies with different objects.* Changes may take place in the suspects/criminals, in the physical clues and other articles of evidence, in the witnesses/complainants, in the scene of crime/occurrence, in the police/prosecutors etc. This is the reason why it is suggested that the sooner the inspection is conducted, the better it is for the administration of criminal justice. One always says that justice delayed means justice denied.

(a) *The Criminal*

He undergoes progressive changes. He may consult legal experts and his version of the involvement may get changed. He may surrender before a Court of Law and try for an anticipatory bail.

Questions by an Investigating Officer about the Individuality of Criminal, Victim etc., to Physical Clues at the Scene of Crime

1. What is this physical clue and what does it indicate in this case?

2. How did it come to the scene and does it indicate anything as to when the crime was committed? Where the crime was committed? How the crime has been committed? Who committed the crime? Why the crime was committed? And what is the motive for committing the crime?

3. Does it show anything as to how the offender entered the scene of crime? How he escaped from the scene of crime? What method did he employ to commit the offence?

4. Does it indicate anything as to how best the crime can be proved by the help of this evidence in a court of law? (The words presence of, location of, size of, position of, use of, misuse of, etc. may be injected in each question to make things clearer. Surely these questions will help the investigating officer to establish the identity of persons, places, method etc. when inspecting a scene of crime).

He may attempt to exert influence upon the investigating officers, win over witnesses etc. Hence, if the crime-doer is not apprehended in time, he may become quite unrecognizable.

(b) *Physical Clues*

The finger prints, foot prints etc. at the scene of crime may be contaminated or destroyed if delay is there to conduct inspection of the scene of crime. Police dogs may be found useless as the smell of the suspects is not likely to last long on physical clues. Sharma writes, "the firearm barrels loosen, metal objects rust, the shoes suffer additional wear and tear and the tools acquire additional surface patterns. The degree of change depends upon the time the upkeep and the use or the misuse of the particular object. In course of time, the object may lose all practical identity vis-a-vis a particular time".[2]

(c) *Witnesses*

It is said: *Even God does not know how human mind works.* With the passage of time, several witnesses may turn hostile to police. They may be influenced, coerced, unduly remunerated by the culprit or his party. The same is the case with the victim too. The victim/his party may feel sympathy or even may attempt to reach a compromise with the culprit. Hence sooner the inspection of the scene of crime is conducted the better it is to interview the witnesses and thereby to elicit maximum information relating to crime and its criminal.

(d) *Scene of Crime*

No doubt the scene of crime will undergo rapid changes. The weather—rain or sun—may cause damages. If the onlookers and curious spectators visit the scene of crime, no doubt, it affects changes. This is the reason why it is insisted that the investigating officers should make arrangements to guard and protect the scene of crime if they are unable to conduct the inspection immediately after the receipt of information.

(e) *The Police*

The investigating officers too are amenable to earthly influences. Their attitudes and approach towards the victim and the criminal may be changed as time passes on.

Principle of Comparison

The principle is *only the likes can be compared.* This principle is important particularly when the investigating officer sends samples and specimens for comparison by a forensic expert. A few examples can be enumerated to make this principle clearer – i.e.,

1. In a murder case, a bullet is recovered from the deceased. The expert opines that the bullet has been fired from a firearm firing high velocity projectiles like a service rifle. It is futile to send shot guns, pistols or revolvers as the possible suspect firearm.
2. The questioned document is found to have been written with a ball pen. To send fountain pen as the likely instrument of writing futile.[3]

Principle of Analysis

The principle is: *The analysis can be no better than the sample analysed.* In other words *'garbage in, garbage out'.* This principle emphacizes the necessity of correct handling, sampling, packing, and transporting of physical clues for expert examination.

Illustrations

1. In a case of alcoholic poisoning, there is no use in sending the vicera in rectified spirit.
2. The investigator sees a finger print on an article at the scene of crime. While handling it, he damages the print, yet sends

it to the expert. Identification is not possible.

3. Blood, semen, soil, glass fragments are put in one packet. On transit, the packet gets broken. The analysis does not yield good result.

Law of Probability

The law is: *All identification—definite or indefinite, are made consciously or unconsciously, on the basis of probability.* For example, the finger prints are identified on the basis of the law of probability and so is the case with the analysis of blood, in the case of determining paternity in disputed cases.

An unknown woman is found murdered. The corpse has one gold plated tooth, a tatoo scar on its left hand and a healed fracture of collar bone. A woman with those characteristics is reported missing. What is the probability of the corpse being of the missing woman? If the occurrence of gold plated teeth in the area is in 5000, collar bone fracture is in 2000 and tatoo-scars is 1 in 100, the chances of the corpse being of another woman are 1 in 10,000,000,000.[4]

Scene of Crime—Locating of Physical Clues

According to Locard's principle of exchange the purpose of inspecting the scene of crime is to find out and collect materials that have been exchanged among objects, persons and places. Hence the information that can be obtained from a scene of crime can be divided principally into four categories:

1. Physical clues left by the criminal at the scene of crime.
2. Physical clues transferred to the criminal by the crime scene.
3. Materials, their location and position affected by the commission of crime.
4. Evidence or information that is ancillary to the crime.

Inspection — Process and Methods

Process means the procedure — i.e., proceeding in a systematic or planned way. Each step is taken with meticulous care and each physical clue is handled without contaminating it. The physical clues are available only once and if the investigating officer alters, adds or destroys the pieces of evidence, it means that its evidentiary value is lost for ever. Likewise, overlooking the physical clue by carelessness or pre-occupation with other things makes the whole purpose of search futile.

Grave crime scenes must be inspected by a team of officers– of course under the close supervision of the investigating officer. The investigating team may consist of finger print experts, technicians from Forensic Science Laboratory, note taker, interviewer and the sketch artist. As stated in the previous chapter, the officers should not be allowed to take up independent searches and enquiries. The role of the investigating officer includes assigning and directing the personnel in the team and thereby assuring the maximum success and systematic procedure for search. He must co-ordinate the activities for all personnel in the team. Some times, it so happens that superior police officers come to the scene when the search is in full swing and more often than not, they assume to themselves the responsibility of investigating the crime. This is indeed bad and superior police officers should allow, in all fairness, the investigating officer to carry on his search without being distrubed. However, he can tell the investigating officer to do something in a specific way, but if the investigating officer shows the least resistance or reluctance to abide by the instructions the superior police officer should in all fairness show due regard to his sentiments, for he is the man who knows what they have done, why they have done so and what more remains to be done.

Methods of Search – Where to Search for?

Before proceeding to search, the investigating officer must know what to search and should form a mental picture as to where to search. The actual search should be conducted only after deciding upon these aspects of crime investigation.

Sl. No.	*What to Look for?*	*Where to Search for?*
1.	Finger Prints.	a) Doors, windows, knobs and handles, glass panes, polished surfaces and locks. b) Transport vehicles – Their doors and handles, steering wheels and mirrors. c) Tumblers, plates, saucers, bottles, cups, spoons, utensils, boxes, furniture, rexine, plastic goods, purses, bags, letters, currency notes, tools, weapons of offence, torch, cells, lantern, watch, etc.
2.	Blood stains, liquor blood, semen, seminal stains, urine, saliva, milk, perspiration, vomitus and purge.	Scene of crime, corpse, victim, criminal, clothes of victim, criminal's objects and articles of furniture.
3.	Documents such as account books cheques receipts, bills, files, books, applications, letters, forms, pens, carbon papers, typewriters, sealing wax, seal stamps, erasers, photographs, and other objects.	In all cases involving documents these items should be searched for in places where they are likely to be found or hidden.
		TYPE OF OFFENCE
4.	Exploded products, fuses, tins, explosives, devices, photographs, objects.	In all cases involving explosives, the search should be conducted at the scene of crime and the places of manufacture, storage etc.
5.	Hairs, fibres, strings, ropes, thread, cloth, rags, leaves, and wood.	Offences against human body textiles, suicides etc.
6.	Bullets, pallets, wads, gunpowder, objects bearing gun firemarks, Photographs, post-mortem reports, guns and their parts.	Offences involving firearms.
7.	Blood, urine, breath, liquor, bottles, tumblers.	Offences against human body, offences against liquor laws, suicides etc.
8.	Bottles, capsules, pills, powders, seeds, leaves, food, fruit, liquor, sweet, tumblers.	Toxicological cases.
9.	Objects, photographs, tools, jimmies, knives and spades.	Cases having tools and tool impressions.
10.	Broken or separated parts, glass, paints, grease, oil, stains, skid, marks, other objects and samples for drunkenness.	Vehicle accidents.

When the search is made, care should be taken to find visible, plastic, and latent prints; and in the case of foot prints, look for surface and semi-sunken prints. Search also should be made for ash, buttons, bricks, cigerettes, earth etc. How should the investigating officer handle, pack and transport these items are dealt with extensively in the next chapter.

Crime Scenes and Methods of Search

As pointed out in the last chapter, a scene of crime may be a room, a cellar or a roof. It can be a road or a road side, an open field, a jungle, a hill, a mountain, a stream, a river, a vehicle, a boat, a train or an aeroplane. Every scene of crime presents physical clues only once and therefore if the inspection is not conducted carefully and minutely, the wealth of information is likely to be lost for ever. The crime scenes are divided into:

1. *Indoor scene of crime* – i.e., inside a room, in a vehicle, train or boat etc.
2. *Outdoor scene of crime* – i.e., on the road, road-sides, open field, jungle etc.
3. *Mobile scene of crime* – i.e., if the items of evidence are seen moving in water, in a stream or river etc.

Depending upon the type of the scene of crime, the investigating officer plans for a thorough search so that all possible evidence is located and collected. A thorough search means a very methodical search. The scene of crime is not confined within the limits of immediate location. It can extend to as much of its surrounding as would enable the investigating officer to appreciate fully the circumstances for the commission of a particular crime. It includes the way of approach and retreat of the culprit. At times it so happens that one and the same crime may have both indoor and outdoor scenes. The investigating officer should therefore inspect very carefully every inch in the scene no matter, where he begins his search, in what direction he conducts his search or where he stops his search.

The method of search usually depends upon:

1. the size or the area of the scene.
2. the nature of the crime.
3. the number of officers conducting the search.

No one can say that a particular method of search is better than other types. One officer may employ spiral search (clock-wise or anti-clock wise) while another may choose to perform a wheel search. So long as the search yields good results — i.e., locating items of evidence, the technique is of a secondary importance.

Random Search

In random search, the investigating officer follows no systematic or methodological pattern. Here, he enters the scene of crime and goes to the first point of interest. When that is over, he walks to the next item of evidence and the process goes on until he thinks that the search is some what over. The author has personally witnessed some of the investigating officers doing random search at very important scenes of crime. At times the head constables who are to assist the investigating officer conducts independent random search, some superior police officers also do the same thing. With such a search the author has seen that the investigator covering the same area three or more times leaving many other parts of the crime scene unexamined. The investigator's overenthusiasm to locate a particular piece of evidence which captures his attention first may cause other items of evidence to literally be lost or overlooked as the investigating officer rushes into the first point of interest. The random search has no pattern to adhere to and therefore it is said to be the poorest of all types of searches and should be discouraged.

Spiral Method of Search

Here the investigating officer makes an ever-widening circle movement in which he starts at the focal point of the scene and circles outward until the friges of the guarded area are reached. The spiral search can also be conducted in such a way that it begins at the outside of the scene and works inwards. Normally this is not employed as one finds it to-be better to begin at the centre of the scene and slowly searching outward in a continuous and ever widening circular path. The search may be conducted either in the clockwise or anti-clockwise direction. Another advantage of the search begun from the centre of the scene is that most of the items of evidence are likely to be seen in or around the centre and therefore a search from the centre can, no doubt, yield quick results.

The spiral method of search is recommended for indoor scenes of crime. It can also be successfully employed for outdoor scenes of crime if the area to be searched is small. However the search should not be conducted by more than one or two officers. If more than two officers conduct the search by this method, there is likelihood for a large number of officers to crowd at the centre of the scene of crime. This can contaminate the material clues available at the scene.

Spiral Search

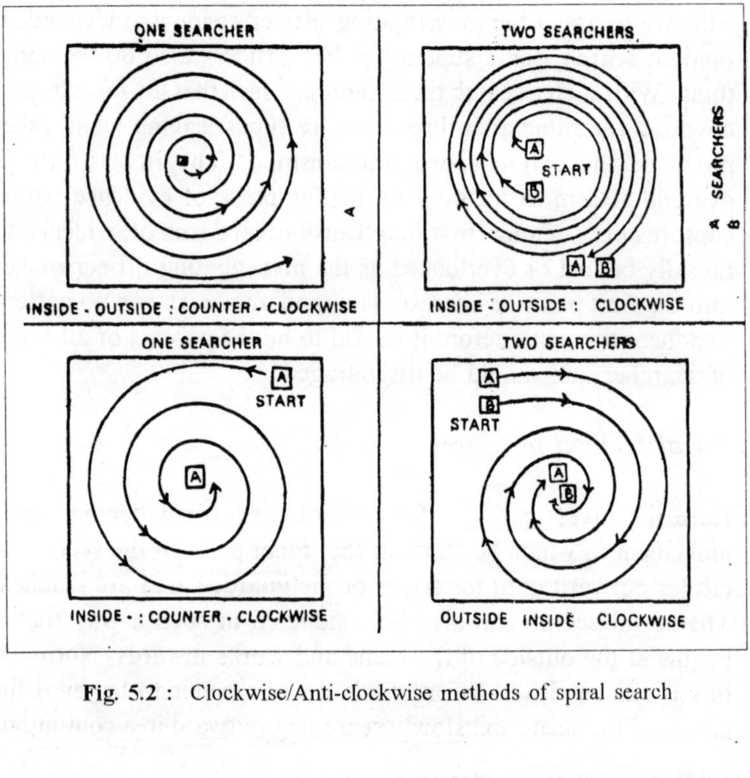

Fig. 5.2 : Clockwise/Anti-clockwise methods of spiral search

Concentric Circle Zones

Spiral method of search can also be employed for searching larger outdoor scenes. Here the area is divided into smaller sections – i.e., concentric circles as sub-divisions. Here a circle, perhaps 8 or 9 yards in diameter is drawn around the centre of the scene. Around that are drawn additional circles taking the same centre as the point, but having a larger radius and the process continues until the perimeter of the scene has been reached.

The central area of the scene may also be searched by using spiral method, following by strip searches of the outer rings.

Strip Method of Search

This is a sector search in which the crime scene is subdivided into segments, each of which searched as an individual unit. This method of search is useful for both indoor and outdoor scenes of crime. But, the outdoor scenes of crime are usually searched by strip method. The method works well if the area to be searched is square or rectangular in shape with clearly marked boundaries. The search may be conducted by one officer, a small group of officers or even by a large number of searchers—depending upon the size of the area to be searched.

Here the area is plotted like a foot-ball field. The search begins at one side and the investigator moves back and forth across the field from one end to the other until every inch is meticulously searched.

While dividing the area into lanes, usually four to seven feet wide, depending upon the area to be searched and the type of evidence to be sought and it may be remembered that the narrower is the lane, the better it is for a thorough search. It would ensure all items of evidence without missing anything. It is advisable that the lanes are to be marked off with rope, twine, or cloth tape laid on the surface or tied to stakes.

Before the search begins it is necessary that unwanted people are prevented from entering the area under search.

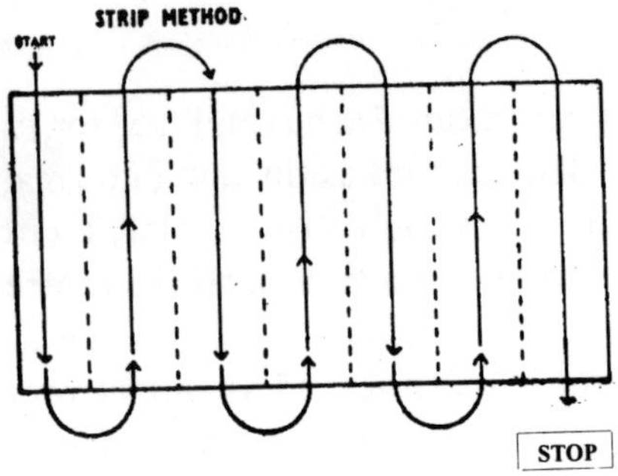

Fig. 5.3 : Strip Method of Search

The searchers line up side by side with appropriate interval between them. One searcher is enough in a particular lane. Upon signal, they walk towards the other end of the scene in straight lines, searching as they walk. When they reach the other end of the scene of crime they move to new lanes and walk back towards the starting point. The process is repeated until the search is over.

Double Strip Method

This method is otherwise called grid search. In this, two strip searches are conducted, the second at right angles to the first. This method proves to be more practical where special lane markers are not laid out-in other words, when the search follows imaginary or pre-existing lines.

Double Strip Method of Search or Grid Search

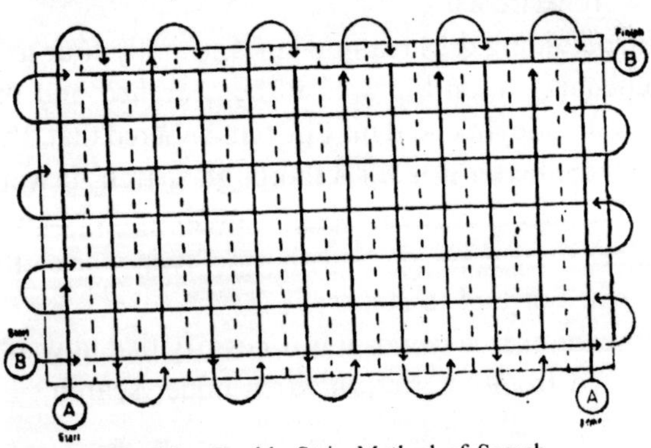

Fig. 5.4 : Double Strip Method of Search

The advantage of grid search is that it permits the searchers to inspect one and the same area twice. It is quite possible that the first searcher does not see everything on his inspection, but the second searcher may find some valuable piece of evidence as he looks at the same area from a different direction and angle. Hence, the chances of overlooking an item of evidence are comparatively less in this method than the same in single strip method.

Double Reverse Strip Search

In this method two officers start their first pass as shown in Fig. 5.5.

Double Reverse Strip Search

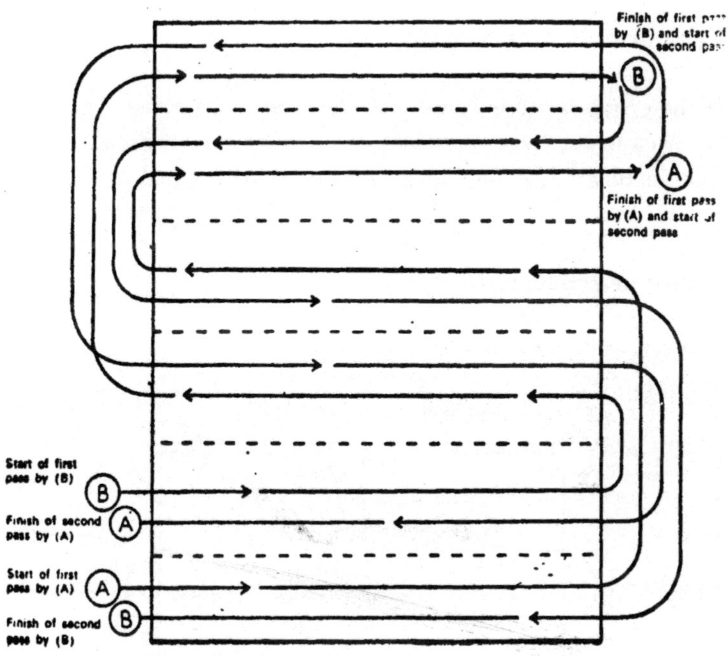

Fig. 5.5 : Double Reverse Strip Method of Search

The searchers continue their search by strip method until they inspect the whole area i.e., beginning from the lower left corner, they proceed from left to right and reach the upper right hand corner. Reaching at the upper right hand corner, they finish their first pass and then the two searchers change lanes there so that each one of them occupies the lane originally searched by the other during the first pass. They now face the opposite direction from that of the original search during the first pass. Upon signal, they conduct the search by strip method, but any given lane is now being searched in the opposite direction by the other searcher. This method eliminates the chances of any evidence being overlooked by the officer who conducts the original search. Also, it provides an opportunity for conducting a thorough search of one and the same area by two officers in the opposite direction.

Zone or Sub–area Search

If the crime scene is large and the number of officers to search the area is small, it is advisable to divide or sub-divide the area into smaller zones. Any of the previously described methods may be employed to inspect the area.

Wheel or Pie Search

The wheel method of search is employed to inspect large outdoor scenes.

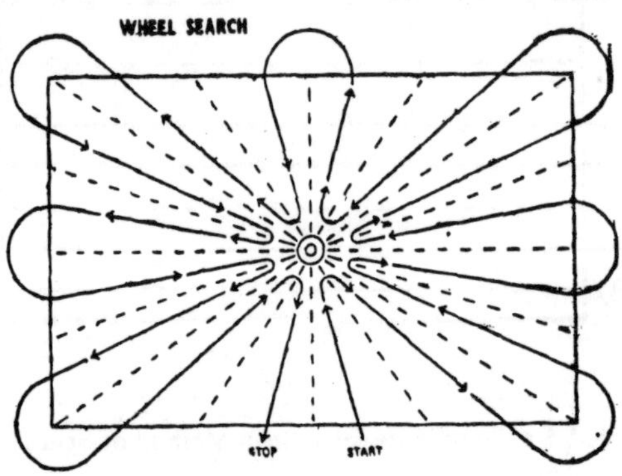

Fig. 5.6 : Wheel or Pie Method of Search

Here the lines are drawn out from the centre point (just like the slices of a pie or the spokes of a wheel) and then each of the wedges is inspected separately or individually. The search begins at the centre and proceeds outward. The method proves to be useful particularly for those crime scenes in which there are different routes of entry and exit.

Close-up and very Close-up Photographs

While the search is in progress, the investigator should, wherever necessary, take close-up and very close-up photographs. In taking very close-up photographs, a measuring tape or scale should be placed where the measurement becomes important. For example, the knifes, wounds, foot-prints etc., should be photographed by keeping the tape/scale in such a way that the length of the item of evidence can be shown clearly in the photographs.

Techniques of Search

The investigator should bear in mind the following guidelines when he conducts crime-scene searches.

1. Take detailed notes of significant details found at the crime scene. Mark the location of each piece of evidence as it is seen by the investigator.
2. Take the photographs (close-up or very close-up photographs) wherever necessary before moving any item of evidence.
3. First make a search for finger prints.
4. Search from the ground to up. Small pieces of evidence are likely to be seen on the ground. Hence the floor or the ground surface of the crime scene assumes greater importance for the search to begin with. Cleaning of all items of evidence and possession of them from the ground surface eliminate the possibility of the evidence being contaminated by stepping on the evidence. If carpet or rug is spread, lift it and examine so that anything which is likely to be underneath can be located. Lifting of the carpet shall be done only after examining the upper side carefully.

5. After inspecting the ground surface of the scene of crime, extend the search to the area from the floor level to approximately waist height. This would mean that the search should be made beneath chair cushions, insides of cabinets, behind the cabinets, desks, backs and bottoms of drawers etc. Search should be made for finger prints, blood stains, bullet holes or any such valuable pieces of evidence and also for inconspicuous forms of evidence.
6. After this, the search should be extended to the area from waist height to ceiling. Inspect the area behind pictures, clocks, book-cases, lamps etc.
7. Finally the ceiling or the roof should be searched.
8. If a team of searchers are employed, the entire searching operation should be commanded by the chief investigator or superior officer. When one of the searchers locates an item of evidence he should loudly announce its recovery for the benefit of his colleagues.
9. Make full, detailed and accurate description of all items of evidence recovered from the scene of crime. This will surely enable the investigating officer to subsequently identify an item of evidence, if that is necessary, from the detailed notes that he has prepared.
10. Some markings should be made on each item of evidence for the purpose of identification later in a court of law. Such markings are given below.

MINIMUM MARKING TO BE MADE ON EACH ITEM OF EVIDENCE FOR IDENTIFICATION PURPOSES*

---

1. Initials of the investigating officer recovering the evidence.
2. Date of recovery.
3. The crime number.
4. An additional code letter or number if the object is one of a series of similar or identical objects. This is necessary for the purpose of individual identification of the item of evidence.

---

* The markings should be permanent and should be on the object itself if that is possible.

If the markings on the evidence may destroy its evindentiary value (or if the item of evidence is very small to make the markings or is not possible to make markings – e.g., powder, dust etc.) then it should be placed in a container. The container may be sealed and the markings may be made on the outside of the container. Evidence tags also can be tied or wired to certain items of evidence and in such cases, the use of containers becomes unnecessary. Table 5.1 gives detailed instructions about markings on each item of evidence for identification purposes.

Table 5.1 : Markings on each Item of Evidence for Identification Purpose

Specimen for Examination	Identification
Abrasives	Use containers-pill box, plastic vial. Identification on outside of the container. Write the type of material, the date obtained. Name or initials of the investigating officer.
Acids	Use containers – pill-box or plastic vial. Identification on outside of the container with type of material, date obtained and name or initials. Use paraffin lined bottle for hydrofluric acid. Pack the container in saw dust.
Adhesive tape	Use containers. The recovered roll in full should be sent. Place it on waxed paper or cellophane. Identification on outside of the container with type of material,. date, name or initials.
Alkalies	Use containers— plastic vial or glass bottle with rubber stopper. Use adhesive tapes. Label alkalies. Identification on outside of containers with date, name or initials.
Ammunition	Identification on outside of container.
Anonymous letters and other letters, papers etc.	Put it in an envelope and write "evidence". Use adhesive transparent cellophane tape. Initial and date on each document.

Contd.

Table 5.1 (*Contd.*)

Specimen for Examination	Identification
Blood	If sent in test tubes or containers, use adhesive tape on outside of test tubes. If the blood is a known sample, then write the name of the donor, date taken, medical officer's name and name or initials of the investigating officer. If the stains are seen on clothing, then use tag or mark directly on clothes.
Bullets	Initial on base.
Catridges	Initial on outside of case near bullet end.
Catridge cases	Intitial on inside or near open end or on out side near open end.
Charred or Burned paper	On outside of container after indicating the fragile nature of evidence. Date obtained and name or initials.
Cheques	Same as in the case of anonymous letters.
Clothing	Mark on garments or use string tag. Name or initials, date and type of evidence. Identification to be marked on outside of package also.
Drugs: (a) Liquids	Affix label to the container, name or initials and date. Use adhesive tape to seal the stopper. Mark "fragile" on the packet.
(b) Powders, pills and solids	Mark on outside of the container. Name or initials and date. Seal to prevent any loss by use of adhesive tape.
Fibres	Mark on outside of the sealed container or on object to which fibres are adhering. Use adhesive tapes.
Fire arms	Attach string tag showing name of the weapon, calibre, serial number, date found, name or initials etc.

(Contd.)

Table 5.1 (*Contd.*)

Specimen for Examination	Identification
Gasoline	Mark on outside of all metal containers. Lebel with type of material. Name or initials and date.
Glass fragments	Use adhesive tape on each piece. Name or initials and date on tape. Mark 'fragile".
Glass particles	Mark on outside of sealed container. Seal and protect against breakage. Name and initials.
Hair	Mark on outside of the container indicating type of material, date etc. Name or initials.
Matches	Mark on outside of the container. Keep away from fire. Label should be marked. Write type of material, date, name or initials.
Medicines	They are sent just like drugs.
Oil	They are marked just like 'matches'. Label accordingly.
Organs of body	Mark on outside of the container with name of the victim, date of death, date of autopsy, name of the medical officer and name or initials. Label "Fragile".
Paint 1. Liquid 2. Solid	Mark on outside of the container. Write the type of material, date, name or initials.
Paint, chips or scrapings	Same as above.
Plaster of paris casts	Mark on the back of the cast before plaster hardens. Put location, date, name or initials.
Shoe print lifts	Mark on lifting tape or paper attached to tape. Name or initials and date.
Tools	Maık on tools if that is possible or use

(Con d.)

Table 5.1 (*Contd.*)

Specimen for Examination	Identification
	string tag. Write type of tool, identifying number, date, name or initials.
Tool marks	Mark on object or on tag attached to. Name or initials.
* Urine or water	Mark on outside of the container, type of material, name of the subject, date taken. Name or initials.

* The list is not all inclusive. In case of doubt, consult the specimen list for an item most similar in nature or contact the nearest laboratory expert.

SUGGESTED READINGS

Fisher, Jacob, *The Art of Detection,* Carlton Press, New York, 1963.

Fricke, Charles William, *Criminal Investigation,* D. W. Smith, Los Angeles, 1933.

Gross, Hans & Adolf Gustav, *Criminal Investigation,* Sweet and Maxwell, London, 1924.

Houts, Marshall, *From Evidence to Proof,* Charle C. Thomas, Springfield, Illinois, 1956.

Liebers, Arthur & Carl Vollmers, *The Investigator's Hand Book,* Arco Publishing Co. New York, 1962.

Mitchell, Charles Ainsworth, *Science and the Criminal,* Sir, I. Pitman and Sons, Ltd., London, 1911.

Morland, Nigel, ed., *Crime and Detection,* Tallis Press, Oxford England, 1966.

Nickolls, Lewis C., *The Scientific Investigation of Crime,* Butter World, London, 1956.

O'Brien, Kevin P., and Robert C. Sullivan, *Criminalistics: Theory and Practice,* Holbrook Press, Boston, Mass, 1972.

Rhodes, Henry Taylor Fowkes, *Clues and Crime. The Science of Criminal Investigation,* J. Murrary, London, 1936.

Richardson, James R. *Scientific Evidence for Police Officers,* W.H. Anderson, Cincinat; Ohoi, 1963.

Samen Charles C., *Major Crime Scene Investigation, Search Patterns Part IV,* Law and Order, November, 1971.

Samen Charles, C., *Major Crime Scene Investigation, Securing the Scene Part I,* Law and Order, August, 1971.

Scott, James, D., *Investigative Methods,* Reston Publishing Company, Inc., Reston, Virginia, 1978.

Soderman, Harry, *Modern Criminal Investigation,* Funk and Wagnalls, New York, 1962.

Svensson, Arne and Otto Wendel, *Techniques of Crime Scene Investigation,* American Elsevier, New York, 1965.

Thorwald, Jurgen, *Crime and Science, The New Frontier, in Criminology,* Harcourt Brace and World, New York, 1967.

Walls, Henry James, *Forensic Science,* An introduction to the Praeger, New York, 1968.

Weston Paul B., and Kenneth M., Wells, *Elements of Criminal Investigation,* Prentice – Hall Inc., Englewood Cliffs, New Jersey, 1971.

Weston Paul B., and Kenneth M., Wells, *Criminal Evidence for Police,*

Prentice – Hall Inc., Englewood Cliffs, New Jersey, 1971.

REFERENCES

1. B.R. Sharma, *Forensic Science in Criminal Investigation and Trials*, Central Law Agency, Allahabad, 1974.
2. B.R. Sharma, *op. cit.*
3. B.R. Sharma, *op. cit.*
4. B.R. Sharma, *op. cit.*

6

MATERIAL EVIDENCE, COLLECTION, PACKING AND TRANSPORTING THEM TO EXPERTS

There are three sources from where exhibits for examination by experts can be obtained. They are: (i) The scene of crime; (ii) the victim and his environment; (iii) the suspect and his environments. The investigating officer should take the following precautions when he handles, packs and transports physical clues to an expert for examination. They are: No clue, if possible, should be touched by hand. Human touch, if carelessly done may destroy finger prints. Use of hand gloves of rubber is recommended. Faces of articles suspected to bear finger prints should be lifted by holding them at their edges. Handle the articles taking special care by holding them only at such parts or places; as are unlikely to have been touched by the hand of the criminal or any other person who could have touched them previously.

Hairs should be lifted by means of paper forcepts.

Wet articles should be allowed to dry at room temperature or under the shade. But, if they are besmeared with volatile substances, they should be secured in firmly corked bottles.

Suspected bombs and explosives should not be removed. Nevertheless, if it is absolutely necessary to change their positions, least movements should be made.

PRECAUTIONS TO BE TAKEN WHILE PACKING OF EXHIBITS TO THE EXPERTS

No contamination of the exhibit should take place either from the packing or from outside materials.

Never allow mechanical damage to the packet owing to jolting, crushing, breakage, explosion or ignition, etc. The article should not be lost while on transit. Hence, wherever possible, send it through a special messenger.

Use only dry, clean and ordourless containers and use suitable containers to prevent leakage or to ensure safety. Take special care when glass bottles or fragile containers are sent. Write 'Glass, Handle with Care' if that needs be.

For powder and dry materials, unless it is specially prescribed, cellopane paper can be used.

Pack each article separately. Use hard wooden box for final packing. Seal the article as a precaution against tampering.

Consult the Laboratory/Expert in case of doubts.

INTERROGATION OF PHYSICAL EVIDENCE*

1. What does ... indicate in this case?
2. Is there anything relating to... in this case? How?
3. How has ...come to the scene of crime?
4. Does.... speak anything as to when, where and how the crime was committed?
5. Does.... say something about the manner in which the crime was committed?
6. What does.... speak about who committed offence?
7. Does.... show anything as to how it helped the culprit to commit the offence?
8. Does.... show as to why the offence was committed?
9. Does.... indicate anything as to the motive of the criminal?
10. Does.... speak of the '*mens rea*' of the criminal?
11. How long is.... here since the commission of the offence?
12. Does.... show as to how difficult or easy was it for the crime-doer to commit the offence with it?
13. Why did the culprit think of employing.... to commit the offence?
14. Does.... say anything as to the deliberations of the criminal?
15. Does.... indicate as to how the offender entered the scene of crime?
16. Does... show anything as to what evidence might have been destroyed by the use of it?
17. Does.... indicate as to the '*modus operandi*' of the offender?
18. Does.... say anything as to what specific method was employed to commit the offence and to conceal the crime?
19. Does.... show anything as to the movement of the offender, his associates, victim or strangers?
20. Does.... show as to how many persons were involved for the commission of the offence?
21. Does.... indicate as to HOW BEST CAN THE CRIME BE PROVED IN A COURT OF LAW

* The investigating officer should ask these questions to himself and try to find out answers to them. Each physical evidence should be put in the blank provided. If he feels necessary, the words presence of, absence of, location of, size of etc. should be inserted in each question to make things clearer.

While picking and packing materials for despatch to the expert, meticulous care should be taken to see that no article is inadvertantly contaminated with extraneous matter or things likely to interfere in its examination. An expert analyses what is sent to him.

Obtain *close-up* or *very close-up* photographs of the items before touching them.

Collect the physical clues without disturbing other material evidence at the scene of crime. In picking up articles, the investigating officer should remember.

a) the possibility of finding out latent, visible or plastic finger prints;
b) the chances of certain microscopic debris adhering to them etc.

Each article must be separately packed and labelled indicating the serial number of items. Never put more than one item in a packet.

The labels must be numbered consecutively and should bear the signature or initials of the forwarding officer and other identification marks.

Signature of the witnesses should be obtained on the parcel containing exhibits sealed before them.

The articles should not be detained for long intervals in the police station.

The result of the examination should be obtained as early as possible so that the investigation may be finalized within 60 days.

Evidence Collection Kit

The Evidence Collection Kit is otherwise called I.O's. Kit (Investigating Officer's Kit). Before going to inspect a scene of crime, the investigating officer should invariably examine whether or not all of the following items are available in the I.O.'s Kit. Now, every police station is provided with Evidence Collection Kit, but it seems that many investigating officers seldom make use of them. This indeed is bad. Experience has shown that an investigator who possesses an Evidence Collection Kit in perfect order, can surely find his work much easier and speedier, for an I.O's Kit usually has the following items for inspection work.

Photographic Equipments

General use camera, spectics camera for photographying finger prints and other trace materials, films, illumination equipments, light meter etc.

Fingerprint Kit

Powder, brushes, atomizer, fuming equipments, iodine crystals, lifting materials, transfer papers and finger print cards etc.

Measuring Kit

Ruler (18"), steel tape measure (50'), pedometer to measure long distances etc.

Other Articles

Magnifying glass, mirrors including a dentist's mirror for examining inaccessible locations – such as beneath automobiles for serial numbers, flash light etc.

Recording Materials

Several sheets of writing paper of the best quality, carbon papers, writing pads, ball pens and pencils, rubber erasure, blade, graph paper, note books, official (printed) blank forms, chalk, cryons, mariner's compass etc.

Storage Materials

Envelops of various sizes, pill boxes, bottles, druggist–folders, filter paper, blotting paper, flat carboards, cord, tape, labels, rubber bands, sealing wax, ball of twine, tissue paper etc.

Tools

Screw drivers, pliers, chisel, tweezers, spatula, scissors, forceps, picks, hammers, sledge-hammer, knife, shovel, pry-bar, saw, wrenches, lock-cutter, pair of compasses, dividers etc.

Other Items

A good electric torch with spare bulbs and cells, two candles of the length and thickness of one's finger, match boxes, soap, towel, rubber gloves, tracing paper and cloth (the cloth is useful for removing traces of blood and in other circumstances when paper is not strong enough), a brush (useful for taking impressions of solid subjects and surfaces with moistened blotting paper), test tubes, bottles of various sizes, gum, a camel hair brush, a bottle or packet of plaster of paris and other accessaries for taking casts.

Hans Gross says: "In selecting the type of wrapping or the container suitable for any given purposes, the first essential is that whatever is used must be scrupulously clean and dry and of such a kind as to avoid any transfer of materials to the specimen. It should also be sufficiently robust to prevent damage in transit. Each article or specimen must be packed separately although there is no objection to the inclusion of a number of items in one parcel provided that care is taken to prevent the transfer of material from one article to another. Such a transfer would, of course, vitiate the whole object of examination".

LAWS RELATING TO THE COLLECTION OF MATERIAL EVIDENCE

1. Section 51 Cr. P.C. – Search of arrested persons.
2. Section 52 Cr. P.C. – Power to seize offensive weapons.
3. Section 157 Cr. P.C. – Procedure for investigation.
4. Section 165 Cr. P.C. – Search by police officers.
5. Section 166 Cr. P.C. – When a officer-in-charge of police station may require another to issue search warrant.
6. Section 27 I.E.A. – Recovery of evidence as a result of confession.

PROCEDURE FOR HANDLING AND PACKING OF PHYSICAL CLUES

Specimen		Other Requirements
AMMUNITION		
Unfired catridges	Place them in small clasp type envelopes or in cellophane papers individually covered. Put them in a hardboard box with sufficient packing materials. Send them through a special messenger.	Submit separately those found in gun from all other evidence catridges.
Discharged bullets	Place each one of them in small clasp type envelope or in cellophane papers individual covered. Put them in a hardboard box with sufficient packing materials. Send them through a special messenger.	To discharged bullet found should be sent.
Bullets from dead bodies	They shall be extracted only by a medical practitioner. He should be asked to establish the location of the bullet through X-rays. Ask him to extract the bullet with hands covered with gloves. If a pair of forceps is to be used, its tips should be covered with rubber or plastic sheets. Packaging of them can be done in the same way as discharged bullets are packed.	Same as above
Bullets found in furniture, wall, wood, floor or earth	Extract them by using a pair of foreceps whose tips are covered with rubber or plastic sheets. If this is not possible, the entire object may be cut and sent to the laboratory or an expert may be called to the scene. Send them in the manner given above for transporting bullets.	All found should be sent.
Shot gun shells	Place them in small clasp type envelopes. Separate envelopes are to be used if found at different locations.	All found should be sent.

Specimen		Other Requirements
Pellets	Same as above. Use a pair of forceps with rubber or plastic covering for picking up the pellets.	All found. It is not necessary to mark pellets on the envelope.
Wadding	Same as given under pellets. But, if taken from dead bodies dry them before sending them to the laboratory.	All found should be sent
Discharge residues	Dishcharged residues are deposited normally on the hands of a person who had fired the gun, or the victim of a suicide. About two milliliter thick molten wax is deposited slowly on the hands of the suspect. The cast is peeled off and placed between two inflexible plastic sheets and jointed with adhesive tape or cement. Pack it in a harboard box and sent it. Also the hands of the suspect are swabbed with clean surgical cotton wool dipped in dilute acetic acid or hydrochloric acid. The diluted acid dissolves the discharged residues which are collected in a clean glass vial. The vial is properly corked, packed and sent through a special messenger to the laboratory.	
Bullet holes	The original article bearing the bullet holes, dents or other marks to be sent. If this is not possible, then the portion containing the bullet holes may be cut of and sent or a cast may be prepared and sent.	If the investigating officer does not know to take a cast, call the expert to the scene.
Burnt bullet and catridges cases	Bullets or catridge cases in a fire (possibly thrown by the culprit himself) may melt themselves. Lead bullets ordinarily loose all indentifiable marks while jacketed	

(Contd.)

Specimen		Other Requirements
	bullets and metal bases of catridges do` not. They may be collected and sent in cellophane papers separately.	
Clothes	The clothes are dried before packing if they are wet and the power patterns and projectile holes, if any, are protected with cellophane sheet. The clothes are packed in sturdy proof-bags or in plastic bags.	
Tissues surrounding gun-shot injuries	Traces of lead may have to be examined and therefore should be sent in lead-free containers, properly corked and by a special messenger.	A specimen of unaffected tissues also will have to be sent separately.
Firearm	The muzzle end of the barrel should be capped and not plugged. In the case of revolvers opening on both the front and rear sides of the chamber, they should be pugged with clean clothes. This should be done at the breach end of the fire arm. The firearm should then be separately wrapped with paper, tied with thread and kept in a wooden box with packing materials such as cotton waste. Send it through a special messenger.	The firearm seized must be sent with the following particulars. 1. The type and make 2. Serial number 3. Calibre, and any other information found to be useful for the expert.

(Contd.)

Specimen		Other Requirements
Before transporting firearm for ballistic examination, assertain whether or not its safety catch is on or off or ensuring whether the firearm is loaded or not. Handle the firearm in such a way that even if it goes off, it does not injure anyone by ensuring that there is no one facing the muzzle end of the firearm. Consider the firearm safe only when one can see through the barrel and when magazine, if any, is detached. Hold the firearm from a place where neither the existing evidence (like the fingerprints) can be destroyed nor new evidence is introduced. The firearm is held from the sling, ring, trigger guard or from the corrugated surfaces of the but. Before packing, search for extraneous evidence like hair, skin, flesh, paint or dust should be made. If the items do not adhere to the firearm firmly, they are detached and packed separately before the firearm is processed for finger prints. Avoid touching inside the barrel. The presence or absence of rust, fouling, dust and other materials can lead to important conclusions. If any thing is introduced into the barrel, the barrel is to be capped.		
CLOTHING	Place in a clean bag. Never use plastic bags. If wet, air-dry it before packing.	All found, Don't cut out the suspect area. Send the whole clothing.
HAIR	Never place loose in an envelope. Use paper forceps for picking up. Druggist fold, pill-box or vial may be used. Hairs collected from different sources should be packed separately. Label the location of the hair. Whenever possible, submit the entire article on which hairs have been found.	All found may be sent as crime-sample. Several dozens, nearly 100 or more hairs should be pulled out, not clipped, from different parts of the body. This is sent as control sample.
Pulled out haris are the best samples where the incriminating hairs have been allegedly pulled out. Hence samples from animals and dead persons should invariably be pulled out in such situations. If this is not possible, hair can be obtained by combing and if combing does not yield sufficient quantity, a considerable number should be clipped from several parts of the body by cutting them close of the skin. The investigating officers should not clean the hair collected. If the hair is wet or smeared with blood, semen or other fluids, they should be dried in room temperature before packing.		

(Contd.)

Specimen		Other Requirements
Hair adhering to objects with blood, semen etc.	The whole object with the hair should be sent. If this is not possible, cut of that portion where hair is stricking and send them.	Hair should be collected both from the suspect and the victim in rape cases, in fatal accidents or similar cases when 'control sample' is sent.
FIBRE	Individual fibres are packed in druggist fold, pill-box or vial. Never place loose in an envelope. Package separately fibres collected from different sources. Whenever possible, submit the entire article on which the fibres have been observed. Sent them through registered mail or by a special messenger.	Entire garment or other cloth-items should be sent as control sample. All fibres, incriminating should be sent.
BLOOD		
Fresh moist stains on clothing, sheets and blankets.	Insert the fabric between clean white paper pads to protect the stains and place them in clean paper bags. Never use plastic bags as they may cause meldew. Before inserting the fabric between white paper pads, allow the stain to dry at room temperature. Never use heat to dry.	The entire cloth will have to be sent. 5 c.c. of blood collected from the suspect and like amount from the victim should be sent as control samples. Do not add any preservative to the *'control blood'*.
Blood in large quantities	Sock it in a filter paper. Allow it to dry in shade at room temperature and send it in an envelope.	All may be sent. Here 5 c.c. of the blood from the suspect & the victim should be sent as *controls*.

(*Contd.*)

Specimen		Other Requirements
Fresh moist stains on solid objects (weapons, wood, furniture, automobiles etc.)	If possible send the entire object to the laboratory. Before sending the object, dry the stain at room temperature. The stains are to be covered with filter paper or with cotton. If, this is not possible, cut off the portion where stain is found and may be sent as said above. Even this is not possible, sock it in a filter paper, allow it to dry in shade — at room temperature — and send it in an envelope.	Here 5 c.c. of the blood from the suspect & the victim must be sent to the laboratory as *'controls'*. If it is not possible to send the entire object to the Laboratory, a portion of the unstained area immediately surrounding the stain should always be forwarded for *control test*. If the stain is on soil, plaster or furniture etc. a portion of (1 gm) of the adjacent unstained area should be scrapped to the same depth as the stained is and send it as *control*. In taking *control samples* near the stain, avoid soakage of the stain. In case of weapons, it is always very desirable that the whole object is sent to the Laboratory so that the *control sample* will be prepared from the washings of the surface of an unstained area by the laboratory.
Liquid blood	Liquid blood in the form of blood pools may be collected as	The vials or test tubes containing

(Contd.)

Specimen		Other Requirements
	under. Two samples- i.e., each about 5 c.c. are collected in clean vials. In one sodium fluoride oxalate or citrate is added and the other is sent without any preservatives.	liquid blood and cooled in crushed ice contained in a thermos bottle. *Control* must be sent
Dried blood stains on clothings, sheets and blankets etc.	Send the entire fabric protecting the stain in between two clean white paper pads. Stich it well.	*Control* also should be sent.
Dried stains on solid objects.	The entire objectg may be sent. If this is not possible, scrap off as much as possible avoiding scrapings of the soild object underneath, particularly if the object is wood or leather etc. Place the scrapings in a test tube, stopper it and send. Even this is not possible, the entire stain may be transferred to a moist filter paper, dry in shade/at room temperature and send it to the laboratory in an envelope.	In the case of blood on earth or earthly material, scrapings should be made deep enough (1") to collect the soaked serum.
Blood stains on dried leaves	Embed them in a mass of plastercene keeping the stained - side upper most. Pack it in a suitable container and send.	*Control* must be sent.
Blood stains in nails	They should be clipped and the clippings packed in a glazed paper may be sent. In clipping nails, care should be taken to avoid cutting the underlying skin of the flesh.	Material sticking to the nail clippings should not be lost in packaing and transit.
Blood in hair	Collect either by combing or by clipping. Put them in a test tube, stopper it and send.	*Control* must be sent.
Blood on the body of a	Filter paper soaked in 9% solution of sodium chloride shall	*Control* must be sent.

(Contd.)

Specimen		Other Requirements
person	be used to remove the stain. Dry it in room temperature and send it in an envelope.	
Blood on grass	Tie the grass with a thread. Cut the tuft. Dry it in room temperature and send it in a glass jar. Washed blood may be sent in any one of the ways mentioned above. The investigating officer may select any method without the blood being contaminated either in packing or in transit.	
Blood-in toxicological cases from living persons	Blood may be collected in a clean test tube or vial. The physician taking sample should add anticoagulant (sodium oxalate) as preservative (sodium fluoride). Refrigerate until delivery to the laboratory.	25 c.c. of blood for drug determination and 5 c.c. for alcoholic content determination must be sent.
Blood-in toxicological cases from a dead body	Same as above	Same as above.
SEMEN		
Fresh moist seminal stains	The stain is allowed to dry at room temperature and a circle is made around the stain with a red pencil. Keep the stain in between two clean white paper pads. Stich them well and send.	The garment of fabric may be folded taking care that the stained area is not disturbed.
Dried Seminal stains	The portion where the stain is found may be marked with a coloured pencil and the stains kept in between two pieces of clean white paper pads. Stich them well and send.	Same as above
Semen on the seat of a vehicle.	Submit the entire seat.	If it is necessary to examine the vehicle, consult the laboratory in advance.

(Contd.)

Specimen		Other Requirements
VAGINAL SPECIMENS	The complainant should be examined as soon as possible for the presence of motile (active or spermatozoa). Inactive sperms can be found in the vagina for extended periods after the intercourse. A thin smear is prepared and allowed to day. Do not use sprays or glazes of any kind on these smears. Upon drying, a cover glass may be placed over the smear and label as such. The smear should be placed in a slide holder to prevent against contamination and breakage. All smears or holders should be labelled with all pertinent data, type of smear, from whom taken, by whom, location and date. The medical officer should rinse the vaginal vault, using a minimum amount of liquid (preferably not more than 5-10 ml of distilled water).	It may be, sometimes necessary, to determine the ABO blood group of seminal material. Hence, it will be necessary to know secret or status and blood group of the people involved. Collect both blood and saliva as *control* from all suspected people. If blood group cannot be directly obtained from a person, an official record —i.e., a hospital or medical record — indicating the blood group will be enough.
	Swabs may be taken. All swabs should be placed in dry test tubes. All test tubes should be properly labelled and initialled for future identification.	The test tubes should be refrigerated until submitted to the laboratory.
Semen from Vagina, from Rectum or oral cavity.	Obtain swabs and place them in dry test tubes properly labelled and initialled.	Swabs should be refrigerated until submitted to the laboratory.
SALIVA		
On article - stamps, clothes, pillow covers, bed sheets etc.	The entire article should be sent after making a mark around it by a coloured pencil. Cover it with white paper, if possible.	When collecting *controls*, be certain that the donor has a good supply of saliva generated in the mouth prior to spitting or have the

(*Contd.*)

Specimen		Other Requirements
Saliva from dead persons.	This should be collected by taking swab and putting it in clean phial. Place in an ice box until submitted to the laboratory. When collecting swab from dead person's mouth, take four samples from four different areas in the mouth.	donor spit in the same area more than once. It is best that the donor is allowed not to have anything in his mouth for an hour prior to giving of the sample including
Saliva from living persons	Ask the donor to spit into a clean absorbent paper towel and outline the area of saliva. Air-dry, initial, fold and place the paper towel into a properly marked envelope. The instruments used to outline the area must not come in contact with the spit.	Cigerettes, beedies, pans etc. Be careful to avoid transfer of prespiration from the hands of the person collecting the sample.
URINE		
From living persons	Collect it in a clean bottle or vial	Take all voided. Refrigerate until delivery to the laboratory.
From dead persons	Collect it in plastic containers	Take all in the bladder. Keep refrigerated until delivery to the laboratory.
STOMACH WASHINGS in toxicology case	Collect it in clean bottle or vial.	Refrigerate it until delivery to the laboratory.
HUMAN FAECES	Collect it in wide-mouthed glass-jars fitted with ground glass stoppers. The jar should have a capacity of not less than 3 pints. The stoppers should be screwed by strips of strong adhesive tape to avoid the possibility of leakage.	No preservatives or disinfectant be added to it. Refrigerate until delivery to the laboratory.

(*Contd.*)

Specimen		Other Requirements
	Vomited and purged matters mixed with earth if dry, may be packed without spirit in any convenient manner. Otherwise, they can be packed with spirit. Vomited and purged matters fallen on the earth should be carefully scarpped upto 1" depth. The superficial scarpings should be packed separately.	
SWEAT, TEARS, NASAL SECRETIONS AND HUMAN MILK	Send the entire article. If on cloth, mark the area by a coloured pencil and insert it in two clean white paper pads. Stich them well and send.	Care should be taken so that perspiration from others does not interfere with the specimens sent for analysis.
INSECTS	Magots of insects may be collected and preserved in formalin or alcohol.	This is necessary to determine the time of death.
TISSUE	Dry at room temperature and put it in a glass jar. Stopper it and send.	Do not put any preservatives. Refrigerate until delivery to the laboratory.
	Fresh or wet tissue can also be kept in glass containers chilled in ice or in a refrigerator and send. Alternatively, such tissues may be preserved in saturated common salt solution in water.	If delay in unavoidable before despatching the tissues, it should be divided into two parts. One part is preserved in 10% formal saline and the other is desiccated (dried) completely.
SKELETAL REMAINS & TEETH	Bones taken from or under the mud (buried ground) should be sent as such without fracturing.	As far as possible skull, teeth, hip girdle and long bones should be

(*Contd.*)

Specimen		Other Requirements
		collected and forwarded completely.
TOXICOLOGY i) Brain, ii) bile, iii) liver, iv) kidney, v) skin around puncture marks.	Collected them in plastic containers separately. Brain (300 gms), bile (all); liver (300 gms), kidney (all); skin around puncture marks (all)	Keep refrigerated until delivery to the laboratory. Besides blood and urine, stomach washings etc. must also be sent in toxicology cases.
i) Alochol; ii) mercury; iii) carbon monoxide-poisoning	50 c.c. blood should be sent. Vomitted matter, if any and faeces should be packed separately and sent after adding rectified spirit as preservative. However, if vomitted or purged matters are mixed with earth in sufficient quality to render them dry and inoffensive, they may be packed without rectified spirit.	
In respired poisons	Lungs should be sent	Lungs in full must be sent.
In alochol, sleeping tablets, opium, chlorofrom.	Brain should be sent.	300 gms should be sent.
Vegetable poisions, mercury, sleeping tablets, lead.	Urine should be collected (24 hours' specimen) and sent.	All available should be collected.
Vegetable poisons, alochol, sleeping tablets, lead	Blood must be sent (10 c.c.)	In cases of poisoning by alcohol, kerosen phosphorous, paraal-dehyde, acetic acid and carbolic acid, rectified spirit should never

(Contd.)

Specimen		Other Requirements
		be used as a preservative. Instead, a saturated solution of common salt should be added as preservative with a layer of salt at the bottom.
Arsenic, lead	Faeces should be sent.	
Bacterial food poisoning and other poisons administered through food.	Food (all) in the stomach must be collected.	If articles of food, medicine etc. are seen, they shall be placed separately and sent. If fruits are seen, they should be sent.
Poisonous seeds and plant parts	Fragments remaining on 'Khalbatta' or 'sil' used for griding should be wrapped in paper and sent.	Plant parts or remnants in poisoning cases should be sent as such.
TOOL AND TOOL MARKS		
Tools	Sent the whole tool after covering it with cotton-wool and tying it with twine.	If the climate is humid and hot, a tool or the mark on a metal article may rust and the mark may get obliterated. A thin oil film is applied over the surface to prevent rusting.
Tool marks	The portion containing tool marks must be sent after covering that portion with soft paper. Then place it in a strong box—i.e., solid container package to prevent damage to the area of the tool mark.	Submit the suspect tools. Pack it in a separate container. Donot attempt to reproduce the markings by casting a mould unless that is

(*Contd.*)

Specimen		Other Requirements
		the only method by which evidence can be preserved.
	If the whole material containing tool marks cannot be sent, cut off the portion bearing tool marks and send it after covering that portion with soft paper and place it in strong wrapping papers. Put it in a strong container and send.	
Tool marks: casts	If the tool marks cannot be transported to the laboratory, cast of the tool marks will have to be made. If the investigating officer has difficulties in making the cast, an expert may be called to the scene of crime for the purpose of making the cast. A lump of plasterence is taken and pressed in between two wet glass plates to give it smooth surfaces. The slightly moistened and smooth area is pressed against the mark.	Cast of tool marks made by plasterence does not pick up fine details and is easily deformed. Hence, plasterence cast is prepared only when it is not required as permanent record or when the area bearing the mark is small.
	Dental mass is kneaded under hot water and when it is soft and uniform in texture, it is passed between two glass plates to give smooth surfaces. The material, while still warm, is pressed against the tool marks and left at the site for some time.	Dental mass like Kerr's dental mass picks up fine details and records the marks permanetly.
	Adhesive tape used to lift finger-prints can be used to lift shallow tool marks.	This does not give good result in deep scrapes.
	Latex and plastic solutions can also be used. The material is poured over the surface bearing marks. It is then allowed to	It is a good material for scrape marks but it is not so good for

(*Contd.*)

Specimen		Other Requirements
	dry for about six hours. The thin film or sheet is then peeled of.	indentations, especially deep ones, as due to stretching, the dimensions of the lifted marks change.
	Wood's metal is melted and poured into the mark. It solidifies on cooling and picks up the details from the marks.	It is good for indentations with appreciable depth on metal surfaces.
GLASS		
Particles	Place in pill-box, druggist fold or vial. Seal and protect against breakage. Do not place loose in envelopes. All fragments found at the scene should be collected.	3" piece of broken item should be sent as *control sample*. Forceps can be used to collect the particles.
Fragements	Place questioned and known fragements in separate solid containers. Avoid breakage. Collect all fragments available.	All glass found at the crime-scene should be recovered and submitted.
Powder	Place it in druggist fold or pill-box or vial. All powder should be collected.	
SOIL	Solid container or druggist fold. Do not place loose in envelope. Pack separately soil collected at different areas. Whenever possible, submit the entire article on which the soil has been observed. Label all samples with proper location (approdimately 8-10 representative samples.)	Collect 1-2 teaspoons of soil at crime scene-top layer only-- as well as representative samples in a 200 feet radius of the crime sample. This is for using as *'control sample'*

(*Contd.*)

Specimen		Other Requirements
POLUTARY, CATTLE FOODS, SAWDUST AND POWDERED DRUGS	Each sample should be separately packed in solid containers. Do not place them loose in envelopes.	Direct sieving through a series of wire sieves of progressively finer mesh will give the investigator a picture of the percentage of particles of any given size or range in the sample, thus enabling a series of samples to be compared or contrasted.
PAINT Paint chips or scrapings	Druggist fold, pill-box or vial. Do not place it loose in envelope or in plastic bag. Whenever possible, submit the entire article on which the paint has been observed. Otherwise, use a clean knife or blade to remove all the layers of paint from the object.	All found at the scene of crime should be collected. At least 1/2 square inch of solid with all layers represented should be sent as *control*.
TABLETS	Druggist fold, pill-box, or vial or glassine envelope—aluminium foil is very acceptable. Separate drugs and pack individually.	All found may be sent.
CAPSULES	Druggist fold, pill-box, or vial or glassine envelope. Separate the capsules and pack them individually.	All found may be sent.
VEGETATION	Plastic or paper bag. Pack vegetations separately. If wet, air-dry thoroughly before submission.	All found may be sent.
EXPLOSIVE RESIDUES	Pack it in solid sealed containers. Collected debris and bomb fragments around suspected origin or explosion should be sent. A laboratory will not accept potentially	All found may be sent. The Chief Inspectors of Explosives have their Head Quarters at Nagpur,

(Contd.)

Specimen		Other Requirements
	exlposive bombs or chemicals. These items should be deactivated by the nearest bomb disposal unit. If necessary, experts should be called.	Agra, Chennai, Kolkatta, Mumbai and Gwalior.
GREASES AND LUBRICANTS	Collect it in a filter paper and put it in a glass-vial. Stropper and send.	
CIGERETTE ENDS AND BEEDI BITS	Take individually and pack them individually in a test tube. Stopper it and send.	Perspiration of the investigator should not be transmitted to it when packing is done.
LIQUIDS	Narrow-necked bottles fitted with glass stoppers are preferable for most of the liquids including acids and inflammable liquids such as pertol, benzene, paraffin etc. Where the sample is an alkaline liquid such as a solution of caustic soda or caustic potash, a glass-stopper is unsuitable and should be replaced by an accurately fitting rubber bung. Care should be taken to avoid the use of stoppers fitted with internal discs of metal foil in the case of acids, and to avoid those fitted with rubber discs in the case of substances such as patrol, benzene, chloroform, paraffin etc.	If bottles with screw capped backelite stoppers are used, it is essential to make sure that the fit of the stopper is sufficiently accurate to prevent leakage. Leakage is usually guarded against by fitting a disc of rubber cork or metal foil on inner surface of the top of the bakelite stopper.
DUST ON CLOTHES	Place the garment in a stout, sealed paper bag and then beat this briskly so that any dust present would accumulate in the bottom of the bag from which it could be collected and examined.	This is a crude method and therefore has been now replaced by making use of a miniature cleaner suction-type vacuum cleaner.

(Contd.)

Specimen		Other Requirements
	Suction - type vacuum cleaner is fitted with a special nozzle permitting the interposition of a fine gauze filter and further back, a filter paper thimble between the mouth of the nozzle and suction unit. Where areas of staining on clothing or other article owing to deposits of foreign matter are obvious and well-defined, but small in amount, it is sometimes, preferable to collect samples by removing selected fragments with a clean-pointed forceps or with a needle lightly moistened with glycerine. The same procedure can, of course, be followed after extraction of dust by means of the miniaute vacuum cleaner.	More recently it has been found advantageous to replace the gauze filter with three grades of bolting silk, a finely woven fabric used among other things.
DUST from pockets, wallets, foot-wear and pocket-knife handles etc.	Collect directly into a suitable container such as petri-dishes by a clean hog bristle brush of suitable size.	
OCCUPATIONAL DUST	Collect it using the 'orange sticks' normally employed in manicuring.	'Orange sticks' are preferable to the use of a knife or scalpel which may bring away minute traces of blood and thus complicate the examination.
TELEGRAPH AND TELEPHONE WIRES	Collect the loosely hanging wires and clearly mark the ends supposed to have been cut by the cuplrit. This is to differentiate it from the cut made by the investigating officer. The ends of the recovered wires should be carefully	The ends cut from the hanging wires should also be wrapped similarly. The wire ends should be enclosed in cotton wool.

(Contd.)

Specimen		Other Requirements
	wrapped in cotton-wool and tied with strong thread so that the delicate surface is not damaged during the transit.	Wrapping should be packed in a moist free container.
FINGER PRINTS	The likely surfaces are carefully examined with a flash light thrown at an oblique angle preferably in semi-dark places. Take the photograph before anything is done on the print. By using camel hair brush or an atomizer or an automatic finger print powder sprayer, the prints may be powdered. Fuming tube also can be used in certain cases.	A magnifying glass is good and useful in locating the print as well as judging the quality of the print.
	1. Black powder is used for all light coloured surfaces, 2. Grey powder is used against dark background. 3. Anthracene powder is used for multicoloured surfaces. The developed prints are photographed with ultraviolet rays. 4. Metalic powders (aluminium copper, brass, gold, antimony) and universal powders can also be used in special situations. 5. Any powder can be used if contrasting colour is kept behind the print –such contracting colour can be given by keeping some paper or pouring some ink.	Camel hair brush powdering is better. Ofcourse atomizers etc. can also be used. Powdering by brush shall be done across the ridges and not against the ridges.

(Contd.)

Specimen		Other Requirements
	6. Liquids such as silver nitrate, osmium tetroxide etc. can also be used. After developing and photographying, the print must be preserved in a light-proof envelope or by chemeical fixing up of hypo.	Liquids may be used as under. The paper containing finger print is immersed in trays containing approximately a 5 % of solution of silver nitrate. Then the paper is hung up to dry over a sink in a dark room. After drying, they are exposed to sunlight or to a powerful artificial light such as carbon arc. The print must then be photographed.
	7. Iodine or osmium tetroxide in vapour form also may be employed.	The iodine crystals are put in a conical flask. It is tightly corked and allowed to vapour out. A tube is inserted until the fume comes out. The latent prints will be darkened as the vapours cling to the secretions. Then a photograph is taken.
	8. If plastic prints —i.e., prints found on soap, fat, butter, tar, paraffin wax etc. — are seen, a plaster cast of the print must be taken after photographying the print.	Woods metal can be used if the surface is not having a low melting point.

(Contd.)

Specimen		Other Requirements
LIFTING UP OF FINGER PRINTS	Only after taking a satisfactory photograph of the print, the print shall be lifted up.	Before lifting up a print, the investigating officer must experiment by placing a new print on the surface and attempting to lift it.
	1. *Rubber Lifters :* A rubber lifter is a sheet of tacky rubber with a celluloid protective strip which clings to the rubber. The celluloid cover is partially stripped from the surface and then hold the exposed end of the tape on one side of the print. The lifter is then rolled slowly over the print and pressed against the print with a finger. The celluloid cover is replaced by placing the lifter face up, holding the end of the cover taut and pressing the cover carefully, but firmly against the rubber. Caution is exercised to avoid air bubbles.	If any difficulty or suspicion occurs in developing and lifting up of the print, then the article itself may be taken (if transferable) to the Finger Print Bureau. Otherwise a finger print expert may be called to the spot of occurrence. Nothing shall be done in a doubtful mood on an experimental or hasty way.
	2. *Transparent tapes :* One end of the tape is held taut and pressed down over the print. The tape is removed by lifting until it is well clear of the position of the print with the end still adhering to the surface. The tape is then cut on the side of the print near the roll. The section bearing the print is then lifted up entirely from the surface and placed on a celluloid cover and sent.	

(*Contd.*)

Specimen		Other Requirements
	3. *Photographic paper :* An exposed printing paper to light is fixed and taken. It is immersed in water and dried up using a blotting paper. It is placed over the print and rolled of by using a pressing rule. It is taken out. Dry and send it in an envelope.	
FOOT PRINTS		
Surface prints	*Tracing :* If the print is made up of perspiration, liquid (or even powder) a glass or celluloid paper is placed over some match boxes. Try to trace the outline of the print. Make a copy of it and transmit it to the Bureau.	Photograph should be taken before tracing the print. No imagination must be permitted to play a role here to fill up the spaces.
	Rubber lifters : This is a sheet of tacky rubber with a celluloid protective strip which clings to the rubber. The lifters are provided in black and white. The surface is first powdered and photographed. The celluloid paper is partially stripped from the surface. The exposed end of the tape is held on one side of the print with one finger. The celluloid cover is replaced by placing the lifter face up and holding the end of the cover taut and pressing the cover carefully, but firmly against the rubber. Caution is exercised to avoid air bubbles.	With regard to all prints, as far as possible, if one can remove the place or object where the print is found, it is advisable to transport it as such to the Finger Print Bureau. Before doing so, a photograph of the print must invariably be taken.

(Contd.)

Specimen		Other Requirements
	Photographic film or papers : Either paper or film may be used. They must be fixed, washed and dried. They are then dipped in water and then dried by the help of a filter paper. It is pressed against the print smoothing it out by the hand and pulled it off.	
SEMI-SUNKEN FOOT-PRINTS	**Plaster-casts**	
	1. *Mixing of the plaster* – Take water to 2/3 of a pan which can contain 2 litres. Spread the plaster over the surface. Allow it to settle gradually. The mixture must be stirred thoroughly with a stiff spatula. It should have the consistency of a No. 20 crank case oil. A little salt (a pinch) is added to get an easy drying.	Never thin the mixture by adding more water as the resulting cast will be chalky. Such casts take much time to get dry and are easily broken.
	The whole surface of the cast should be poured out one time eventhough the first layer be very thin. Then place a wire gauze and pour the rest. It will be always advisable to round the cast with a flexible piece of metal sheet.	Never use dry pieces of wood instead of wire gauge as it would absorb water well and split the casts.
	If water is found in the impression, it should be drawn out. If a considerable amount still remains, dry plaster may be sprinkled over the surface until the water is absorbed. Then a batch of plaster poured as previously outlined.	A large syringe may be used for this purpose.

(*Contd.*)

Specimen		Other Requirements
	If the imprints are found on dust or sand, never pour the mixture directly into the print. In such cases, the imprints will lose their details. Before pouring the plaster, spray with a 50-50 mixture of orange shellac and methyl (wood) alcohol by using a spraying pump. When the print is taken, there will be a coating of shellac adhering to it. This can be removed by spraying the impression with a light coating of very thin oil after the shellac coating has hardened and before pouring the cast. If it is not done, a shellac coating adheres to the cast which may be removed with wood alcohol. Before pouring the plaster of paris solution, a spray of talcuum powder may be sprayed over the shellac solution.	The addresses of the premises, the officer, the case number, left or right foot etc. should be marked behind the cast. When more than one print is taken number the cast as (1), (2), (3) etc. They should also be written in the officer's diary as it may be washed off when the cast is washed with water.
	Dig all the earth in the side of cast. Gentle flow of a tap is the best method to clean the cast. A wooden box may be used to transport the cast.	The casts of tyre impressions in mud can be taken just like this.
DOCUMENTS : Partly burnt documents	They are collected in a hardboard box of convenient size. A cotton wool padding is placed at the bottom and the document is gently brought into the box. Another cotton padding is gently palced at the top.	Burnt documents are found in the wilful destruction of documents, in arson and accidental fire cases. They may be partly burnt, carborized, or ashed. Burnt documents are extremely fragile and if mishandled, they change into small bits and become

(Contd.)

Specimen		Other Requirements
		useless or evaluation purposes.
	Sometimes, partly burnt documents need strengthening before they can be collected. It is done by spraying dilute solution of polyvinyl acetate. In collecting the document, one should : (a) as far as possible, avoid handling of the burnt document; (b) avoid straightening the folds; (c) collect partly charred documents or their ashes from different places in different boxes; (d) prevent the scattering of the partly burnt documents by strong wind or air from fans.	Hence, whenever possible, an expert should be called to collect burnt documents.
Fragile documents	Place the same in two transparent plastic sheets. The sheets are held together with an adhesive tape or cement. If necessary the document is reinforced with polyvinyl acetate solution. While handling the document, never make an attempt to fold it.	Old documents or those exposed to sun heat or action of chemicals become fragile.
Damaged or torn documents	For damaged or torn documents recovered before complete destruction, the following methods may be used— i.e.,	This happens when a suspect tears the incriminating documents in small bits and throws them in water closets or chews and eats

(*Contd.*)

Specimen		Other Requirements
	(a) If the collected document is wet, it should be dried at room temperature before packing.	
	(b) The pieces of documents should be collected from different places in separate packets.	
	(c) No document should be carried in the pockets as it is likely to be damaged. Never expose the document to strong light, heat or moisture. When documents are required to be preserved in humid climate for a long time, they should be placed in a closed space with some anti-moist substances. A document should not be cut, trimmed, torn, pinned, punched, tagged or joined by adhesive tapes. When the documents are to be put together, use an envelope to put them together. The documents should not be folded and unfolded unnecessarily. This is to avoid new folds.	A record of the questioned document is kept by photographs whenever possible. If facilities for photography are not available a certified true copy of the document is kept for the purpose of a record. A copy of the document should not be prepared by tracing the writing on the questioned document.
Request Documents	For the purpose of investigation, sometimes request documents are to be prepared. If the questioned item is a signature, about 30 signatures should be obtained on 3 or 4 sheets of paper. If the questioned material is a long text, selected paragraphs are dictated to get writing on 3 or 4 sheets of paper. They are written at different speeds. The writing speed should be adjusted by dictation speed. Each sheet should be removed when it is completed	If the questioned document is a cheque or a lined paper, then similar blank cheques or envelopes or lined paper sheets should be provided. If printed blank forms are not available, electrostastic copies of the blank forms should be provided.

(Contd.)

Specimen		Other Requirements
	and the suspect, if possible, should not be aware of why he is asked to write. He should never be shown the original questioned writing when the investigating officer takes the request document. The spellings and punctuations should not be dictated. It is effective to frame a paragraph describing a paragraph or event or filling a story unrelated to the crime in hand. While doing so, all the essential letters, digits and their combinations in the paragraph should be introduced.	The suspect should not be given prior notice for taking specimens. The investi-gating officers should put his signature or initials on each sheet with date and particulars of the case.
Type-written documents	They should be collected by any one of the most suitable ways explained above.	
Type-script specimens	When taking the type-script specimens for comparison purposes, the following methods should be adopted If the type faces are dirty, five sheets of specimens should be obtained each before and after cleaning the dirty faces. If the ribbon is worn out, five sheets of specimens each with the worn out ribbon and with new ribbon should be obtained.	

(*Contd.*)

Specimen	Other Requirements
	If the pattern of the type-writer is uneven, remember that it does not give even the type-scripts. Even specimens are obtained if the paper being typed is padded with a few sheets of paper. Five sheets of specimens each before and after the insertion of sheets should be obtained.
	Whenever possible, questioned text should be typed for specimens.
	Exemplar type-script immediately before or after the date on which the questioned document was typed should be collected.
	If typed carbon copies are the questioned documents, some carbon copies should be prepared.
	The number, make and model of the type-writer, the name of the typist etc. should be put on each typed specimens.

(Contd.)

Experts and Their Utility

Every investigating officer should know (i) who is the proper expert; (ii) through what agency the article or the matter to be referred to him; (iii) what documents should accompany while referring the matter; and (iv) what problems can not be fruitfully dealt with by the experts.

Different States may have formulated their own rules for sending exhibits to experts and the investigating officers should carefully study these rules. This will doubtlessly help them to fulfill all the requirements and formalities for sending exhibits to experts. The law does not specifically say anything about who can be the expert and who cannot be. Nevertheless, section 45, Indian Evidence Act, 1872 says who is an expert. Hence, the investigating officers should keep in mind that private experts of doubtful repute are not to be consulted and should always go to government experts at the Forensic Science Laboratories. Of course the investigating officer can take the help from any reliable and honest expert in cases, if there is no government expert for making a very specialised examination. Government experts can be of two kinds: they are (i) State Government Experts, and (ii) Central Government Experts.

1. State Government Experts

(a) Medical Officer

The medical officer of a district and his assistants are qualified to examine and report on (i) injuries, the weapons with which they could be caused and their duration; (ii) symptoms of poison, effects of drugs and narcotics and intoxicants; (iii) probable cause of death and time of and after death. In case of injuries from firearms, the doctor may be asked to observe the size of the wounds charring or blackening or tatooing around a wound and dispersion of shots on different parts of the body. He can say the range of fire and angle of firing and sometimes the type of firearms.

(b) Director, State Forensic Science Laboratory

In States where there is no separate Chemical Examiner, the following examinations are taken up in the State Forensic Science Laboratory. Remember that many of the Forensic Science Laboratories have divisions in Biology, Ballistics, Physics, Chemistry and Questioned Documents. This may be consulted on:

1. Determination of blood and its origin.
2. Determination of semen, saliva or other biological specimens.
3. Examination of hairs, fibres, dust, debris, dirt etc.
4. Soil analysis.
5. All problems of toxicology.
6. Blood and semen grouping. If this is not done in the State F.S.L., the matter may be referred to the serologist, Government of India, Calcutta.
7. Problems relating to firearms.
8. Problems relating to tool marks.
9. Problems relating to secret writings and sympathetic inks.
10. Problems relating to questioned documents.
11. Problems relating to partial establishment of personal identity, and calcinated human remains.
12. Problems relating to broken windows, glass chips etc.
13. Traces of motor vehicles.
14. Dyes and stains.
15. Examination of metals, organic substances and their residues.

(c) Chemical Examiner to Government

1. Liquors.
2. Vicera in toxicological cases.
3. Opium and other narcotic drugs. This can also be sent to Forensic Science Laboratory.

4. Substances falling in the category of explosives can be sent to the Inspector of Explosives; and examination of opium and other narcotic drugs may be sent to the Directors of Narcotic Factories.

(d) Director, Finger Print Bureau

1. Articles containing finger prints.
2. Foot prints.
3. Chance prints.

(e) State Laboratory of Public Works Department

1. Building materials.
2. Cement.
3. Girders and other technical advice in this regard.

(f) Motor Vehicle Inspector

Consulted in cases of motor vehicle accidents to know the mechanical conditions of vehicles, approximate speed of the vehicle at the time of accident, conditions of breaks and mechanical failures etc.

(g) Director of Fire Services

He may be consulted in matters of cause and origin of fire.

(h) Dentist

He may be consulted to know the age and sex of persons by examining teeth or jaws (bones) and also to establish identity of an individual by examining the teeth.

(i) Engineer, State Electricity Board

He can be consulted in all cases of property (stolen cases etc.) belonging to the State Electricity Board.

2. Experts of Central Government

(a) Serologist

He analyses blood, semen, saliva, bones and other human remains and determines their group as A, B, AB, O and sub-groups as M,N, MN, Rh+ive and Rh –ive etc.

(b) Controller or Deputy Controller of Explosives or Chief Inspector of Explosives

They are the agencies for disposal and removal of bombs. In emergency cases, the services of Bomb and Mines Disposal Squads of Military Department can be utilized by the investigating officers.

Officers attached to Department of Explosives (Government of India) examine bombs and explosives and give their opinion.

(c) Superintendent, Security Printing, Nasik

He gives opinion about forged currency notes, court fee, revenue and general stamps, lottery tickets of government, Government bonds, postal stamps, cash certificates, Government paper or parchment or other origin and the date of issue in each case. He can be consulted on any other problems relating to printing and paper, pulp, off-set printing and any other special difficulties regarding them.

Some Forensic Science Laboratories (States) in India have examiners of questioned documents. They too can be contacted in similar cases. Examiner of questioned documents, Government of India too can be consulted in these cases.

(d) Mint Master, Calcutta, Bombay and Hyderabad

He gives opinion regarding counterfeit coins and exhibits to all offences described in Chapter XII of the Indian Panel Code. Some State Forensic Science Laboratories too have facilities to do the same thing.

(e) Director, Central Finger Print Bureau, Calcutta

He can be consulted for getting previous conviction of foreigners. Preserved and undisposed F.P. records of persons needed by INTERPOL and other governments, absconded offenders, interstate criminals etc. can be obtained from there.

(f) Examiner of Questioned Documents, Simla, Calcutta, and Hyderabad

He examines documents – hand-written and type-written.

(g) Director (Superintendent), Narcotics Factory, Gazipur

He gives opinion about the origin of opium and its derivatives. All alkalloids and their derivatives like morphine (marijuana) and heroin etc. can be analysed in a chemical laboratory.

(h) Director, Central Forensic Science Laboratory Hyderabad, New Delhi and Calcutta

All items which are examined in State Government Laboratories are examined in the Central Forensic Science Laboratories as well. Their services can be effectively utilized in those things for which no facilities exist in State Forensic Science Laboratories.

(i) Engineer, Telephone Department

He can be consulted in case of copper-wire thefts belonging to the telegraph department.

(j) Engineer, Railways

He can be consulted in all cases of property belonging to Indian Railways.

(k) Textile Experts

They are consulted in the identification of cloths.

Samples for Chemico-Legal Examinations

The investigating officer should bear in mind that the Chemical Examiner needs the following information for his analysis. Therefore, he should inform the medical officer to furnish details of (in case of poisoning):

1. What material was there between the last eating or drinking and the first appearance of symptoms of poisoning?
2. What interval was there between the last eating or drinking and death if death has resulted by consumption of poisoning?
3. What were the first symptom seen in the patient?
4. The medical officer should be requested to say whether or not the following symptoms were seen – viz.,
   (a) vomiting and purging;
   (b) deep sleep;
   (c) tingling of the skin and throat;
   (d) convulsion or twitching of the muscles;
   (e) delirium and clutching at imaginary objects;
   (f) any other symptoms worth mentioning etc.

The substances for chemico-legal examination should not ordinarily be forwarded by Medical Officers to the Chemical Examiner except upon the written requisition of a Magistrate or Police Officer. Nevertheless, if the Medical Officer is of opinion that the sample to be examined by the Chemical Examiner is likely to be decomposed, he can send it to the Chemical Examiner in anticipation of the requisition of the Magistrate/Police Officer. Vicera and other highly decomposable articles should not be kept by the Medical Officer longer than 24 hours. In cases where the Medical Officer has sent the samples for chemico-legal opinion, the Magistrate or the Police Officer should furnish to the Chemical Examiner (i) a brief summary of the history of the case; (ii) date and hour of the time of death; (iii) date and time of collection of material objects; (iv) the urgency in the examination; (v) return of the article after the examination etc. These pieces of information should be furnished in all cases requiring chemico-legal examination.

Relevancy of Expert Opinions

In this regard section 45 of the Indian Evidence Act, 1872 provides:

> "When a Court has to form an opinion upon a point of foreign law, or of science or art or as to identity of hand writing or finger impressions, the opinions upon that point of persons specially skilled in such foreign law, science or art or in questions as to identity of handwriting or finger impressions are relevant facts.
>
> Such persons are called Experts.

Thus according to Indian Evidence Act, experts are persons *specially* skilled in matters of foreign law, science, art, identity of handwriting or finger impressions. The basic test for an expert is his possessing of a *special skill* in the subject matter of opinion. If we take a broad view, the definition of 'expert' in law would cover all branches of human knowledge requiring a course of special study and acquisition of special skill, experience of a trade, handcraft or profession. Thus, medical-men, artists, engineers, surveyors, engravers, mechanics, artisans and the diverse classes of specially skilled workmen would all be experts within the meaning of this section, of course each in his own walk of life.[1]

Section 46, Indian Evidence Act, 1872 says that when the opinion of an *'expert'* is relevant, then the facts bearing upon that opinion and the grounds on which the opinion is based are also relevant.

Whatever may be the law regarding relevancy of expert testimony, there is a feeling among some police officers that courts in India are reluctant to accept expert testimony in criminal cases. This was so, perhaps, in the early decades of the present country. But, as evidence from the case-laws given at the end of this chapter would show, the expert opinion are given due weight provided such opinions are valid in the cases. In Hari Singh *vs.* Saradarni Lachmi Devi, it was held by the court that. "It must be borne in mind that expert witness, however impartial he may wish to be, is likely to be unconsciously prejudiced in favour of the side which calls him. The mere fact of opposition on the other side is apt to create a spirit of partisanship and rivalry so that expert witness is unconsciously impelled to support the view taken by his own side. Besides, it must be remembered that an expert is often called by one side simply and solely because it has been ascertained that he holds views favourable to its interests.[2] This view taken in 1921, by the courts have been changed to day by the increased use of experts in criminal investigation. A number of case laws are quoted at the end of this chapter to make things clearer in this regard.

Physical Clues – Labelling

The reason for labelling is to enable the investigating officer to identify the exhibit whenever necessary. The investigating officers, besides examining the exhibits with proper care and caution must see to it that they do not destroy any possible evidence.

INGREDIENTS OF A LABEL

The label should contain the following information, namely:

A number for the label.

Police station, District and State.

Case reference, date and section of law.

A brief description of the article.

Date and time of seizure.

Place and circumstance of seizure.

Signature of witnesses.

Signature of the officer making the seizure.

The label should be prepared in duplicate and the original be tied with the exhibit. The copy of the label must be forwarded with a covering latter to the expert. The following precautions should be taken for tying the label —that is :

(a) The tying should not interfere with the examination of the exhibit by the expert.
(b) It should not be destroyed or lost in transit.

In case the exhibit is of a minute size, then it must be put in a suitable container and the container should be marked.[3]

Sealing of Exhibits

All knots and fastenings should be sealed with distinction seals. Remember that one and the same seal is used in all the articles seized in connection with a crime and throughout the entire process of investigation. Cases have come to the notice of experts of investigating officers using coins to imprint the seal on wax. This is not permitted and should be avoided. The experts used to return the exhibits in such cases and necessarily it may cause further delay for examining the exhibits. Care should also be taken not to imprint the seal on the naked face of the exhibit or on the naked brim of the container.

The investigating officer should see that the packet containing exhibits are sent to the court by a special police messenger and from there again by a police messenger. If this not possible it may be sent only by registered post and in all such cases a receipt from the postal authorities should be obtained. Such receipts will have to be produced in court of law and when necessary to prove the chain of possession. The forwarding letter should be sent in a separate sealed cover either by a special messenger or by post as the case may be. Remember that all the exhibits must be sent to experts through the concerned court of law. On the packet, write *CAUTION* and indicate top and the bottom of bottles, glass etc. in the packet by putting an arrow and inscribing above it *THIS SIDE UP.*

FORMALITIES TO BE OBSERVED WHEN TRANSPORTING EXHIBITS TO EXPERTS

1. Same seal should be used throughout on the same lot of articles and on the forwarding report.
2. The specimen seal on the forwarding report should be on sealing wax and *not in ink* or on anything else.
3. A copy of the label in writing or made by carbon process should accompany the report.
4. The forwarding report should be sent separately in a sealed over and a copy thereof should be placed inside the parcel.
5. Receipt granted by the Laboratory for the exhibits should be preserved. If the parcel is sent by post, it should be *'Registered with Acknowledgement Due'* and, if by a messenger, a command certificate should be issued. The postal receipts and the command certificate should be preserved for production in court if necessary.[4]

FORWARDING NOTE

In all cases where the examination of any material is required at the ...... FORENSIC SCIENCE LABORATORY, a copy of this form duly filled in should accompany the exhibits.

Case No............................ Police Station:

District.....................

State........................

Section of Law

I. NATURE OF CRIME

(This should cover nature of charge, brief history and any relevant details).

II. LIST OF EXHIBITS SENT FOR EXAMINATION

Sl. No.	Description of the exhibits	How, when and by whom found?	Source of the exhibits*	Remarks

III. NATURE OF EXAMINATION REQUIRED**

(Including any information which will assist the examination).

Memo No...........................Dated, the.........................

Forwarding to the Director.........................Forensic Science Laboratory.

Signature and Designation of the
Forwarding Officer..................

SPECIMEN SEAL IMPRESSION

* 1. The exact place from where the exhibits were collected.

2. If these exhibits were in the possession of a person (Victim/suspect/witness). The other details of the owners should be furnished.

** See *Scientific Aids to Investigation,* Intelligence Bureau, Govt. of India.

Note— In the "Nature of Crime" and "Nature of Examination" care should be taken to ensure that all necessary information regarding individual samples submitted is included.

In the packing of material for expert examination, it is important that the specimen samples should be well protected against contamination from outside sources. The specimen when received at the laboratory must be a true unadulterated sample of the material found at the scene of the crime.

The exhibits should be collected, packed and transported according to the directions issued in the instruction sheet supplied to all investigating officers. Methods describe under each type of exhibit should be meticulously observed.

The specimen must be in a separate clean, glass-stoppered bottles and sealed

Specimen seal impression should be on sealing wax.

Certificate to be signed by a competent forwarding authority and forwarded to the Director............ Forensic Science Laboratory..................with Exhibits.

CERTIFIED that the DIRECTOR............. FORENSIC LABORATORY.................has the authority to examine the exhibits sent to him in connection with the case of State versus...

....

....

under section...................................and if necessary, to take them to pieces or remove portions for the purpose of the said examination.

Signature and Designation of
Forwarding Authority.

Date.............
Place.............

Chain of Possession of Evidence

It must be remembered that the chain of possession of evidence should be maintained. This should be maintained from collection to preservation to transport and production etc.

Special Provisions regarding the Attendance of Experts in Courts

By virtue of sections 292 and 293 of the Code of Criminal Procedure,1973, some categories of experts need not come to court to give their testimony. Such experts include.

(i) Gazetted officers of the Mint or of the India Security Press (including the office of the Controller of Stamps and Stationary) as the Central Government, by notification, specify in this behalf;
(ii) Any Chemical Examiner or Assistant Chemical Examiner to Government ;
(iii) The Chief Inspector of Explosives;
(iv) The Director of the Finger Print Bureau;
(v) The Director, Halfkeine Institute, Bombay;
(vi) The Director of a Central Forensic Science Laboratory or State Forensic Science Laboratory;
(vii) The Serologist to the Government.

The law also says that when any Expert, as mentioned in Sl. No. (ii) to (vii) above, is summouned to appear before a court to give oral evidence with reference to the report of the Expert, an officer subordinate to the Expert, who is conversant with the facts of the case, may be deputed unless the Court expressly requires the presence of the Expert himself.

The Code of Criminal Procedure, 1973 makes the report of such experts admissible as evidence in any inquiry, trial or other proccedings provided the report relates to any matter or thing duly submitted to them for examination or analysis and the report is in the course of any proceedings under the Code of Criminal Procedure.

Expert Evidence –Case Laws

1. "The alleged weapon of the offence should be shown to the medical witness in order to ascertain as to whether all or any of the injuries could be caused with that weapon"[5].
2. "The man of medicine has his own limitation and his failure to give definite opinion should not be considered as an end of the case"[6].
3. "If the prosecution evidence conflicts with the evidence of an expert, i.e., medical or ballistic, it is most fundamental defect and unless reasonably explained, it is sufficient to discredit the entire case"[7].
4. Prosecution case as emerges from the seizure recovery memo is that the accused caused injuries with the dagger. Prosecution cannot now contend that the injury might have been caused by some other dagger, in order to get out of the effect of the evidence of the doctor that the injuries cannot be caused by the dagger shown to him"[8].
5. "The very fact that the medical officer found marks of injuries from which he could definitely opine about the cause of death shows that the decomposition was not so advanced as to defy identification"[9].
6. "In a case where death is due to injuries caused by a lethal weapon it is the duty of the prosecution to prove by expert evidence that it was likely or possible for the injuries to have been caused with the weapon with which and in the manner in which they are alleged to have been caused."[10]
7. "The expert bases his opinion on observing rifling marks on the bullets provided the same are not defaced by the entry in the bodies of the victims. Since the accused had used a country made pistol, the expert would not have found identifying mark on the bullet. Non-examination of the expert is not fatal."[11]
8. "When a catridge is fired, gases are generated by the combination of the powder, creating a presure of 2 to 20 tons per square inch. Under the effect of this pressure, the cap and the paper tube of the catridge cling firmly with the

breach face striking pin and chamber and being of a softer matter the individualities of these parts are impressed upon them. The expert after doing necessary tests came to the conclusion that the crime cartridge found near the dead body was fired from the pistol belonging to the accused."[12]

9. "The prosecution proceeded on the basis there is no ambiguity about it—that Ex.III was the weapon that was used in the commission of the offence. The Ballistic Expert was positive that the seized empties as well as the misfired catridge could not have been fired from Ex III. To hold that, by some mistake a revolver different from that seized from the accused might have been sent to the expert has no basis. It is just a speculation, a process not open to courts."[13]
10. "Expert found that the firing pin impression of the crime catridge and missed catridge tallied with the firing pin impression of the rifle seized from the accused. This shows that the rifle was used at the time of incident".[14]
11. "The chemical examiner's duty is to indicate the number of blood stains found by him on each exhibit and the extent of each stain unless they are too minute or too numerous to be described in detail."[15]
12. "From the microscopic examination of the hair it is possible to say whether they are of the same or of different colour or sizes and from the examination it may help in deciding where the hairs come from."[16]
13. "The two negatives, i.e., one of the photo of the deceased and the other in respect of the skull found were then superimposed to determine the identity of the skull. This evidence is admissible under section 9 of the Evidence Act."[17]
14. "A court would not be justified in rejecting the opinion of the expert who has examined the markings under the comparison microscope simply for the reason that he has not thought it necessary to take the photographs."[18]
15. "The evidence of a handwriting expert is generally of a frail character and its fallibilities have been quite often noticed. The Courts should, therefore, be wary to give too much weight to the evidence of handwriting expert."[19]

16. "Even if originals be not forthcoming, opinions as to handwriting can be formed from the photographs. It is of course always admissible to prove the contents of the document, but subject to the safeguards indicated to prove the authorship. This is all the more so in India under section 10 of the Evidence Act to prove participation in a conspiracy. But evidence of photographs to prove writing or handwriting can only be received if the original cannot be obtained and the photographic reproduction is faithful and not faked or false."[20]
17. "The science of identification of foot prints no doubt a rudimentary science and not much reliance can be placed on the result of such identification. The track evidence, however, can be relied upon as a circumstance which, along with other circumstances, would point to the identity of the culprit though by itself it would not be enough to carry conviction in the minds of the Court."[21]
18. "Expert's opinion must always be received with great caution and perhaps none so with more caution than the opinion of a handwriting expert."[22]
19. "A conviction cannot be based solely on expert opinion without substantial corroboration. This being opinion evidence is, by its very nature, weak and infirm and can not be of itself form the basis of a conviction."[23]
20. "The positive evidence in the case is that of the eye-witness. The evidence of an expert is merely an opinion which lends corroboration to the direct evidence in the case."[24]
21. "No adverse inference can be drawn against the accused if prosecution fails to obtain the opinion of an anatomy expert."[25]
22. "It is not proper way to rely on mere theories of expert witnesses of any sort against facts positively proved."[26]
23. "Direct evidence cannot be branded as untrustworthy because of its inconsistancy with medical evidence."[27]
24. "In a murder case, the place of occurrence is often disputed. A failure of the police to send the blood for chemical analyser is to be deprecated."[28]
25. "Failure to send blood stained earth from the place of occurrence to the Chemical Analyser may indicate that the defence version may be true."[29]

SUGGESTED READINGS

Burrard, G., *The Identification of Firearms and Forensic Ballistics,* Jenkins, London, 1934.

Crown, David, A., *The Forensic Examination of Paints and Pigments,* Charles C. Thomas, Springfield, 1968.

Gunther, J.D. and Ch. O. Gunther, *Identification of Firearms,* Institute of Applied Science, Chicago.

Harrison, W.R., *Suspect Documents,* Praeger, New York, 1958.

Kirk, P.L., *Crime Investigation, Physical Evidence and the Police Laboratory,* Interscience, New York, 1953.

Moenssens, A.A., Ray E. Moses and F.R. Inbau, *Scientific Evidence in Criminal Cases,* Foundation Press, Mineola, N.Y. 1973.

Nicholls, L.G., *The Scientific Investigation of Crime,* Butterworth, London, 1956.

Rhodes, H.T.F., *Forensic Chemistry,* Chapman and Hall, London, 1946.

Saferstein, R., *Criminalistics: An Introduction to Forensic Medicine,* Pretice-Hall, Englewood Cliffs, New Jersey, 1977.

Sharma, B.R., *Forensic Science in Criminal Investigation and Trials,* Central Law Agency, Allahabad, 1974.

Soderman, H. and J.S., O'Connell, *Modern Criminal Investigation,* Funk and Wagnalls, New York, 1932.

Svensson, A and O. Wendel, *Crime Detection: Modern Methods of Criminal Investigator,* Elsevier, New York, 1955.

Williams, R.L., *Forensic Science: The Present and Future,* Analytical Chemistry, 45 No. 13 (1973), 1067 A.

REFERENCES

1. *Crime Investigation,* Directorate of Training, B.P.R. & D., New Delhi.
2. Hari Singh *vs.* Saradarni Lachmi Devi, A.I.R. 1921 Lah. 126.
3. See also, *Crime Investigation,* Directorate of Training, B.P.R. & D. Government of India, 1981, New Delhi.
4. See *Crime Investigation,* B.P.R. & D. *op. cit.*

5. Kartar *vs.* State of Uttar Pradesh, A.I.R. 1976 S.C. 76:1976 Cr. L.J.13: Mohinder Singh *vs.* Narain Singh *vs.* State of Punjab, A.I.R. 1975 S.C. 1727: 1975 Cr. L.J. 1500.
6. A.C Lagu *vs.* State of Bombay, A.I.R. 1960, S.C. 500: 1960 Cr.L.J. 1500.
7. Ram Narain *vs.* State of Punjab, A.I.R. 1975 S.C. 1727:1975 Cr. L.J. 1500.
8. Swaran Singh *vs.* State of Punjab, A.I.R. 1976 S.C. 464:1972 Cr. L.J. 262.
9. Har Dayal *vs.* State of Uttar Pradesh, A.I.R. 1976 S.C. 2055:1976 Cr.L.J. 1578.
10. Mohinder Singh *vs.* State of Punjab, A.I.R. 1953 S.C. 415: 1953 Cr. L.J. 1961.
11. Chatar Singh *vs.* State of Haryana, A.I.R. 1976 S.C. 2474: 1976 Cr. L.J. 1891.
12. Kalua *vs.* State of Uttar Pradesh, A.I.R. 1958 S.C. 180: 1958 Cr. L.J. 300.
13. Mohar Rai *vs.* State of Bihar, 1968 Cr. L.J. 1979.
14. Halim Miani *vs.* State of Bhiar, A.I.R. 1971 S.C. 1864: 1971 Cr. L.J. 1298; Mukhtiar Singh *vs.* State of Punjab A.I.R. 1971 S.C. 1864: 1971 Cr. L.J. 1298.
15. Prabhu *vs.* State of Bombay, A.I.R. 1956 S.C. 51: 1956 Cr. L.J. 147.
16. K.K. Jhadaw *vs.* State of Gujarat, A.I.R. 1966 S.C. 821: 1966. Cr. L.J. 605.
17. Ram Lochan *vs.* State of West Bengal, A.I.R. 1963 S.C. 1074: 1963. (2) Cr. L.J. 170.
18. Ramanathan *vs.* State of Tamil Nadu, A.I.R. 1978 S.C. 1204.
19. Bhagwan Kau *vs.* M.K. Sharma, A.I.R. 1973 S.C. 1346: 1973 Cr. L.J. 1143.
20. L. Choraria *vs.* State of Maharashtra, A.I.R. 1968 S.C. 938: 1968 Cr. L.J. 1124.
21. Pritam Singh *vs.* State of Punjab, A.I.R. 1956 S.C. 415: 1956 Cr. L.J. 805.
22. A.I.R. 1977 S.C. 1091.
23. Magan Bihari Lal *vs.* State of Punjab, A.I.R. 1977 S.C. 1091: 1977 Cr. L.J. 711.
24. Piara Singh *vs.* State of Punjab, A.I.R. 1977 S.C. 2274.
25. State of Punjab *vs.* Bhajan Singh, A.I.R 1975 S.C. 258: 1975 Cr. L.J. 282.
26. Piara Singh *vs.* State of Punjab *op. cit.*
27. Bajwa *vs.* State of Uttar Pradesh, A.I.R. 1973 S.C. 1204: 1973 Cr. L.J. 729.
28. Raghunandan *vs.* State of Uttar Pradesh, 1974 Cr. L.J. 453: A.I.R. 1974 S.C. 463.
29. Lakashmi Singh *vs.* State of Bihar, A.I.R. 1976 S.C. 2263: 1976 Cr. L.J. 1736.

7

SOURCES, MEANS AND AGENTS OF INFORMATION

Investigation of any crime needs collection of massive data about the crime-doer, victim, circumstances leading to the commission of the offence etc., prior to, during and after the occurrence of crime. Collection of information is not an easy task as it is laborious, time consuming, painstaking, and many a time unrewarding. Patrolling, surveillance, shadowing, employment of sources and agents etc. are, doubtlessly, some means by which every investigator tries to collect information. The resourcefulness of the crime investigator in this regard is considered to be an asset in his professional career. This chapter, therefore, deals with sources of information and agents for investigative works.

Information may be defined as "the knowledge produced from people and things"[1] and an informant may be defined as "an individual who, for a particular reason, provides information."[2] Information can be classified into three categories. They are:

i) Information of direct value.
ii) Information of indirect value.
iii) Information of no value.

The first refers to that information which has some direct bearing on the case-say, the crime itself—i.e. statement of suspects victims, witnesses, material evidence etc. They are of direct value as doubtlessly they help to identify, exclude, focus suspicion or provide a basis for further information. The second category means that which is ancillary to the crime. In this category belongs the statements, background information of an offender and the relationship that exists between the culprit and the victim etc. This information can definitely help the investigating officer to formulate theories. The third category is that which provides nothing of importance to the investigation. In every case, virtually, there will come a lot of information, which proves to be useless and often misleading—they are the anonymous tips, irrelevant clues, witness with poor perception etc.[3]

But, it should be remembered that an information, which seems to be apparently of no value at a particular stage of investigation, can be of immense importance at a subsequent stage. Therefore it is not wise or prudent to discard entirely that which the investigating officer thinks to be of no value. This being the case, the investigator may maintain a separate file for keeping this sort of information in the rear of the case folder, so that he can peruse them if that needs be—particularly when the investigation has come to a standstill or to a dead end.[4]

SOURCES

Casual Source	**Cultivated Source**
The casual source supplies information out of their civic sense or hostility jealously, vengeance etc., towards the accused or conversely sympathy, consideration, love etc, towards the victim. Mostly, they would like to remain anonymous and in many instances the police get letters from anonymous sources.	They are the informants or agents cultivated by the department. They are generally called *confidential informants of police.*

Information for investigative works can be collected from many sources or agents. The source in investigation means the source of supply of information and agent means a person cultivated by the department for the purpose of collecting information of which the investigating officer cannot or does not find accessibility in the normal course of his work.

Agents

"Agents" in police work can be classified as: (i) confidential agents, (ii) the one time-agent, and (iii) involuntary agents. These agents generally do not want their identities exposed. They want to remain secret and secret always. Remember that these secret agents supply information regarding crime and criminals, most often, to get something in return—may be money, or favours or special consideration from police or to get prestige etc. Accordingly the secret agents are subdivided into various classes.

Professional decency and ethics demand that the investigator must keep the secret information furnished by these agents confidential. He should not divulge the source even to his associates in the department. If he does so he is sure to loose his credibility. Remember that an investigator's success depends considerably upon the reputation he earns in keeping secret of the sources of information. New ones may be afraid to enrol their names in the confidential lists maintained by the investigator if they understand that the investigator is not a reliable person. In case of acute necessity, the investigator can divulge the source of information, but only after informing the informant that his name would be revealed and getting permission from the agents to do so. Section 125 Indian Evidence Act, 1872 gives protection to police officers and the *investigating police officer* is not compelled to disclose the source of his information. In case of his transfer, the investigating officer must entrust the "confidential list" to his successor who is bound to keep the secrecy of it.

SECTION 125, INDIAN EVIDENCE ACT, 1872

Section 125, Indian Evidence Act reads:

"No Magistrate or Police Officer shall be compelled to say whence he got (any) information as to the commission of any offence, and no Revenue Officer shall be compelled to say whence he got any information as to the commission of any offence against the public revenue".

This privilege is essential for the conduct of any criminal cases. This is the reason why the law has been enacted. "It is the duty of every citizen to communicate to his Government any information which he has of the commission of an offence against the laws. To encourage him in performing this duty without fear of consequences, the law holds such information to be among secrets of the State. Courts of Justice therefore will not compel or allow the discovery of such information, either by the subordinate officer to whom it is given by the informant himself, or by any other person, without the permission of the Government."[5]

In R.V. Hardy, 24 How. St. Tr. 808, EYRE L.C.J. stated:

> "It is perfectly right that all opportunities should be afforded to discuss the truth of the evidence given against a prisoner; but there is a rule, which has universally obtained on account of its importance to the public for the detection of crimes, that those persons, who are the channel by means of which that detection is made, should not be unnecessarily disclosed; if it can be made to appear that really and truly it is necessary to the investigation of the truth of the case that the name of the person should be disclosed, I should be very unwilling to stop it, but it does not appear to me that it is within the ordinary course to do it".

However there are some limitations for this privilege and they are:

1. It applies to the identity of the informant, and not to the contents of his statements as such, for, by hypothesis the contents of the communication are to be used and published in the course of prosecution. Much less does the privilege apply to prevent merely the proof of contents which has already been *de facto*

disclosed, —as in an action against the informer for libel (see Majju *vs.* Lachman, 46 A. 671).

2. If the identity of the informer is *admitted or known*, then there is no reason for pretended concealment, and the privilege of secrecy would be merely an artificial obstacle to proof.
3. The privilege applies to communications to such officers only as have a *responsibility or duty* to investigate or to prevent public wrongs, and not to officials in general. This ordinarily signifies the *police* and officials of criminal justice generally. But it may also include *administrative officials* having a duty of inspection or of law enforcement in their particular spheres.
4. Even where the privilege is strictly applicable, the *trial court may compel disclosure*, if it appears necessary in order to avoid the risk of false testimony or to secure useful testimony.[6]

SECTION 172, CODE OF CRIMINAL PROCEDURE, 1973

Section 172, Cr. P.C. entitles a police officer to refuse to disclose the source of his information as to the commission of any offence. It reads:

1. Every police officer making an investigation under this chapter shall day by day enter his proceedings of the investigation in a diary, setting forth the time at which the information reached him, the time at which he began and closed his investigation, the place or places visited by him, and a statement of the circumstances ascertained through his investigation.
2. Any Criminal Court may send for the police diaries of a case under inquiry or trial in such Court, and may use such diaries, not as evidence in the case, but to aid it in such inquiry or trial.
3. Neither the accused nor his agents shall be entitled to call for such diaries, not shall he or they be entitled to see them merely because they are referred to by the Court; but, if they are used by the police officer who made them to refresh

his memory, or if the Court uses them for the purpose of contradicting such police officer the provisions of section 161 or section 145, as the case may be, of the Indian Evidence Act, 1872 (1 of 1872) shall apply.

AGENTS

PAID AGENTS

He is paid for each information he supplies to the police either on piece meal or on salary-wise. He makes an income out of it. Provisions to appoint agents on salary-wise are not in practice in India. Mostly, they are paid on piece meal basis from the secret fund.

Criminal Agents

They are ex-criminals or those involving in anti-social acts—He wants to get favours such as overlooking an illegal act or operation in which he is deeply/ partly involved.

Agents whose sole purpose is to cement friendship

Their intention is just to maintain their friendship they established long back or in the recent past. By this they want to be more friendly with individual police officers.

Agents who work for special favours & considerations

They want to get favours and considerations. They may be small-scale politicians, social workers or popular leaders. Some of them may make money not from police but from their customers.

Prestige Seeking Agents

They want to show to others that they are having association with police officers. They want to get prestige.

Agents who work out of civic mindedness.

They are very few in India. Still, there can be this group as well.

Agents, as stated earlier, can be of many kinds. The chart above gives a list of such agents who can beneficially be employed by the police during various stages of investigation.

1. Casual Source

It is not advisable to ignore totally the casual sources. Anonymous telephone calls, letters etc. may help the investigator to unearth certain mysteries connected with crime. The principle to be followed is that there will be a grain of truth in all anonymous information coming to the police. Likewise, news in a paper or a casual conservation with people may reveal secrets which police may need. It is also possible that some people may try to misguide the investigation by supplying false information. Does not matter. Such things are the inevitable evils in all walks of human life and police are no exception to it. Making an awareness among the public that the information supplied by them—in an anonymous way or otherwise—will be seriously pursued and follow-up action will be initiated will prove to be beneficial to reach the goal in investigative processes.

2. Paid Agents

They, as said earlier, are the cultivated source. The police have to get in touch with them as frequently as possible. But where? They should be contacted in secrecy by arrangement at odd hours of the night at their residence or in an inconspicuous way in a restaurant, lavatory etc. The investigator should change the meeting places as often as possible and if that is not possible, then encourage them to write letters in the name cover to the investigator. Of course they are paid agents. Although their services are paid, it does not mean that money or payments make everything in human relations. It is quite likely that the informants may take freedom with the investigating offices, and the freedom they take may make the constables to suspect the investigator-agent relationship. This is not going to serve anything good and therefore they should be properly warned and instructed at the time they are recruited to take necessary precautions against their overt behaviour with the investigator. The investigator should see to that they are not called to police station for supplying information. It is and should be secret business transaction.

Use only Code Names or Code Numbers to identify a particular informant. A model of the Index Card with Code Name and Number can be as under. The police department should see that sufficient number of Index Cards are provided in every police station.

INFORMATION (AGENT) INDEX CARD
HOUSE BREAKING AND THEFT (Chalai Bazar Area) Code Name: **Sparrow** Code No. **A. 89** Location – T.C. 17/1897, Opposite to Paul Jacobs & Co., Bazar Road, Chalai. Information : Knows house breaking and theft in Chalai Bazar. May be able to provide information on Gopal, Ravi and Jose.

The card shows that "Sparrow', Agent No. A. 89, can be located in Bazar Road, Chalai for collecting information about house breaking and theft. He can also furnish information about Gopal, Ravi and Jose. Here the investigating officer should have a location file under 'Chalai Bazar Area'. A notation to see Agent No. A. 89 also must be made in the suspect file, if the police station has any such file for Gopal, Ravi and Jose.

As the agents in this category are paid ones, it should be seen that prompt payment is made for the services rendered by these agents as many of them have nothing other than mercenary considerations for their services done to the police department. The police department has enough money in their 'Sector Service Fund' and the money spent form this fund is exempted from external audit. If the agent is prepared to give a receipt for the money, there is no harm in getting it, but never insist for a receipt if he is reluctant to do so.

As stated earlier, all paid agents furnish information, many a time, for mercenary considerations. Therefore, they are likely to furnish 'false information'. Hence all information from these agents must be viewed with suspicion and should be verified through other sources. For the first time they are detected for giving false information, they should be warned and payment should not be made and if they continue again providing false information, there names should be deleted from the Index Card.

LIST OF INFORMERS WHO CAN BE RECRUITED AS SECRET AGENTS

1. Hotel Keepers
2. Sarai-Keepers
3. Managers of Dharma-shalas
4. Servants and those work-ing as scavengers
5. Electricians
6. Telephone testers
7. Servants of public catering house, tea-shops, restaurants
8. People employed in toddy/arrack selling shops
9. Doctors, dentists, nurses & druggists.
10. Rickshaw pullers, taxi-drives, auto-rickshaw drivers and bus conductors
11. Station-masters, booking clerks and other railway employees and employees at bus stands.
12. Panwalas, bidiwalas
13. Village grocers, village leaders, patwaris, landlords
14. News paper reporters and correspondents, news paper selling boys
15. Prostitutes, primps procurers, managers of brothels
16. Managers of gambling dens
17. Astrologers, sooth-sayers
18. Poojaris of temples, temple servants, priests, sacristians
19. School teachers, college lecturers, student leaders
20. Tailors, carpenters, cobblers smithies
21. Government servants, factory employees, quasi-government employees
22. Sports-stars, scout members, N.C.C. cadets.
23. Road-side sellers
24. Employees in theatres
25. Ex-convicts
26. Society women, social workers so on.

3. Criminal Agents

Catch a thief to fetch a thief is an at times employed police craft in criminal investigation. Therefore, the investigator can profitably recruit a number of agents from the jail or from those who are ex-convicts. So long as a person is in the jail, police need not have to take precautions in arranging visits with him. Offering a cigerette or conveying some messages about his family or children etc. can establish the needed rapport between the convict and the officer. The close relationship can be continued even after the convict's release from the prison. This has, many a time, some corrective value also. An ex-convict may not think of relapsing into crime or becoming a recidivist if he has healthy relationship with the police officer. This needs not be true always. For, those who are ex-convicts may create problems for the investigating officers. He may furnish information, perhaps, just to see that his recidivist activities are not seriously taken note of or they are overlooked. Therefore it should be to the interest of the investigator that his rapport or relationship with the ex-convict is not misused. The ex-convict should not take it for granted that his relation with the investigator is a licence for him to involve in further committing crimes. This is the reason why Richard H. Ward says:

"The decision by police to overlook a crime in return for information is not to be lightly taken, and further developments may place the investigator's position in jeopardy. As a rule, the investigator must realize that an informant is working for the police department and while he may belong to a particular investigator, his ultimate value is measured in terms of accomplishing the investigative goal. For this reason, there should be a departmental policy concerning the use of informants and some one other than the investigator (preferably superior officer) should be aware of the circumstances surrounding the use of each informant. If the department is not willing to overlook a particular crime for certain type of information, the investigator should not take the burden of doing so on his shoulders".

4. Friendship Agents

Police officers do and should establish good and healthy friendship with a number of people in their jurisdiction—may be government servants, officers in other departments like the Excise, Forest,

Weights and Measures, Income-tax, Health Services etc. This friendship can profitably be utilized for investigative purposes without any loss of money. Many of these officers have their own resource personnel whose service can be beneficially made use of provided the investigating officers have good friendship/relations with them. Once a medical doctor made use of his patients to collect information for his colleague in the police department.

5. Prestige-Seeking Agents

Information supplied by prestige-seeking agents may proceed from various motives—immediate or ulterior. Prestige seeking agents may be a textile owner, an upstart in society or a wealthy estate owner and so on. They want prestige and for this purpose they would like to have association with police officers. They may freely offer their cars for the personal use of the police officer or may like to travel along with the investigating officers. They may invite the police officers for lunch at their homes or even make family visits. Establishment of friendship with them may be good, but too much of anything is bad and friendship with them is just for the purpose of investigation and nothing else.

Prestige-seeking agents, from experience, seem to be dangerous people. They may often exaggerate or over-exaggerate things. Hence it is very necessary to compare and verify the information supplied by them on the same point from various sources and check them up. These prestige-seeking agents may tell others about their association or contact with police officers. This may be with the intention of showing others that they are very influential people. As such, at times these agents are more harmful than useful. Due caution should be exercised in the recruitment of these people.

6. Agents Who Work for Special Favours/Considerations

Petty politicians (local level), so called social workers, local agents/ correspondents of news papers, political workers etc. may furnish information to police—the purpose being to get some special favours or consideration from the police officers. If they are offered a seat in the police station/a cup of tea/some good words etc., they may feel highly elevated and more often than not they may try to misuse it. Whenever a petition enquiry is conducted or a witness is called or an accused is brought to police station they may accompany them, preferably in cars and may insist on being entertained in good hotels or remunerated in cash or in kind. Local level politicians may advance very valuable information if the accused belongs to a political party which is not theirs and so is their attitude to the victims/witnesses/complainants etc. Therefore these agents are harmful, if not useless.

7. Agents Who Work Out of Civic Consciousness

They are comparatively very few in our country. But if the police are able to cultivate a source of this nature, it will prove to be highly useful during investigation work. Really civic minded people may advance information. But many a time, the so-called civic minded people volunteer information, perhaps, with ulterior motives. It so happens that they for some reason or other, come forward with information and in such cases, on depth analysis, it may be found that their motive is not civic mindedness, but jealousy, vengeance, intimate relations, personal enimity etc. to the crime-doer or his victim. As such, the information furnished by them may be fabricated, distorted, exaggerated or falsely interpreted. Verification is called for in such instances. This type of informants cannot come under the cultivated source. They may belong to the casual source. Similar is the case of people who know every thing about crime and criminals, and are reluctant to come forward because they are afraid of police or the opposite party. There may be a number of causes as well. In case the police comes across such informants through casual or cultivated sources, every effort must be made to get their full cooperation which ultimately can or will unearth secrets about the crime and its criminals.

Recruitment of Sources

How to recruit agents to the list of cultivated source of informants?

The considerations for recruitment should be:

1. Ascertain the motive first—the motive may be monetary, political, personal etc.
2. Ascertain his contacts with people and methods of his collection of information.
3. Ascertain his aptitude and interest in the work.
4. Ascertain his reputation, social standing, character etc. Character is something which a man has in himself and reputation is what other people say about him.
5. Ascertain his capacity to keep secrets and ability to understand and appreciate the problems of the investigator in a particular situation.

If these conditions are satisfactory there is no harm in recruiting him as a member of the cultivated source of the department.

Management of Cultivated Source

Some methods and techniques for the management of cultivated source/agents are given in the next page. Here are a few more rules for developing a good rapport between the investigating officer and the informant. The relationship between the investigator to the informant must be like the attitude of a good salesman to his customers. The author once entered a good shoe-market just to see the new arrivals. As soon as a he entered a shop, the salesman came similing, spoke nicely, behaved courtesely, so much so that the author felt like purchasing a pair of shoes and he did so. Hence, it goes without saying that the investigator, if he desires success, should know the dynamics of human behaviour, understand the psychology of each informant and his wants and demands. This is necessary for his business-relationship with his customers—say the informants. 'Business-relationship' means only 'business-relationship' and nothing more—in other words he should not become too friendly although he must show respect to his informant and his sentiments. The source traits of the investigators should be those which he prossesses in him for the ultimate goal of his investigative works and the surface traits are all those qualities which he may show on his face and behaviour so as to achieve his goals. All the principles for maintaining good business man-customer relationship can be employed here remembering that all these are necessary means to achieve his end—the end being success in investigation.

METHODS AND TECHNIQUES OF MANAGING CULTIVATED AGENTS

1. Keep the informant happy and in good humour.
2. Maintain a business-like relationship with the agents.
3. Show respect to the agent and his sentiments, but never try to become very friendly with him.
4. Keep the information always 'confidential' remembering that secrecy is the most important thing in this regard.
5. Don't show to the informant that the investigating officer knows the motive of his supplying information. This makes him 'cheap' or 'less'.
6. Be plain to the informant if the investigating officer cannot fulfill a promise.
7. Try to maintain frequent contacts.
8. Remember that good informants are always the property of the department and an expenditure on this aspect is an investment on human resources of the department.
9. Establish good 'rapport' with the informants.
10. Never allow the subordinates to know the names and addresses of the agents and also the agents among themselves.
11. Never call the agents to the police station and do not meet them in places where others may watch the activities in suspicion.
12. If found useless, delete the agent's name from the list without telling him the reason for doing so.

Briefing the Successor

Briefing the successor about the agents is of very great importance. Many a time, this may not be possible and in such situations, the successor should be given facility to have complete background information about the agents. For this purpose, it is better to maintain the following *Background Information Sheets* about the agents in police stations.

Remember that an agent is virtually a betrayer. This means that if he can be a betrayer once, he can always be a betrayer.

Therefore, it is necessary to collect information about the agent as much as possible. Once an agent is recruited, it should be seen that he is instructed to collect information without being overzealous or ostentatious. He should not give information on mere gossip or rumour. He should be asked to substantiate his statements on facts and documents. Objectivity and accuracy in details should be ensured. Absence of information is always better than misinformation.

BACKGROUND INFORMATION SHEET OF AGENTS

Code Name: **Sparrow** Code No. **A.89**

1. Motive for becoming an agent ....
2. Background information such as: married or unmarried; number of children; parents alive or not; address to which communications to be sent; sources of getting information about the agent in case of his absence; qualifications; any other important information etc.
3. Rate of remuneration per information supplied Rs ....
4. Reliability of the agent ....
5. Methods to verify the information supplied by the agent ....
6. Secret place/s to meet the agent ....
7. Identifying marks ....
8. Other remarks ....

Section 125 Indian Evidence Act—Case Laws

1. "Statements made to the police are in their nature confidential and section 162, Cr. P.C illustrates the limited purposes for which their production should be required. Under section 125 Evidence Act, a police officer can not be compelled to say whence he got any information as to the commission of any offence. Therefore, the discretion under section 94 Cr. P.Code to order production of a document should be exercised in such a way as not to conflict with the policy in section 125." (R.*vs.* Bilal Md. 1940 Bom. 768)[7]

2. "The accused was convicted of criminal breach of trust in respect of three gold bangles. The evidence went to show that

the accused insured a parcel in the post office as containing these gold bangles, but, shortly after delivery to the addressee, the parcel was found to contain only a piece of steel. One of the witnesses deposed that he sold the steel to the accused. The accused's counsel asked the Superintendent of Post Offices the name of the person who had informed him about the sale of steel to the accused but the Sessions Judge refused to allow the question to be put—Held that neither section 124 nor section 125 had any application to the case and that the question should have been allowed" (R. *vs*. Ramdhan, 2 Bom. L.R. 329 (Folld. in Harbans *vs*. R., 16 W. N. 431)[8].

3. "This section rests upon public policy and protects the name of a spy or informant and the nature of the information and it has no application to an informant who lays sworn information and thereby initiates criminal proceedings" (Liladhar *vs*. R. 8 S.L.R. 309: 291.C.79)[9]

4. Examination of spy or informant of the police is neither necessary nor desirable (S.*vs*. Dhanpat, A 1960, P. 582).[10]

Other Sources of Information

All of us live in a society that is noted for collecting information. From the time an individual is born, a lot of information is collected and recorded. Many of the children born in Hindu families get their horoscopes written. This will be a good source of information for knowing the date of birth. Similarly, the hospital records reveal the birth and time of birth of a child. Panchayats/Muncipalities/ Corporations too record the births and deaths of people. Archives of the Christian churches have records of baptism. The Schools, the Clubs, Insurance Companies, Post and Telegraph departments have their records. In certain cases a criminal record is also maintained in police stations. Finger prints and the bio-data of some of the criminals are available with the Director of Finger Print Bureau. The service book will reveal a lot of information about government, quasi-government servants. Private companies do maintain records of their employees. Voters' list is another source of information. Title deeds, contract deeds or sale deeds can reveal information needed by police. The friends and relatives of the offender can be a good source of information. Thus, in short, the effective use of these sources of information is dependent on the initiative and drive which an investigator has in him. The investigating officer should try to locate an individual through these informational sources.

RECORDS AS SOURCES OF THIN INFORMATION

Name of the record	**Purpose**
1. Telephone Directory	To know the names, addresses and telephone numbers of all persons having telephones.
2. Other Directories of a Church, Organisation, Club etc.	To know the names, addresses and other matters about persons belonging to a particular organi-sation, club etc.
Name of the agencies	
1. Department of Agriculture	To know details regarding people applied for loans and similar matters connected with agricultural departments.
2. Post Offices	To know all persons receiving mail at a given address; to trace people whose addresses are known to postal authorities.
3. Passport Division	To get details of people who have applied for passports from their applications.
4. Office of the Excise Commissioner	To get details about abkari contrac-tors, distillers, brewers, and persons/firms handling alcohol as side line/main product.
5. Customs and Central Excise	To collect details of importers and exporters, customs house brokers, custom house truckers etc.
6. Drug Controller	To collect details relating to medical shop owners, druggists and pharmacists etc.
7. Transport Commissioner	To collect details regarding automobiles, drivers etc.
8. Census Department	To take details about people whose names are included in the census report by looking to the back files.

9. Court Records	To know about criminal and civil-case-matters regarding a particular individual.
10. Hospitals	To know the health records of people treated.
11. Inspector General of Registration	To collect copies of deeds or documents.
12. Income-tax Department	To know the property and income of an individual.
13. Voters' Register	To collect details of people who are in the voters' list by perusing the back files.
14. Employment Office	To know details of persons registered in the employment offices.

15. Libraries, Schools, Banks, Money Lenders, Insurance com-panies, Gas-distribution Agencies, Electricity Board, Water Supply Agencies, Social Welfare Boards, Bonding Companies, Churches, Commercial Credit Agencies, Finance and Loan Companies, Political Party Offices, Hotels and Motels, Laundry and Dry Cleaning Establishments, Magazines, News paper and Book Clubs, Trade Unions etc. will be useful in furnishing information relating to people and organizations.

Sources and Prevention of Crime

Police can make use of their agents and sources for prevention of crime as well. Sections 106 to 110, 114 to 152, Code of Criminal Procedure, 1973 are important from this point of view.

Police Patrol, Surveillance, Beat etc. for Investigation Work

Preventive maintenance, doubtlessly, is an important objective of police patrolling. Prevention of crime may be effected through patrolling—by means of eliminating or reducing the desire of potential criminals to commit crimes. Repression of crimes and thereby maintenance of law and order and public peace can be resulted if the police department is keen in its patrolling. How far patrolling will be useful in crime investigation works?

Collection of information regarding the crime and criminals are of paramount importance during various stages of investigation. The patrol man on duty, therefore, can and should keep a special eye on any suspicious people and others so that he can gather a lot of information. He can also make enquiries about the suspects if that needs be. The beat patrol constable can collect information about the movements of strangers, and characters, suspects in a crime and their activities. He can watch all sorts of people from all walks of life and contact his agents for the purpose of collecting information. Thomas F. Adams writes in this context: "The officer on patrol should develop informants. He will cultivate informants among the criminal ranks, the vice operators who provide information concerning criminal activities of others for various reasons and those who have criminal records, but choose to 'live it straight' now that have been rehabilitated. The officer will seek informants among the members of people who obey the laws themselves and who sincerely wish to assist the police in identifying and prosecuting other people in the community who choose to disobey the laws of the community and the state"[11].

Surveillance, as defined, is the secret or open watching of particular bad characters and thereby collections of information about their activities—i.e., those who involve or are likely to involve in the commission of crimes. All persons who are known or suspected to have committed an offence can be and should be placed under surveillance although there are special and specific rules guiding the procedure and conduct of surveillance in different States. Open surveillance on people may be controlled by specific rules, but secret surveillance can be and should be done if the department wants of collect information about persons who are suspected to have involved in the commissions of crimes.

Surveillance and the techniques of surveillance should not be taken in their strict legal sense for the purpose of investigation works. Secret picketing, verification of movements of the suspects in crimes, shadowing or unobstrusive trailing of suspects etc. are some of the techniques which can be successfully employed in investigation work by an officer who is skillful in the art of secret surveillance.

Secret Picketing —A Case Law

"It is obvious that the secrecy here referred to is secrecy from the subject. In other words, its purpose is to ascertain the identity of the person or persons who visit the house of the suspect so that the police may have a record of the nature of the activities in which the suspect is engaged. This, ofcourse, can not in any from affect either the right on the part of the suspect to move "freely" nor can it be held to deprive him of his "personal liberty" within Art. 21."[12]

SUGGESTED READINGS

Chapman, Samuel G., *Police Patrol Readings,* Charles C. Thomas, Springfield, Illinois, 1964.

Deinstein, William, *Techniques for the Crime Investigator,* Charles C. Thomas, Springfield, Illinois, 1970.

Directorate of Training, *Crime Investigation,* ed. R.K. Nigam, B. P. R. & D, New Delhi.

Harney Milachi, L., *The Informer in Law Enforcement,* Charles C. Thomas, Springfield, Illinois 1962.

Holcomb, R.L., *Police Patrol,* Charles C. Thomas, Springfield, Illinois, 1964.

McCann, Michael G., *Police and the Confidential Informant,* Indiana University Press, Bloomington, 1957.

McCormic Mona, *Who-What-Where-How-Why-Made Easy,* The New York Times Co., New York, 1971.

Rmanujam, T., *Prevention and Detection of Crimes,* Madras Agency, Madras 1972.

Schultz, Donald, O., *Police Operational Intelligence,* Charles C. Thomas Springfield, Illinois, 1968.

Ward, Richard, H., *Introduction to Criminal Investigation,* Addison-Wesley Publishing Company, Phillipines, 1975.

Wilson, O.W., *Police Administration,* 2nd ed., McGraw Hill Book Co., New York, 1963.

Whisenand, Paul, M., and Tug. T. Tamaru, *Automated Police Information Systems,* John Wiley and Sons, New York, 1970.

REFERENCES

1. Richard H. Ward, *Introduction to Criminal Investigation,* Addison-Wesley Publishing Co., Phillippines, 1975.
2. Richard H. Ward, *Introduciton to Criminal Investigation, op. cit.*
3. Richard H. Ward, *Introduciton to Criminal Investigation, op. cit.*
4. See also Richard H. Ward, *Introduciton to Criminal Investigation, op. cit.*
5. Grey C.J. in Worthington *vs.* Scribner, 109 Mass, 487, 489 (Am.).
6. See S.C. Sarkar, *Sarkar's Law of Evidence,* S.C. Sarkar & Sons (Private) Ltd., Calcutta, 1965.
7. Section 94 Cr. P. Code, 1898 corresponds to section 91 of the Cr. P. Code, 1973. For the case law referred to see S.C. Sarkar, *Sarkar's Law of Evidence, op. cit.*
8. S.C. Sarkar, *Sarkar's Law of Evidence, op. cit.*
9. S.C. Sarkar, *op. cit.*
10. S.C. Sarkar, *op. cit.*
11. Thomas P. Adams, *Police Patrol : Tactics and Techniques,* Prentice-Hall Inc. Englewood Cliffs, N.J., 1971.
12. Kharak Singh *vs.* State of Uttar Pradesh, (Writ Petition No. 356 of 1961), 1963 All. L. J., 729.

8

POLICE RECORDS, REGISTERS AND DIARIES

The role that records and registers play during the conduct of criminal investigation is really very important. The police records and registers are the mainspring for the success of investigation. Report writing is said to be an art, but seldom do some of the investigators recognize it. For, sometimes, they entrust this task to ill-qualified or underqualified head constables. The H. Cs do the entire writing exercise during the various stages of investigation. This practice, if it exists, should be discouraged by investigating officers and superior police officers alike. The report is a word picture of all activities and findings which the investigating officer can communicate to his successors, colleagues and supervisory officers. It is the basic reference for anyone and is the basis for the prosecution and resultingly the public prosecutor depends heavily on these reports. The reports should, therefore, ensure accuracy, completeness, bravity, fairness, etc.

1. Roznamah or Hozamcha or General Diary or Station Diary

This is used by police to write:

a) all happenings in the station;
b) coming and going of the officers;

c) the purpose for which the officers have come and gone out;
d) all information the station receives etc.

They will be entered in the General Diary day after day and hour after hour. The Station House Officer is entrusted with the responsibility of maintaining the General Diary.

2. Case-Diary

This is a Diary in which every proceedings of a particular case is recorded in a chronological order. Different officers who are put in charge of the investigation of a particular case write the developments of investigation in this. Hence the diary is opened as soon as a particular case is registered in the Station House. The Diary contains the crime number of a particular case and includes every step taken during the process of investigation.

3. The Pocket Note-Book

Every investigating officer is supplied with a Pocket Note-Book and he records his actions and movements in the course of his duty as a police officer. This is a book of confidential nature and a Court of Law can not and will not look into the contents recorded in the Note-Book. If necessary superior police officers can peruse it.

The objective of maintaining these diaries is: (i) to preserve knowledge, (ii) to provide accurate details, (iii) to aid other personnel and agencies and (iv) to co-ordinate the activities of a police organization—says J. C. Hazelet.

General Diary—What Should it Contain?

Section 44, Police Act, 1861 insists every officer-in-charge of a police station to maintain a General Diary and to register therein all complaints and charges preferred, names of all persons apprehended, the names of complainants, offences charged against the accused, the weapon or property that has been seized and the names of all persons who have been examined as witnesses. When a F.I.R. about a cognizable offence is registered, section 154, Criminal Procedure Code, 1973 prescribes that the contents of the information relating to a cognizable offence to be written in the General Diary. If the information relates to the commission of a non-cognizable offence, then the contents of the information is entered in the G. D. as per section 155, Cr. P.C., 1973. What action is initiated on the receipt of the information is also written in the G. D. with the name of the officer and the time of leaving the station together with the purpose for which the officer left etc.

Example: 8.30 a.m. Received the information × relating to the commission of the offence [State here the substance of the information]. Registered a case as Crime No..........The Sub-Inspector...........leaves the station to the scene of crime at..........(area) at..............O'clock to investigate.

9.30 a.m. Sub-Inspector returned to the station with AB arrested in connection with Crime No. .... Property seized under a mahazar and brought to the station is........... etc.

The statement of witnesses and the various steps taken during the investigation of a particular case need not be written in the G.D. They should find a place in the Case-Diary relating to the case under investigation. Nevertheless, the informer's address, his fathers' name etc. are entered in the G. D. This is to enable the officer to make easy reference. Also, the General Diary should contain:

i) the names of all persons arrested;

ii) the time and place of arrest;

iii) the weapons/property seized from the accused or else—where;

iv) the names of witnesses who were examined;

v) any matter of importance relating to the work of a police station.

General Diary —Use in a Court of Law

The General Diary can be used by the Court or the accused without any restriction. It is a chronological record showing the time of receipt of information, the time when any weapons or articles connected to a crime are brought to the police station or the arrival of persons injured during the commission of a crime etc. The General Diary is used in a Court of Law:

i) to prove the time of receipt of an information relating to a cognizable/non-cognizable offence. In private complaints, the G. D. entry, if there is, is summoned to the court to prove the genuineness of the complaints and also to prove that an information was lodged to the police immediately after the commission of the offence;
ii) to prove the time of seizure of any incriminating articles/ weapons. The entry in the G. D. corroborates the Mahazar or search list;
iii) to use as record of the injuries noticed by the police officer on the person of a victim of offence.

"The absence of an entry in the General Diary in any important case and any discrepancy between the entries in the General Diary and prosecution evidence in court regarding the time of receipt of F.I.R. will have serious adverse consequences for the case in a court of law"writes K. Krishnamurti[1]. The superior police officers and the District Magistrates (see section 44, Police Act,1861) should see to it that they call for and inspect the General Diary as often as possible so that mistakes in maintaining the G.D. are rectified at the earliest available opportunity.

Case-Diary

Section 172 Code of Criminal Procedure reads:

1. "Every police officer making an investigation under this Chapter shall day by day enter his proceedings in the

investigation in a diary setting forth the time at which the information reached him, the time at which he began and closed his investigation, the place and places visited by him, and a statement of the circumstances, ascertained through his investigation.

2. Any Criminal Court may send for the police diaries of a case under inquiry or trial in such Court, and may use such diaries, not as evidence in the case, but to aid it in such inquiry or trial.
3. Neither the accused nor his agents shall be entitled to call for such diaries, nor shall he or they be entitled to see them merely because they are referred to by the Court, but, if they are used by the police officer who made them to refresh his memory or if the Court uses them for the purpose of contradicting such officer, the provisions of section 161 or section 145, as the case may be, of the Indian Evidence Act, 1872 (1 of 1872) shall apply."

The Case-Diary of a particular case is a complete record of investigation and is by its very nature confidential, but can be used to a limited extent under the certain circumstances explained under section 172 Cr. P.C., 1973. The use of the Case-Diary by the Court or by the accused etc. are dealt with at length in the pages that follow.

The Case-Diary serves the following purposes:

i) It is a full and complete record of an investigation of a particular case.
ii) It is a means by which police work is effectively regularised and continuity of investigation is ascertained when investigation in done by several officers.
iii) It is a means by which superior police officers do exercise effective supervision and check up the progress of investigation. They can direct the investigation in the proper way. In order to enable this, the copies of the case diary is sent to superior police officers every day.
iv) It is a record which can be perused by Courts of Law

under section 167 Cr. P.C., 1973 at the time when the remand of the accused is prayed for by the police and under section 172 Cr. P.C., 1973 during the trial of a criminal case.

v) It is a record which can be used by the investigating officer to refresh his memory, if that need be.

vi) It is considered as an evidence if it is used by the Court of Law for contradicting the police officer under section 172 Cr. P.C 1973.

vii) Since supervision is exercised by superior police officers on the progress of investigation by perusing the Case-Diary, it improves the quality of investigation.

How to Write a Case-Diary?

The following points should be borne in mind when the case-diary is written[2]:

i) "Facts should be written down in the order of their occurrence.

ii) Absolute accuracy should be observed.

iii) The exact hour, day of the week and date on which anything is reported to have taken place should be given.

iv) All necessary details and facts should be given so as to avoid the necessity of making a subsequent supplementary or explanatory report.

v) The writer should make it clear what he saw, heard or did himself.

vi) When reporting what he has been told by others, the writer should make it clear that he is reporting what he has heard from others.

vii) While preparing site-plan of the locality where a crime has been committed, the investigating officer should invariably record all the material distances in the site plan and also in the Case-Diary.

viii) If any article is recovered or seized by the investigating officer in the course of investigation, he must record adequate detail of the circumstances in which and the place/person etc. from where the recovery or seizure was made"

How to Write a Case-Diary? A Few Do's

1. Write the Case-Diary by the investigator himself in his own hand. If this is not possible, get it be writen by his Head Constable in his presence and signed by himself and the H. C. In such cases, the reason for not writing the Case-Diary by the investigator should be recorded.
2. Write the Case-Diary on the books supplied by the Government/ Department with serially numbered and perforated pages. Write the Case-Diary in triplicate.
3. Send one copy of the Case-Diary to superior police officers. One copy should be preserved for being forwarded to the Court, if that need be.
4. Write only on one side of the paper and the writing should be clear and legible.
5. Don't write the theories, opinions or conjectures in the Case-Diary. Likewise no irresponsible rumours, village gossips, possible/hypothetical ways of solving crime should find a place in the Case-Diary.
6. Write the Case-Diary in the normal language.
7. Write the Case-Diary in two parts—one portion containing the narrative portion of the investigation and the other part containing the statements of witnesses taken by the police under section 161 Cr. P.C. 1973. One additional copy each of the second part should be made for giving it to all accused and it should be furnished to each of them before the trial begins.

The investigating officer should see that the Case-Diary is written from day to day. The writing should not be postponed. This is to avoid the possibility of omission in details. If the investigation is not done, then one needs not write the Case-Diary on that day. At the end of each day's Diary, there should be mention about further action to be initiated on the case.

If the investigating officer does not like to divulge the sources of information, he needs to commence his Case-Diary without revealing his sources of information. He can in such instances start writing 'from information received that A has committed such and such offences at such places at such time (write the details here), I proceeded to such and such places at such time to investigate the offence etc.' Under section 125 Indian Evidence Act, 1872 the investigating officer gets full protection for his action and no Court of Law can compel the investigator to disclose the name of the informant. In such instances, the investigating officer is bound to reduce the information into writings as the accused has a right to know the information which led the law into motion against him.

Remember that the entries in the Case-Diary is of a confidential nature and the responsibility of the entries lies squarely on the investigator himself. Usually, the practice seems to be that the Case Diaries are written by the Head Constables/Station Writers with an endorsement below by the Sub-inspector that he also did the same things and finds no difference from what the Head Constable/Station Writer has written and therefore he is not writing it again. This, indeed, is bad particularly when the truth is otherwise.

Remember that the "want of pagination of the sheets of Case-Diary or jumbing of serial numbers or dates of the Diaries therein create serious suspicion"[3]. Even if some statements are taken on loose sheets and rough notes prepared, they must be copied into the Case-Diary but the original notes and papers must also be preserved to avoid any contraversy[4].

In grave crimes and cases in which police officers are accused of, then more copies of the Case-Diary are to be prepared and if so required should be sent to the Sub-Divisional Police Officer. Diaries of cases investigated by Crime Investigation Branch are sent to the superior officers of the Crime Investigation Branch. In such cases, if necessary, a copy of the Case-Diary is also sent to the Superintendent of Police of the District for favour of information.

The last Diary of a particular case must state whether a

prima facie case has been made out or not. It should also contain the number and date of the charge-sheet or final report. It should also contain the despatch of exhibits to Court and the usual intimation to the informant regarding the disposal.

Cases for which Case-Diaries are Written by the Police

Case-Diaries are to be written in the following cases:

1. All cognizable cases investigated by the police under Chapter XII of the Code of Criminal Procedure, 1973.
2. All non-cognizable cases investigated by the police under the orders of a competent Megistrate.
3. All investigations under Cr. P.C. into the apparent causes of death. In some States, no Case-Diaries are written in accidental deaths.
4. In some States, Case-Diaries are written in cases where security proceedings for keeping peace and good behaviour under the Code of Criminal Procedure is taken.

Witness-Statement in Case-Diary

Witness statements are written in the Case-Diary itself as explained earlier in this chapter or are written on separate sheets of paper which are to be attached to the appropriate Case-Diary. The following points may be noted regarding the recording of witness-statements.

(i) Under no circumstances, should a witness be asked to sign his statement. It is illegal under section 162 Cr. P.C., 1973. to do so.
(ii) Statements of every witness should be separately written even if the statements of different witnesses do corroborate one another.
(iii) Omissions in witness-statements are considered to be serious defects and therefore omissions of important details must not occur under any circumstances.

(iv) If witness-statements are taken in separate sheets of paper, then the names of witnesses examined should be mentioned in the Case-Diary.

A Case-Diary: Points to Remember

In writing a Case-Diary, the following points may be borne in mind. They are :

1. What is the time at which the information regarding the commission of a crime reached the police station?
2. What is the time at which the investigating officer began and closed his investigation?
3. What are the place and places visited by the investigating officer during the process of investigation?
4. What is investigating officer's statement regarding the circumstances ascertained through his investigation?
5. Do the Case-Diary contain the following information?
   a) The reference made to station crime-records, i.e., crime directory, crime-map, gang chart, village crime note-book, equipment required to be taken to the crime scene, records to be picked up, stationaries to be provided for, man-power required for assistance etc.
   b) Information sent to the superior police officers about the occurrence of the crime and the mode of information—i.e., through special messenger, express report or telegraphic information, wireless-message etc .
   c) Services of experts requisitioned—i.e., the services of medical officer, photographer, plan-drawer, finger-print/ foot print expert, scientific expert, dog-squad etc.
6. Have you made a full and faithful description of—
   a) scene of crime and its surroundings?
   b) line of approach and retreat of the offender/s?
   c) traces noticed and absence of traces which are likely to be found at the scene of crime?
   d) seizures made, photographs taken and the scene sketch prepared with distance correctly measured?

7. Does the Case-Diary contain information relating to—
   a) particulars of witnesses examined?
   b) particulars of suspects and accused persons interrogated?
   c) particulars of informants contacted?
   d) searches made of persons and places with grounds for search and the result thereof?
   e) property recovered during the searches, locked up in the station house or despatched to the Magistrate etc.?
8. Does the Case-Diary contain information relating to—
   a) various theories formed as a result of investigation?
   b) steps taken to verify each and every theory formed and the results obtained?
   c) any further line of investigation suggested by superior police officers?
9. What are the steps taken in furtherance of investigation? This must include information relating to: (a) issue of inquiry slips, (b) hue and cry notice, (c) verifying the complicity of criminals addicted to similar *modus operandi* and other probable criminals, (d) references to District Intelligence Bureau, M.O.B. and the like.
10. What are the other relevant information to be included in the Case-Diary?

Use of the Case-Diary in a Court

First Part of the Case-Diary

This part is usually treated as confidential. Nevertheless, in special circumstances the document will have to be produced. For, section 167(i) Cr. P.C. reads: (a) "Whenever any person is arrested and detained in custody, and it appears that the investigation cannot be completed within the period of twenty-four hours fixed by section 57, and there are grounds for believing that the accusation or information is well founded, the officer-in-charge of the police station or the police officer making the investigation, if he is not below the rank of a sub-inspector, fourthwith transmit to the Judicial Magistrate a copy of the entries in the Diary...." In such instances, the Magistrate looks into the Case-Diary and if he is satisfied that the detention of the accused is proper, may authorize further detention of the accused.

Sub-section 2 of section 172 Cr. P.C. 1973, reads: "Any Criminal Court may send for the police Diaries of a case under inquiry or trial in such Court, and may use such Diaries, not as evidence in the case, but to aid it in such inquiry or trial.

Under sections 228 and 240 Cr. P.C., 1973, when the police file the charge-sheet, the Court may call for the Case-Diaries and look into them for the purpose of framing a charge if the Court has some doubt which cannot be cleared without having a perusal into the police Diaries. Again in order to decide whether or not cognizance of an offence should be taken, the Magistrate can peruse the Case-Diary including the statement of witnesses recorded under section 161 Cr. P.C. and if he is convinced that there is *prima facie* case against one or more accused, he can issue process. In such instances, the police report submitted under section 173 Cr. P.C. also should be looked into to see whether or not the facts contained in the report constitute an offence.[5]

Thus the Case-Diary is used by the Court:

i) to see whether or not there are any suspicious circumstances in the conduct of investigation. It cannot use the Diary to corroborate the police officer's testimony, rather only to contradict him;
ii) to clarify doubts or some points which need further explanation;
iii) to find out the indication of sources of information and evidence, the lines of enquiry and the names of persons whose evidence may be material;
iv) to ensure fairness in trials and to bring on record by evidence any material facts that come to the knowledge of the Judge by perusing the Case-Diary.
v) to treat a particular witness as hostile at the request of the prosecution to find out whether or not there is any reason for granting the request;

vi) to remand a person into the custody at the request of the police;
vii) to drop out an investigation (already completed) for want of sufficient evidence;
viii) to grant bail to the accused;
ix) to order further investigation if the Magistrate is not satisfied with the investigation.

The Courts are not to treat the materials in a Case-Diary as evidence in a criminal case.

Second Part of the Case-Diary

The second part consists of statements of witnesses and the accused and their use in the Court is controlled by section 162 Cr.P.C., 1973 and section 27, I.E.A. 1872.

Section 162 Cr.P.C. 1973 reads:

(1) No statement made by any person to a police officer in the course of an investigation under this Chapter, shall if reduced to writing be signed by the person making it, nor shall any such statement or any record thereof, whether in a police Diary or otherwise, or any part of such statement or record, be used for any purpose, save as herein after provided, at any inquiry or trial in respect of any offence under investigation at the time when such statement was made:

Provided that when any witness is called for the prosecution in such inquiry or trial whose statement has been reduced into writing as aforesaid, any part of his statement, if duly proved, may be used by the accused, and with the permission of the Court, by the prosecution, to contradict such witness in the manner provided by section 145 of the Indian Evidence Act, 1872 (1 of 1872); and when any part of such statement is so used any part thereof may also be used in the re-examination of such witness, but for the purpose only of explaining any matter referred to in his cross-examination.

(2) Nothing in this section shall be deemed to apply to any statement falling within the provisions of clause (1) of section 32 of the Indian Evidence Act, 1872 (1 of 1872) or to affect the provisions of section 27 of this Act.

Explanation— An omission to state a fact or circumstances in the statement referred to in sub-section (1) may amount to contradiction if the same appears to be significant and otherwise relevant having regard to the context in which such omission occurs and whether any omission amounts to a contradiction in the particular context shall be a question of fact".

The Code of Criminal Procedure makes it a statutory obligation on police to supply all the statements recorded under section 162 Cr.P.C. 1973 along with the copy of the F.I.R., copy of the report forwarded under sub-section (1) of section 173 and all other documents or relevant extracts thereof on which the prosecution proposes to rely including confessional statements if any, recorded under section 164 Cr.P.C. 1973. In addition, it has been made mandatory for the Court to see that the copies of such statements are granted to the accused at the commencement of any inquiry or trial. If the copies are not given to the accused, then the whole trial will be vitiated.

Remember here that (i) Statements taken under section 162 Cr.P.C. are not substantive evidence and nothing is proved or disproved by these statements. (ii) The statements of witnesses cannot be used at all for any purpose other than contradicting the witness and the contradictory portion of the statement can be used by the Court just to prove that the witness has given a prior contradictory statement to the police. (iii) The contradiction in the statement of a particular witness who is examined in the court only can be proved. This is to say that a contradictory statement of another witness can not be put to any particular witness and proved. (iv) A contradictory statement to the police by a defence witness cannot be proved[6].

The prosecution can use the statements of witness to contradict its own witness with the permission of the Court if the witness turns hostile. In this eventuality, one should not think that the entire witness testimony is of no value. For, the Division Bench of the Orissa High Court has held: "But it is well settled by the authorities that the evidence of a hostile witness is not necessarily to be rejected either in part or in whole...... It is also not to be rejected so far as it is in favour of the party which called in the witness, not it is to be rejected so far as it is in favour of the opposite party"[7].

The defence can use the statements of witness to police to contradict the maker of the statement when he is examined in the Court on behalf of the prosecution. Here the prosecution can also use the statement to explain away any such contradictions.

Coming to confessions made by the accused, Section 25 of the Indian Evidence Act reads:

"No confession made to a police officer shall be proved against a person accused of any offence". Section 27 I.E.A. further reads. "Provided that, when any fact is deposed to as discovered in consequence of information received from a person accused of any offence, in the custody of a police officer, so much of such information whether it amounts to a confession or not, as relates distinctly to the fact thereby discovered, may be proved."

Here it must be noted that the section 25 of the Evidence Act emphasises a particular aspect of section 162 Cr.P.C. 1973, i.e., no confession to a police officer is admissible in law. Section 26, I.E.A., 1872 lays down that no confession to a police officer by an accused person in his custody is admissible unless it is made in the immediate presence of the Magistrate. Section 24 I.E.A. says that no police officer or person in authority shall offer any inducement, threat or promise to any accused person to make a confession and Section 28 I.E.A. lays down that any confession to a person other than a police officer is irrelevant if the Court is satisfied that such confession is the result of inducement, threat or a promise by a person in authority. Section 29 I.E.A. makes such confessions relevant if the effect of inducement, threat or fraud has been completely and fully removed from the mind of the accused when he makes the confession and finally section 30 I.E.A. lays down that a confession is not affected simply because it was made against a promise of secrecy or as a result of deceptions or by a person when he was drunk.

The police officer has to bear in mind all these provisions of the Indian Evidence Act when he records the confessional statements of accused persons in a crime.

Use of the Case-Diary by the Accused

The law does not give any right to the accused to inspect the Case-Diaries. This is so because the Diary contains matters of a confidential nature relating to the investigation of a particular crime. Nevertheless, section 172 Cr.P.C., 1973 confers rights on the accused to make use of the Diary when it is used by the investigating officer to refresh his memory in the court or when the court uses the Case-Diary to contradict the police investigator. Sections 159 to 161, Indian Evidence Act, 1872 also confer the same powers to the accused in the use of Case-Diaries. However, the accused person's rights to inspect the Case-Diary and to cross-examine the investigator are limited to only if the Case-Diary has been used by the investigating officer to refresh his memory. The accused has no right to insist that a police officer should look into his Case-Diary to refresh his memory and reply[8].

The condition under which a police investigator may refresh his memory by perusing the Case-Diary are:

1. The Case-Diary must have been written by the investigating officer himself immediately after he took the steps mentioned in the entries.
2. The Case-Diary, if has been written by some one else other than the investigator, should have been read by the investigator immediately after he took the steps mentioned in the Diary and he should be aware that the contents were correct when he read them.
3. The police investigator should be sure that the Case-Diary was correctly written, but he fails to recollect the contents of the Diary, i.e., the investigating officer has seen the record and known that the contents were correct.

As stated earlier the Case-Diary can be used by the Court

to contradict the police officer who wrote it. In that case, the particular portion of the Case-Diary used by the Court to contradict the maker of the Diary partially loses its previlege. Here, the defence can use that portion of the Diary used by the Court for the purpose of cross-examining the police investigator.

Disposal of Case-Diaries

The Case-Diary is a confidential report always kept by the investigating officer under lock and key in his personal possession. But, when a case is charge-sheeted, the investigating officer must entrust the original Case-Diary to the Assistant Public Prosecutor or the Public Prosecutor as the case may be. However in some States, the practice is to keep the Case-Diary in the personal custody of the investigating officer even after the charge-sheeting. In such cases, the Diary will be made available to the Prosecutor whenever he needs it. On the disposal of the case by the Court, if the Case-Diary is with the A.P.P./P.P. it must be taken back by the investigating officers who will destroy it after three years. The rules about the destruction of Case-Diaries are not uniform in all States in India.

Pocket Note-Book

Pocket note-book maintained by every police officer is a confidential record and can not be used in a court of law. It can be looked into by superior police officers for checking the work of a particular police officer. The book contains not only investigation done by the police officer, but also many details of his work carried out as a police officer. It is an hourly record of an individual police officer's activities.

Other Registers Maintained by Police

Other important registers connected with police investigation and maintained by police officers are:

i) The Village Crime Note-Book including the Surveillance Register, Bad Character Roles or Enquiry Slips.

ii) Crime Register and Crime Maps showing the incidence area, etc., offences against specific sections of the Indian Penal Code, 1860.

iii) Absconders and Escaped Convicts Register.

iv) Gang Register.

v) Report Register.

vi) Register of Stolen Property.

vii) Property Register which contains information concerning property brought into the police station or taken out of it. The property relating to any crime under investigation and also property of the accused seized from him at the time of arrest and brought to the station are also entered in this register with particulars.

viii) Sentry Relief Book – which may contain along with other things entries regarding the number of accused in the lock-up.

ix) F.I.R. Book.

x) History-Sheets of Habitual Offenders.

These registers are meant for supervision and check by superior police officers. They may assume importance in some cases about which one can not predict. These registers can be of great use in crime investigation – particularly relating to property offences. Hence they should be maintained with meticulous accuracy and precision in details.

SUGGESTED READINGS

Krishnamurti, K., "*Police Diaries, Statements, Reports, Investigations and Arrests etc.* Law Book Co., Allabahad, 1973.

Deinstein, W., *How to Write a Narrative Investigation Report,* Charles C. Thomas, Springfield, 1959.

Deinstein, W., *Techniques for the Crime Investigator,* Charles C. Thomas, Springfield, 1952.

Gammage, Allen, Z., *Basic Report – Writing,* Charles C. Thomas, Springfield, 1960.

Hazelet, John C., *Police Report Writing,* Charles C. Thomas, Springfield, 1958.

Leonard, V.A., *The Police Record System,* Charles C. Thomas, Springfield, 1970.

Ramanujam, T. *Prevention & Detection of Crimes,* Madras Book Agency, Madras, 1972.

Wilson, O.W., *Police Records and Their Installation.* Public Administration Service, 1951.

REFERENCES

1. K. Krishnamurti, *Police Diaries, Statements, Reports, Investigation and Arrests etc.,* Law Book Co., Allahabad, 1973.
2. K. Krishnamurti, *Police Diaries, Statements, Reports, Investigations and Arrests etc. op. cit.*
3. Priyalal Barman *vs.* State, 1970 Cr. L.J. 1599.
4. Bhaiya Lal Singh *vs.* State, 1952 V.P. 7; 1952 Cr. L.J. 143.
5. A.K. Roy *vs.* State of West Bengal, 1962 Cal 135 (F.B.) 1 Cr. L.J. 285.
6. K. Krishnamurti, *Police Diaries, Statements, Reports, Investigation and Arrests. op. cit.*
7. Rama Naik and other *vs.* the State, 1965 (1) Cr. L.J. 315; 1965 Orissa 31; (1964) 6 Orissa J.D. 184; 30 Cut. L.J. 517.
8. Mohinder Singh *vs.* Emperor, 1932 Lah. 103: 33 Cr. L.J. 97: 33 Punj L.R. 891.

9

ARREST, BAIL, DETENTION AND IDENTIFICATION PARADE

Arrest means taking into custody of a person under the authority of law for having committed an offence or in connection with an expected violation of law. Infact, no statutes in India define 'arrest' although every one knows that it consists of the actual seizure or touching of a person's body with a view to his detention[1].

Arrest in law, therefore, has the objectives as:

1. to ensure the presence of the accused in a court of law in case he is charge-sheeted for having violated the law;
2. to incapacitate him or her from continuing further his or her unlawful activities in special cases.

Arrest means and includes a serious interference with the personal liberty of citizens and therefore the curtailment of this fundamental freedom is ensured and guaranteed by the Constitution of India. The arrest should be made strictly in accordance with the law in force. "Indeed the law relating to the exercise of the power of arrest should be as strictly construed as possible so that light or flippant interference with the most valued of the fundamental rights by the Constitution may be rendered difficult if not impossible" says Krishnamurthi[2]. This is the reason why Supreme Court of

India has laid down clearly what is meant by the terms *"arrested and detained in custody"* occuring in Article 22 of the Constitution of India as:

"Arrest may be classified into two categories – arrest warrants issued by a Court and arrests otherwise than under such warrant. The warrant contains a clear accusation against the person to be arrested. Section 80 Cr.P.C., requires that the police officer executing the warrant must notify the substance thereof to the person arrested and if so required shall show him the warrant. Similarly, a warrant issued by a Court under the Code of Civil Procedure quite plainty discloses the reason for the arrest in that it sets out of an accusation of default apprehended or actual and that the person to be arrested is made acquainted with the reason for his arrest before he is actually arrested. Two things are to be noted, viz., arrest without warrant under the Code of Criminal Procedure as well as under Special Acts like Sea Customs Act and the Forest Act, proceeds upon an accusation that the person arrested is reasonably suspected of having committed an offence and in this case there is no provision (in the Criminal Procedure Code) for communicating to the person arrested the grounds for his arrest. The physical restraint put upon an abducted person in the process of recovering and taking that person into custody without any allegation or accusation of any actual or suspected or apprehended commission by that person of any offence of a criminal or quasi-criminal nature or of any act prejudicial to the State or the public interest and delivery of the person into the custody of the officer-in-charge of the nearest camp under section 4 of the Abducted Persons and Restoration Act cannot be regarded as Arrest and Detention within the meaning of Art. 22 (1) of the Constitution of India"[3].

It is clear from the forgoing decision of the Supreme Court that arrest means an arrest in connection with an alleged violation of the penal laws and which cannot be redressed except by the judicial process of bail. Hence arrest in strict legal sense applicable in criminal proceedings means taking into custody or detention under the authority of law in connection with the alleged violation of the provisions of the penal law of the country or under the preventive provisions of law which may apply to certain classes of expected or anticipated violation of law.

Arrest and Detention

As stated earlier "an arrest is the seizing of a person and detaining him in the custody of law"[4]. The sole purpose of an arrest in criminal proceedings, therefore, is to route the person arrested before a Magistrate or Court so that proper legal proceedings can be initiated for the determination of guilt or innocence of the crime charged[5].

Section 46 (1) of the Code of Criminal Procedure, 1973 stipulates: "In making an arrest, the police officer or other person making the same shall actually touch or confine the body of the person to be arrested unless there is submission to the custody by word or action". An arrest can be made with or without a warrant from a Court of Law. In cognizable cases, an arrest is made without a warrant. Clause (1) of Sub-section 41 of the Code of Criminal Procedure, 1973 mentions persons who can be arrested. They are:

a) Those concerned in a cognizable offence.
b) Persons against whom a reasonable complaint for having committed a cognizable offence has been made.
c) A person regarding whom a credible information of having committed a cognizable offence has been received.
d) A person against whom a reasonable suspicion as to the commission of a cognizable offence exists.

Section 46, Code of Criminal Procedure makes it clear that the police officer should not use force to effect an arrest. Nevertheless, if the person to be arrested forcibly resists or attempts to evade the arrest, force may be applied to effect the arrest. Here, the police officer has no right to cause the death of the person while apprehending him unless he is accused of an offence punishable with death or imprisonment for life. Resistance to lawful arrest is punishable under sections 224, 225 and 225-B, of the Indian Penal Code, 1860.

Section 49, Cr.P.C. reads: "The person arrested shall not be subjected to more restraint than is necessary to prevent his escape and section 51 Cr.P.C. empowers the police officer to search persons arrested and taken into custody for any articles that might be found upon him. Section 52, Cr.P.C. deals with the power to seize offensive weapons. Section 53 Cr.P.C. is about the examination of the persons arrested by a medical practitioner at the request of a police officer and Section 54 Cr.P.C. concerns examination of an arrested person by a medical practitioner at the request of the person arrested.

Section 48 Cr.P.C. empowers a police officer to pursue a person to any place in India for the purpose of arrest even without a warrant. Section 60 Cr.P.C. confers on a police officer same powers above on escape of a person to pursue and retake him. Section 77 Cr.P.C. is about arrest with warrant and lays down the provision that the arrest with warrant can be executed anywhere in India and section 79 Cr.P.C. reads that a warrant of arrest can be directed to police officers for execution outside jurisdiction. Section 47, Cr.P.C. is about the search of place entered into by the suspect with right to climb on grills and open doors or windows for that purpose even by breaking them. But, according to section 47 (2) Cr.P.C., notice to withdraw is to be given before breaking it open and entering into a place if it is an apartment in the occupancy of a woman who does not appear in public and section 47 (3) Cr.P.C. permits a police officer or other person authorised to arrest a person to break open any other or inner door or window of any place in order to liberate himself.

Section 50, Code of Criminal Procedure reads: (1) "Every police officer or other person arresting any person without warrant shall forthwith communicate to him full particulars of the offence for which he is arrested or other grounds for such arrest. (2) where a police officer arrests without warrant any person other than a person accused of a non-bailable offence, he shall inform the person arrested that he is entitled to be released on bail and that he may arrange for sureties on his behalf".

Who May Arrest?

Under the Code of Criminal Procedure, 1973, the following persons are empowered to arrest.

Who May Arrest? (1)	Section of Law (2)	Under What Circumstances? (3)
Private Persons	a) s. 37 Cr.P.C.	While assisting a Magistrate or a police officer in taking or arresting persons or in case of breach of peace or preventing to any injury on railway, canal, telegraph or public property.
	b) s. 43 Cr.P.C.	Any person who in his presence commits a non-bailable and cognizable offence or any proclaimed offender.
	c) s. 44 Cr.P.C.	When an offence is committed in the presence of a Magistrate (Executive and Judicial) within his jurisdiction.
Private Persons	d) s. 72 Cr.P.C.	When a warrant of arrest is issued by a Court for which no police officer is available for its immediate execution and therefore it is directed to a private person.
	e) s. 73 Cr.P.C.	In the case of escaped convict, proclaimed offender or a person accused

(1)	(2)	(3)
		of a non-bailable offence and is evading arrest and a warrant of arrest is directed to a private person.

The private persons when they effect an arrest shall make over or cause to be made over any person so arrested to a police officer, or in the absence of a police officer, take such person or cause him to be taken in custody to the nearest police station.

Police Officers a) Arrest Without Warrant	a) s. 41 Cr.P.C.	1. Any person for being concerned in a cognizable offence. 2. Any person for possession of any thing reasonably suspected to be stolen property. 3. Any person who obstructs a police officer on duty. 4. Any person who has deserted from the Armed Forces. 5. Any person who is wanted under any law relating to extradiction.
Arrest Without Warrant		6. Any person who, being a released convict, commits a breach of any rule. 7. Any person who is arrested on any requisition weather written or oral.

(1)	(2)	(3)
Police Officers	b) s. 151 Cr.P.C.	Any person who designs to commit any cognizable offence.
	c) s. 432 (3) Cr.P.C.	Any peson whose suspension or remission of sentence has been cancelled by the Government.
b) Police Officers Arrest with Warrant	a) S. 72 Cr.P.C.	When a warrant of arrest is directed to him by a Magistrate
	b) s. 74 Cr.P.C.	When a warrant is endorsed by the police officer to whom it was directed to another.
	c) s. 55 (1) Cr.P.C.	In connection with a case investigated by an officer-in-charge of a police station or the investigating officer, he can by an order in writing depute a subordinate officer for the purpose of effecting an arrest.
Police Officers Arrest without Warrant	d) s. 157 (1) Cr.P.C.	Under written order from the officer-in-charge of a police station or the investigating officer, a police officer can effect the arrest of an offender who is wanted in a cognizable case which is being investigated into.
	e) s. 44 (1) Cr.P.C.	Under the orders of a Magistrate for an offence

(1)	(2)	(3)
		committed in the presence of him.
	f) s. 44 (2) Cr.P.C.	Arrest under direction of a Magistrate of a person for whose arrest the Magistrate is competent to issue warrant.
	g) s. 42 Cr.P.C.	Effect arrest without warrant in a non-cognizable case if the offender refuses to give his name and residence.
	h) s. 42 (2) Cr.P.C.	Arrest of vagabonds etc. This special power of arrest is given to the officer-in-charge of a police station.
	i) s. 129 (2) Cr.P.C.	The Sub-Inspectors may arrest people for the purpose of dispersal of assembly by force.
Police Officers Arrest Without Warrant	g) s. 36 Cr. P.C	Superior police officers derive the powers of an officer-in-charge of a police station throughout the local area to which they have jurisdiction.

Arrest can also be made by Military officers, Trying Magistrates and High Courts under certain circumstances. In case a private person effects an arrest and hands over the arrested to the police, the police officer to whom the arrested is handed over has to rearrest the person already arrested by the private person. Any police officer mentioned in the section 41 Cr.P.C.

means any police officer and there is no restriction on the status of the police officer to effect an arrest without warrant. Hence it follows that even a constable can exercise this power. Uniform of the police officer is not essential as it will not by itself affect the legality or regularity of arrest. In any case, the police have the duty to disclose their identity in such instances.

Arrest of Women

Women shall be arrested, whether with or without warrant, by a police officer who is not below the rank of an Assistant Sub-Inspector and when the services of such an officer is not available, the arrest can be made by a Head Constable in the presence of responsible male relatives or village or town officials. But it is always advisable to take women police if the arrest of women is anticipated. Whenever a woman is arrested, the matter should be reported to superior police officers as well. If a Head Constable arrests a woman, the reason should be explained in the report. After the arrest, if the woman should be searched under section 51 Cr.P.C., it should be done only by another woman and with strict regard to deceny.

Arrest of Public Servant

Whenever a public servant is to be arrested, the matter should be intimated to superior officers, if possible, before the arrest and in any case immediately after the arrest. In case of the members of the Armed Forces – Army, Navy or Air-Force —intimation should be sent to the Officer Commanding the Unit to which the member belongs and it should be done immediately after the arrest is effected. Within the military area, members of the Armed Forces can not be arrested unless they are handed over to the police authorities by the military authorities after observance of the formalities and procedures necessary for the purpose.

Arrest of a Member of Parliament/Member of Legislative Assembly

Under Rule 229 of the Procedure and Conduct of Business in Lok Sabha, when a Member is arrested on a criminal charge or is detained under an executive order of the Magistrate, the executive authorities must inform without delay such fact to the Speaker. As soon as any arrest, detention, conviction or release is effected, intimation should invariably be sent to the Government concerned concurrently with the intimation sent to the Speaker/Chairman of the Legislative Assembly/Council/Lok Sabha/Rajya Sabha. This should be sent through telegrammes and also by post and the intimation should not be delayed on the ground of holiday.

In the case of the arrest of a M.P. the intimation should be as under.*

Place ....
Date ....

To

The Speaker,
Lok Sabha,
New Delhi.

Dear Mr. Speaker,

I have the honour to inform you that I have found it my duty, in the exercise of my powers under section .... of the ....(Act) to direct that Shri .... Member of Lok Sabha, be arrested/detained for .... (reasons for the arrest or detention, as the case may be.)

Shri .... M.P., was accordingly arrested/taken into custody at .... (time) on .... (date) and is at present lodged in the .... (place).

Yours faithfully,

* See Rule 230, Appendix, Third schedule.

In the case of conviction, the intimation should be as follows:.

I have the honour to inform you that Shri .... Member of the Lok Sabha, who was convicted on .... (date) and imprisoned for .... (period) for .... (reason for conviction was) released on bail, pending appeal (or released on the sentence being set aside on appeal as the case may be) on the ....(date).

Yours faithfully,
Judge, Magistrate or Executive Authority.

Apprehension of Juvenile Offenders

Arrest, strictly speaking of the juvenile delinquents, is called apprehension in criminology. In India we do not have any special procedure for the arrest of delinquent children. The Code of Criminal Procedure, 1973 under section 49 lays down that "the person arrested shall not be subjected to more restraint than is necessary to prevent this escape". This means that children should not be handcuffed or fettered after arrest. However, it is up to the police to implement such provisions with reformative and preventive perspectives in mind. Again under section 58, Code of Criminal procedure, 1973 it is laid down that: "Officers-in-charge of police stations shall report to the District Magistrate or, if he so directs, to the Sub-Divisional Magistrate, the cases of all persons arrested without warrant, within the limit of their respective stations whether such persons have been admitted to bail or otherwise". The Juvenile Justice (Care and Protection of Children) Act-2000 further lays down that police officers apprehending juveniles shall inform their parents/guardians and the probation officers about the apprehension of the children immediately after having arrested them. The police officers must remember that the principle behind juvenile legislations is purely correction and therefore when police officers handle juveniles roughly by handcuffing or jailing or when they resort to profanity or otherwise abuse youngsters, children often develop a negative attitude to the law enforcement agencies. They become very antagonistic and feel humiliated. This surely has a bad psychological effect which may counteract the reformation of young offenders. The Magistrates, parents/guardians, probation officers and so on must immediately be informed by the police about the apprehension. This is meant to prevent the misuse of children by police and to stop unnecessary strain and difficulties put to the juveniles. The parents/guardians must be in the know of the where abouts of their children.

Detention of juveniles usually refers to the provisional custody of a juvenile before the final disposition of his case by a Judge or other competent body and does not include institutionlization for observation or long-term treatment. In India, the Juvenile Justice (Care and Protection of Children) Act-2000 lay down the following provisions as to the detention of young children: i.e. having taken charge of the child, the police officer is authorized to release him on bail, if he is arrested for the commission of an offence and sufficient security is forthcoming. However if such release is likely to defeat the ends of justice or to go against the moral and social welfare of the young offender, the police officer is not supposed to grant bail. In the case of destitute, neglected or victimized children, if the child is not released on bail, he/she is taken to Remand Home (in some States it may be called by some other name) for detention and the Probation officer or the officer-in-charge of the Remand Home is informed. The children should not be detained in police stations. Within 24 hours of detention, every child must be produced before the appropriate authority.

Arrest – Case Laws*

1. Timely arrest of the accused persons in serious cases is an essential step in investigation; failute in this regard considerably weakens the position of the presecution[6].
2. Where the master saw a thief cutting and removing some trees and raised an alarm at which the servant came up on the scene and arrested the thief, it was held that the servant

* Quoted in K. Krishnamurthi, *Police Diaries, Statements, Reports.....*, *op. cit.*

who had not actually seen the theft being committed had no right to arrest the thief[7].

3. When a person stabbed another and ran away, the person who did not see the stabbing but only heard the cry of the victim and saw the accused run away had no right to arrest the offender[8].
4. Where a person commits a non-bailable and cognizable offence and tries to escape, the whole transaction is to be treated as one single transaction and that a person who sees an offender committing the offence as well as the person who sees him running away immediately after the offence has the right to arrest the offender[9].
5. Reasonable suspicion is understood to mean a *bonafide* belief that an offence had been or is about to be committed necessitating the arrest of the person concerned[10].
6. What is a reasonable complaint or suspicion, no doubt, depends upon the circumstances of each case; but it must be founded upon some tangible proof which is sufficient to establish in the mind of a reasonable police officer the reasonableness or credibility of the charge, information or suspicion[11].
7. Section 54 Cr.P.C. does not suggest that the arresting police officer is to be the final Judge of what is reasonable or credible[12].
8. Where there was a warrant of arrest, the sub-inspector of police and a police constable proceeded to arrest the person concerned without being armed with the warrant. It was held that he had credible information as defined in section 54 (1) Cr.P.C.[13].
9. Where, besides being armed with an order under section 56. Cr.P.C. the arresting police officer is in possession of information under section 54 Cr.P.C., his arrest would be legal even if the formalities under section 56 Cr.P.C., are not fully complied with[14].
10. Where the only information on which the police arrested some persons, was that these persons were bad characters sitting and talking together on a river bank, it was held that

the arrest could not be justified under the law eventhough some implement of house breaking was recovered from them after arrest[15].

Bail

The criminal justice system in India provides for a person taken into custody, prior to his trial by a competent Court of Law, to be released on bail. In the First Schedule of the Code of Criminal Procedure, 1973, offences under the Indian Penal Code have been classified as bailable and non-bailable offences. *Bail is a right and not a favour*. Section 437 of the Code of Criminal Procedure, 1973 contains the provision regarding grant of bail to persons accused of non-bailable offences. Except in cases for which the punishment prescribed is death or imprisonment for life, both police and Court have concurrent jurisdiction in the matter of granting bail while the cases are under investigation. During the stage of investigation, Courts are empowered to release on bail children below 16 years of age and women accused of offences punishable with death or life imprisonment. Under section 437 (2) of the Code of Criminal Procedure, 1973, police officers are empowered to grant bail to an accused person if they find that the accused is not liable to be prosecuted against further for non-bailable offences. The police, as a rule, should not be either stingy or liberal in granting bail to the accused in a crime[16].

The Code of Criminal Procedure, 1973 under section 437 (3) lays down the provision to the effect that, in certain specified classes of serious offences – i.e., offences punishable with imprisonment which may extend to seven years or more or of an offence under Chapter VI, Chapter XVI or Chapter XVII of the Indian Penal Code, 1860 or abetment of or conspiracy or attempt to commit any such offence – if the offender is released on bail, the Court may impose any conditions necessary for ensuring attendance, non-repetition of the offence or in the interest of justice.

Section 167 (2) of the Code of Criminal Procedure, 1973 states that irrespective of whether the offence is bailable or not, a facility is provided for granting of bail in cases of prolonged investigation. This applies to cases where the police do not submit a charge-sheet within sixty days of taking an accused in custody[17].

Also the Code of Criminal Procedure, 1973 provides that in cases triable by Magistrates and where the trial of a person accused of a non-bailable offence is not concluded within a period of sixty days from its initiation, such person if he is in custody during the whole of the said period shall be released on bail unless the Magistrate directs otherwise the reasons which must be recorded in writing by him. Besides, the Court shall release an accused person in custody on the execution of a bond without sureties to guarantee appearance to hear judgement if, at any time after the conclusion of the trial and before judgement is delivered, there exists reason to believe that the accused is not guilty.

The High Courts or the Courts of Session are empowered to grant anticipatory bail to persons apprehending arrests subject to the conditions under section 438 of the Code of Criminal Procedure, 1973. Regarding anticipatory bail, section 438, Code of Criminal Procedure lays down:

"(1) whenever any person has reason to believe that he may be arrested on an accusation of having committed a non-bailable offence, he may apply to the High Court or the Court of Session for a direction under this section and that the Court may, if it thinks fit, direct that in the event of such arrest, he shall be released on bail.

(2) When the High Court or the Court of Session makes a direction under sub-section (1), it may include such conditions in such direction in the light of the facts of the particular case, as it thinks fit, including:

i) a condition that the person shall make himself available for interrogation by a police officer as and when required;

ii) a condition that the person shall not, directly or indirectly, make any inducement, threat or promise to any person acquainted with the facts of the case so as to dissuade him from disclosing such facts of the Court or to any police officer;

iii) a condition that the person shall not leave India without the prior permission of the Court;

iv) Such other conditions as may be imposed under sub-section (3) of section 437, as if the bail were granted under that section.

(3) If such person is thereafter arrested without warrant by an officer-in-charge of a police station on such accusation and is prepared either at the time of arrest or at any time while in custody of such officer to give bail, he shall be released on bail; and if a Magistrate taking cognizance of such offence decides that a warrant should be issued in the first instance against that person he shall issue a bailable warrant in confirmity with the direction of the Court under sub-section (1)".

The power of the Court to grant bail is judicial and is governed by precedents and established principles of law. Courts of session and High Courts enjoy special powers to grant bail under section 439 Cr.P.C., 1973. A person already released on bail can be retaken into custody and also a person not granted bail can be released or the amount of bail may be reduced or enhanced if that needs be.

Detention of the Accused

As per section 57 of the Criminal Procedure Code, 1973, no police officer shall detain in custody a person arrested for a longer period than under all circumstances of the case are reasonable and such period shall not, in the absence of a special order of a Magistrate, under section 167 Cr.P.C., 1973 exceed twenty four hours exclusive of the time necessary for the journey from the place of arrest to the Court of the Magistrate. This restriction of the period is a fundamental right under the Constitution of India.

Section 167, Cr.P.C., 1973 is about the procedure when investigation cannot be completed within 24 hours. The section reads:

"(1) Whenever any person is arrested and detained in custody and it appears that investigation cannot be completed within the period of 24 hours fixed by section 57, and there are grounds for believing that the accusation or information is well founded, the officer-in-charge of the police station or the police officer making the investigation if he is not below the rank of sub-inspector shall forthwith transmit to the nearest Judicial Magistrate a copy of the entries in the diary hereinafter prescribed relating to the case and shall at the same time forward the accused to such Magistrate.

(2) The Magistrate to whom an accused person is forwarded under this section may, whether he has or has not jurisdiction to try the case, from time to time, authorize the detention of the accused in such custody as such Magistrate thinks fit, for a term not exceeding fifteen days in the whole and if he has no jurisdiction to try the case or commit it for trial, and considers further detention unnecessary he may order the accused to be forwarded to a Magistrate having such jurisdiction:

Provided that —

(a) the Magistrate may authorize the detention of the accused persons otherwise than in the custody of the police beyond the period of fifteen days if he is satisfied that adequate ground exists for doing so, but no Magistrate shall authorize the detention of the accused person in custody under this section for a total period exceedings–

(i) ninety days, where the investigation relates to an offence punishable with death, imprisonment for life or imprisonment for a term of not less than ten years;

(ii) sixty days, where the investigation relates to any other offence, and on the expiry of the said period of ninety days or sixty days as the case may be, the accused person shall be released on bail if he is prepared to and does furnish bail and every person released on bail under this sub-section shall be deemed to be so released under the provisions of Chapter XXXIII for the purpose of that Chapter.

(b) no Magistrate shall authorize detention in any custody under this section unless the accused is produced before him;

(c) no Magistrate of the second class, not specially empowered in this behalf by the High Court, shall authorize detention in the custody of the police.

Explanation I – For the avoidance of doubts, it is hereby declared that not withstanding the expiry of the period specified in paragraph (a), the accused shall be detained in custody so long as he does not furnish bail.

Explanation II – If any question arises whether an accused person was produced before the Magistrate as required under paragraph (b), the production of accused person may be proved by his signature on the order authorising detention.

(2A) Not withstanding anything contained in sub-section (1) or sub-section (2), the officer-in-charge of the police station or the police officer making the investigation, if he is not below the rank of a sub-inspector, may, where a Judicial Magistrate is not available, transmit to the nearest Executive Magistrate on whom the powers of a Judicial Magistrate, or Metropolitan Magistrate have been conferred, a copy of the entry in the diary hereinafter prescribed relating to the case, and shall, at the same time, forward the accused to such Executive Magistrate, and thereupon such Executive Magistrate, may, for reasons to be recorded in writing, authorize the detention of the accused person in such custody as he may think fit for a term not exceeding seven days in the aggregate; and on the expiry of the period of detention so authorised, the accused person shall be released on bail except where an order for further detention of the accused person has been made by a Magistrate competent to make such order; and where an order for such further detention is made, the period during which the accused person was detained in custody under the orders made by an Executive Magistrate under this sub-section, shall be taken into account in computing the period specified in paragraph (a) of the proviso to sub-section (2):

....

....

Provided that before the expiry of the period aforesaid, the Executive Magistrate shall transmit to the nearest Judicial Magistrate the records of the case together with a copy of the entries in the diary relating to the case which was transmitted to him by the officer-in-charge of the police station or the police officer making the investigation, as the case may be.

(5) If in any case triable by a Magistrate as a summons case, the investigation is not concluded within a period of six months from the date on which the accused was arrested, the Magistrate shall make an order stopping further investigation into the offence unless the officer making the investigation satisfies the Magistrate that for special reasons and in the interest of justice the continuation of the investigation beyond the period of six months is necessary.

(6) Where any other order stopping further investigation into an offence has been made under sub-section (5), the Sessions Judge may, if he is satisfied, on an application made to him or otherwise, that further investigation to the offence ought to be made, vacate the order made under sub-section (5) and direct further investigation to be made into the offence subject to such directions with regard to bail and other matters as he may specify".

In Banta Ram *vs.* State of Himachal Pradesh, the Supreme Court observed; "While calculating the period of 90 days or 60 days under clauses (i) and (ii) of paragraph (a) of sub-section (2) of section 167 of the Code of Criminal Procedure, the period of detention authorized by the Magistrate under sub-section (2) of section 167 must be included"[18].

Bail and Detention: Case-Laws

1. "The High Court has inherent power to cancel bail. Even in bailable offence, the bail can be cancelled. This jurisdiction springs from the over-riding inherent powers of the High Court"[19].
2. "If appeal cannot be heard in a reasonable period of time, bail should be granted"[20].
3. "The intention of the Legislature seems to be to grant no discretion to the Court and to make it obligatory for it to

release the accused on bail if the investigation cannot be completed within 60 days. This applies even to serious cases like criminal conspiracy, murder etc."[21].

4. "An adjournment requires an order in writing and so does an order of remand. The Magistrate while adjourning the case under section 344 Cr.P.C. did not make an order remanding the person to custody, hence detention was held illegal"[22].
5. "In the case of a bailable offence, bail is a matter of right and not a favour by the police officer or the Court"[23].

Identification Parade

Identification of a suspect can be made by photographs, fingerprints, voice prints (this is not conclusively determined as acceptable means of identification yet) and a line-up. Section 9 of the Indian Evidence Act, 1872 makes relevant any facts which establish the identity of a person or thing whose identity is relevant. Line-up or identification parade means a method of proving the identity of a person or article before the Court. Ramanujam writes: "with regard to criminal offences, identification has two-fold objects – first to satisfy investigating authorities before sending a case for trial to Court that the person arrested, but not previously known to the witnesses, was one of those who committed the crime or the property concerned was the subject of such crime; and secondly to satisfy the Court that the accused was the real offender or the article was really the one concerned in the crime which is being tried"[24].

Identification Parade: Case-Laws

The case-laws below show certain guidelines that should be followed while conducting identification parade.

1. "Identification held by police officers would be hit by section 162 Cr.P.C.[25].
2. "Prosecution was not justified in declining the request of the accused to hold identification parade"[26].

3. "No rule of law requires that the oral testimony of a witness should be corroborated by evidence of identification. In fact the evidence of identification is itself a weak type of evidence.[27]"
4. "If the intention is to rely on the identification of the suspects by the witnesses, his ability to identify should be tested without showing him the suspect or his photographs or furnishing him the date for identification[28]".
5. "It can be laid down as a proposition of law that after the lapse of a long period, witnesses would, in no case, be able to identify the dacoits they had seen in the course of a dacoity committed during the night. However, the Courts will have to be extremely cautious when such evidence is before them[29]".
6. "Identification of the accused was held reliable because (1) in F.I.R. it was mentioned that they would identify dacoits if shown (2) that the witness saw dacoits in adequate light for about half an hour[30]".
7. "Brahmanand was brought by the police and made to sit outside the Court of the Magistrate where these witnesses also waited. Before the identification parade began, the Magistrate took no precautions to see whether other similar bearded men joined the parade. The identification proceedings was therefore rightly described by the Trial Court as a farce[31]".
8. "Failure to hold an identification parade would not make inadmissible the evidence of identification in Court[32]".
9. "Absence of test identification is not necessarily fatal[33]".
10. "Necessity to hold the parade arises when the accused are not personally known to the witness[34]".
11. "Prosecution should hold an identification parade specially if an accused says that the alleged eye-witnesses did not know him previously[35]".
12. "It is true that the evidence about identification of a person by the sound of his voice depending upon subtle variations in the overtones, when the person recognizing is not familiar with the person recognized, may be somewhat risky in a criminal trial. But if the accused is intimately known to the witness, it can not be said that identification of the assailant

by the witness from what he heard was so improbable[36]".

Identification Parade—Objects

The objects of holding identification parade have been thus put by the Supreme Court – i.e.,

(1) "The identification is not a substantive evidence in law and it can be used for corroborating or contradicting the evidence of the witness. (2) If there is no substantive evidence at all, the evidence of identification parade is of no assistance to the prosecution. (3) It furnishes an opportunity to the investigating officers to know whether the investigation is proceeding on the right line. (4) The chances of the eye-witness's memory fading are reduced. (5) It can be used under section 157 or 145 of the Indian Evidence Act. (6) It should be arranged without delay[37]".

Hence if identification of the suspect or property is made at the scene of crime or shortly after the crime has been committed, there is normally no legal problem, at least in so far as the admissibility of testimony is concerned. Nevertheless, "when an eye-witness failed to pick up an accused both in the identification parade as well as in the Committing Magistrate's Court, it should be entirely incorrect to rely upon his belated identification in the Sessions Court[38]". Again "the evidence of mere identification of the accused persons at the trial for the first time is from its very nature inherently of a weak character. The evidence in order to carry conviction should ordinarily clarify as to how and under what circumstances he came and the details of the part which the accused played in the crime in question with reasonable particularity. The purpose of a prior test identification, therefore, seems to be to test and strengthen the trustworthiness of that evidence. The persons required to identify an accused should have had no opportunity of seeing him after the commission of the crime and before identification, and secondly that no mistakes are made by them or the mistakes made are negligible. The identification to be of value should be held without delay. The number of persons mixed up with the accused should be reasonably large and their bearing and general appearance not glaringly dissimilar[39]".

How to Hold an Identification Parade?

The Supreme Court of India, in Ramakrishna *vs.* State of Bombay has clearly laid down how identification parade is to be held by the police or at their request, by the Magistrate in the course of the investigation of an offence for the purpose of enabling the witnesses to identify the persons who are concerned with the offence or the properties which are its subject matter. Here the witnesses are explained the purpose of holding the parade and are asked to identify the persons or the properties which are concerned in the offence[40]".

The manner of holding an identification parade should never be one open to criticism. Remember that if the identification parade is not conducted properly, the defence will be able to develop successfully inconsistencies in the procedure. Hence:

i) Put up each suspect separately for identification. The suspect should be mixed up with as many persons as possible. A dozen of people will be ideal, if not less.

ii) Witnesses should not be allowed to see the suspects prior to the identification parade. One should always remember that the identification is held to test the power or capacity of the witnesses to identity the suspect, animal or things which they claim to identify.

iii) If there is only one suspect, his position should be changed when each witness is called out. Each witness should be asked to identify the suspect and other witnesses should not see the identification done by a particular witness.

iv) If necessary, a suspect may be asked to exhibit in a certain way i.e., wear certain clothing, make a gesture or take a stance and he may be asked to say certain words. But this should be asked to all persons in the line-up.

v) If the suspect is a lame person and the witness says that he will identify only if the accused walks in which case all the persons in the line-up should be asked to walk. In such cases, it is better to have lame persons in the line-ups, if that is possible.

CONDUCT OF IDENTIFICATION PARADE – A FEW DON'TS FOR POLICE

1. Never present the suspect in some manner that might be deemed prejudicial.
2. Never allow the suspect to dress or present or exhibit himself in such a way as to make him stand out from others.
3. Never make any statement that might lead the witness for easy identification.
4. Never try to be present when identification parade is held by a Magistrate.
5. Never coach the witnesses as to how to identify a suspect—such as visible marks on the face of the suspect or some peculiarities which the suspect has etc.
6. Never allow other witnesses to see the identification made by a particular witness.
7. Never conduct identification parade under conditions which are not identical with those of the crime under investigation.
8. Never show the suspect to witnesses from the time of his arrest of his admission to the jail.
9. Never postpone the identification parade.
10. Never refuse the counsel of the accused to be present if a request is made to this end. But never allow him to take part in the actual proceedings.
11. Never forget to record the position of the subject if identification is made.

vi) If the suspect possesses a scar, a mole, a pierced nose or ear, a blind eye, a split lip or any other distinctive marks, then such visible scar/mole/mark should be covered with paper or similar materials. The same part of the body of all persons in the line-up should be similarly covered.

Identification Parade by Police

Theoretically speaking, there is no legal objection to a test identification being conducted by the police. But in such instances, any statement made by the witnesses will be hit by section 162 Cr.P.C. and therefore the statements can be used only for the limited purpose of contradicting the witnesses under section 145 of the Indian Evidence Act. As a result, the purpose of using the identification for corroborating the statement of the identifier before the Court is defeated. Because of this, it is never advisable for the police to conduct a test identification parade.

In Narayan Singh *vs.* Madhya Pradesh, it is held that an identification parade should not be conducted by police officers who may take too much or undue interest or by the Magistrate who will be reduced to the position of ordinary witnesses and may have to give evidence[41].

Identification Parade by Private Citizens

There is no legal objection for a private or ordinary citizen to conduct an identification parade even in cases the line-up is arranged by the police. Section 162 Cr.P.C. does not apply to the identification parade held by private citizens. In Ramkishan *vs.* State of Bombay, the Supreme Court has held that private citizens can under their direction and supervision conduct identification parade[42]. In any case, such procedures are viewed with suspicion and are open to criticism. Therefore, it is not desirable nor advisable that an identification parade is arranged under the direction and supervision of private or ordinary citizens.

Identification Parade by Magistrates

If a Magistrate of the First Class or of the Second Class especially empowered for the purpose of holding an identification parade conducts the parade, section 164 Cr.P.C. applies and his identification memo becomes admissible in evidence under section 80, Indian Evidence Act, 1872 without any further proof. But if any other Magistrate holds it, he must be called to prove his memo. If the proceedings are held before a Magistrate of the Second Class not specially empowered, then the statements irrespective of the powers of the Magistrate before whom it is made, remain formal statements of the witnesses and can be used for contradicting him under section 145 or under section 155, Indian Evidence Act or for corroborating him under section 157 Evidence Act.

SUGGESTED READINGS

Aubry, Jr., A.S. *The Officer in the Small Department*, Charles C. Thomas, Springfield, 1961.

Campbell, D., *Police: The Exercise of Power*, Macdonald and Evans, 1978.

Gupta, R.L., *Law of Identification*, Eastern Book Co., Lucknow, 1963.

Houts, M., *From Arrest to Release*, Charles C. Thomas, Springfield, 1958.

Khan, M.K.A., *Law of Identification*, Law Book Co., Lahore, 1947.

Prasad, V., *The Law of Bail*, Supreme Court Criminal Ruling Office, Allahabad, 1978.

REFERENCES

1. See also 9 H.L.E. Second Edition, Para III, page 84:10 H.L.E. Third Edition, Para 631, page 342.
2. K. Krishnamurthi, *Police Diaries, Statements, Reports, Investigation and Arrests etc.*, Law Book Co., Allahabad, 1973.
3. Quoted in K. Krishnamurthi, *Police Diaries Statements, Reports....., op. cit.* Seciton 80 Cr. P.C. (old) is section 75 in the new Code of Criminal Procedure, 1973.
4. Long *vs.* Ansell, 293 U.S. 75, 55 S. Ct. 21, 79 L. Ed. 208.

5. Henry *vs.* United States 361 U.S. 98 103; 80 S. Ct. 168, 171; 4 L. Ed. 2nd 134.
6. Rambal Singh *vs.* State, 1959 M.P. 380: 1958 Cr. L.J. 1402.
7. Boli Dc *vs.* Emperor, 35 Cal. 38: 7 Cr. L.J. 188.
8. Abdul Aziz *vs.* Emperor, 1933 Pat. 508: 35 Cr. L. J. 725.
9. Sheo Balak Dusadh *vs.* Emperor, 1948 All. 103: 49 Cr. L. J. 62.
10. K. V. Mohammed *vs.* Chakappanyan, 1943 Mad. 218.
11. Harachand Patnaik *vs.* Emperor, 1939 Pat. 129: 18 Pat. 121: 40 Cr. L. J. 500.
12. Premila Gupta *vs.* Hopkyn, 1932 Cal. 470 The corresponding section for section 54 Cr. P. C. (old) is section 41 Cr. P. C. 1973.
13. Emperor *vs.* Gopal Singh, 36 All. 6: 11 A. L. J. 957.
14. Emperor *vs.* Abdul Hamid, 198 I. C. 264: 1942 All. 74: Cr. L. J. 338: I. L. R. 1942 All. 35; 1042 A. L. J. 32: 1941 A. W. R. H. C. 352. The corresponding section for section 56 Cr. P. C. (old) is section 55 Cr. P. C. (new).
15. Emperor *vs.* Abdul Hamid, *op. cit.*
16. Section 436, Cr. P. C., 1973 reads :
    (1) When any person other than a person accused of a non-bailable offence is arrested or detained without warrant by an officer-in-charge of a police station, or appears or is brought before a Court and is prepared at any time while in custody of such officer or at any stage of the proceeding before such Court to give bail, such person shall be relesed on bail:
    Provided that such officer or Court, if he or it thinks fit, may instead of taking bail from such person, discharge him on executing a bond without sureties for his appearance as hereinafter provided:
    Provided further that nothing in this section shall be deemed to affect the provisions of sub-section (3) of section 116.
    (2) Not withstanding anything contained in sub-section (1) where a person has failed to comply with the conditions of the bail bond as regards the time and place of attendance, the Court may refuse to relese him on bail, when on subsequent occasion in the same case he appears before the Court or is brought in custody and any such refusal shall be without prejudice of the powers, bound by such bond to pay the penalty thereof under section 446.
17. See Banta Ram *vs.* State of Himachal Pradesh, 1980, Cr. L. J. 748.
18. Banta Ram *vs.* State of Himachal Pradesh, *op. cit.*
19. R. B. Mitheny *vs.* Assistant Collector, A.I.R., 1967 S.C. 1639: T.H. Hussain *vs.* M. P. Mondkar, A. I. R. 1958 S. C. 376: 1958 Cr. L. J. 701.
20. Kashmira Singh *vs.* State of Punjab, A. I. R. 1977 S. C. 2147: 1977 Cr. L. J. 1746.
21. Natabar Parida *vs.* State of Orissa, 1975 Cr. L. J. 1212: A. I. R. 1975 S. C. 1465.
22. Ram Naravan Singh *vs.* State of Delhi, A.I.R. 1953, S.C. 277: 1953 Cr.L.J.

1113.

23. Dowlat Singh, 14 All. 45.
24. Ramanujam, *Prevention and Detection of Crimes,* Madras Book Agency, 1972.
25. Harnath Singh *vs.* State of Uttar Pradesh, 1970 Cr. L. J. 1422: A. I. R. 1970, S. C. 1619; Budh Sen *vs.* State of Uttar Pradesh A. I. R. 1970 S.C. 1321: 1970 Cr. L. J. 1149.
26. Shri. Ram *vs.* State of Uttar Pradesh A.I.R. 1975 S.C. 175: 1975 Cr.L.J. 240.
27. Shri Ram *vs.* State of Uttar Pradesh, *op cit.*
28. L. Choraria *vs.* Maharashtra, A.I.R. 1968 S.C. 938 Cr.L.J. 1124.
29. Delhi Administration *vs.* Balakrishnan, A.I.R. 1972 S.C. 3: 1972 Cr.L.J.1.
30. Chander Singh *vs.* State of Uttat Pradesh, A.I.R. 1973 S.C. 1200: 1973 Cr. L.J. 1252.
31. Yeshwant *vs.* State of Maharashtra A.I.R. 1973 S.C. 337: 1972 Cr.L.J. 1252.
32. Kanta Prasad *vs.* Delhi Administration, A.I.R. 1958 S.C. 350: 1958 Cr.L.J. 698.
33. Harbhajan Singh *vs.* State of Jammu and Kashmir, A.I.R. 1971 S.C. 363: 1971 Cr.L.J. 305.
34. Mehtab Singh *vs.* State of Madhya Pradesh, A.I.R. 1975 S.C. 275: 1975, Cr.L.J. 290.
35. Jabu Nath *vs.* State of Uttar Pradesh, A.I.R. 1971 S.C. 363: 1971 Cr.L.J. 305.
36. Kripal Singh *vs.* State of Uttar Pradesh, A.I.R. 1965 S.C. 712.
37. Vaikutam *vs.* State of Andhra Pradesh, A.I.R. 1977 S.C. 1340: 1970 Cr.L.J. 1984; Matru *vs.* State of Uttar Pradesh, A.I.R. 1971 S.C. 1050: 1971 Cr.L.J. 913; S. T. Shinde *vs.* State of Maharashtra, A.I.R., 1974 S.C. 791: 1974 Cr.L.J. 674; Hasib *vs.* State of Bihar A.I.R. 1972 S.C. 282: 1972 Cr.L.J. 233; Rameshwar *vs.* State of Jammu and Kashmir, A.I.R. 1972 S.C. 102: 1972 Cr.L.J. 14.
38. Vaikuntam Chandrappa *vs.* State of Andhra Pradesh, A.I.R. 1960 S.C. 1340: 1960 Cr.L.J. 1681.
39. Budh Sen *vs.* State of Uttar Pradesh, A.I.R. 1970, S.C. 1321: 1970 Cr.L.J. 1149.
40. Ramkrishan *vs.* State of Bombay, A.I.R. 1955, S.C. 104.
41. Narayan Singh *vs.* State of Madhya Pradesh, A.I.R. 1965, M.P. 225: 1965 Cr.L.J. 507.
42. Ramkishan *vs.* State of Bombay, *op. cit.*

10

INTERROGATION AND INTERVIEW BY POLICE

Interrogation is a skillful method of questioning. "It is a conversion, but one which is very tightly controlled by the police officer, between himself and a suspect"[1]. The object of interrogation is to ascertain facts, to disclose truth and to unveil the mystery in a crime by putting a series of questions to the suspect in a crime. The questions are to be pertinent, tangible and relevant to the facts. The content and mode of examination of the accused or of the suspect by police is governed by sections 163, 164, 281 and 316 of the Code of Criminal Procedure, 1973 and sections 24 to 30 of the Indian Evidence Act, 1872. Of these, sections 164, Cr.P.C. and section 26 of the Indian Evidence Act go together and deal with confessions made to a Magistrate[2].

A review of the rulings by the Courts of India makes it clear that they have paid keen and continuous attention to the admissibility of confessions obtained by police in criminal cases. Through the years the views of the Courts have become more and more clear with respect to the circumstances under which the confession is obtained, imposing severe restrictions on its admissibility as evidence. Accordingly, every confession made by a suspect or accused should be voluntary. Therefore, as stated earlier, a confession caused by inducement, threat or promise is made inadmissible. Similarly confessions made to a police officer while the accused is in custody are made irrelevant. Nevertheless, when any fact is deposed to as discovered in consequence of information received from a person accused of any offence in the custody of a police officer, so much of such information, whether it amounts to a confession or not as relates distinctly to the fact thereby discovered may be proved. In the system of criminal justice administration prevalent in some countries in the west, a confession made by an accused, if it is voluntary, whether to a police officer or others, is made admissible in evidence against him in his subsequent trial. For instance, in English law, the statement of an accused person to the police could be tendered in evidence provided he has been cautioned and the exact words of the accused are deposed to.

In India, confessions are to be recorded by Magistrates. Section 164 of Cr. P.C. empowers Metropolitan and Judicial Magistrates to record any confession or statement made to them in the course of an investigation or at any time afterwards before the commencement of the inquiry or trial. However, the Magistrates must record it only after cautioning the suspect making confession that the latter is not bound to make the confession and also ascertaining that the suspect makes the confession voluntarily. If the suspect, in spite of the caution, makes the confession, it may be used against him if the confession is recorded as provided in section 281 of the Code of Criminal Procedure, 1973. Instances there are of retracted confessions in criminal proceedings. The rule in this case is that the retraction by itself cause doubt on the truth of a confession. Such retracted confessions can, however, be proved, in Court and admitted in evidence; but they cannot be acted upon unless they receive general corroboration by other evidence.

Interviewing During Investigation

Besides interrogating the suspects in a criminal investigation, the police have to interview several persons who know about the facts of the case. Hence, "an interview is a conversation between the policeman and a witness or a victim which is controlled somewhat by the police officer"[3]. Remember that the witnesses whom the police examine are potentially witnesses for prosecution. Section

161 of the Code of Criminal Procedure, 1973 makes the following provisions *for* examination of witnesses:

(1) "Any police officer making an investigation under this chapter or any police officer not below such rank as the State Government may, by general or special order, prescribe in this behalf acting on the requisition of such officer, may examine orally any person supposed to be acquainted with the facts and circumstances of the case.

(2) Such person shall be bound to answer truly all questions relating to such case put to him by such officer, other than questions the answers to which would have a tendency to expose him to a criminal charge or to a penalty or forfeiture.

(3) The police officer may reduce into writing any statement made to him in the course of an examination under this section and when he does so, he shall makes a separate and true record of the statement of each such person whose statements he records".

Under section 160, Cr. P.C. a police officer has the power to require the attendance of witnesses.

I

Police Interrogation

Interrogating suspects or those accused of crime is perhaps the most difficult among the duties of crime investigators. Hence a basic understanding of the various defence mechanisms in operation among suspects/interrogators during interrogation becomes necessary for police investigators. Defence mechanisms in police interrogation are nothing but the escape mechanisms by virtue of which a suspect in a crime or a police interrogator resolves or attempts to resolve his frustrations or inner conflicts during the process of police interrogation[4].

Defence Mechanisms in Suspects

Often it so happens that a suspect in a crime makes his own forecasts about the possible evil consequences of his act. No doubt he experiences anxiety. Detection psychologists argue that the knowledge of the after-effects or better the consequences of being judged guilty—no matter the suspect in a crime is guilty or innocent—leads certainly to fear and anxiety of the consequences in the form of punishment, court action, police harrassment, social stigma, financial loss and loss of prestige or personal status. The manifestation of fear and anxiety is usually found more in a really guilty man than it is in an innocent one. Necessarily the fear and anxiety cause frustrations and inner conflicts in a suspect and as such, he may normally resort to various defence mechanisms to save himself from the frustrating situations.

"Policeman"—says Gerber—"has been presented to the general public not as the defender of law and person of justice, but as someone who is out to get you. The end result of this has been that many people, from the time they are children, dislike police officers and feel that they are essentially sadistic, cruel individuals who are going to take every chance they can to stick them in jail.... They shake in their boots". Why do people fear the custodians of law and order?

The fear of the public to the custodians of law and order is predominantly a learned response. It may depend upon the painful or unpleasant experiences which they might have had from police officers. Police mustache – even little children amidst us know it well, for, they look like a policeman when they play the game "Police and Thief". They would very much have to appear as *ferocious* as they can towards their "little thief". They like to have a "police look" and to speak as "the policeman speaks" – to show a "police attitude" and to cut short, they *walk, talk* and *behave* like a policeman does. It, therefore, follows that if infants and little children have formed peculiar images about their policeman in their infantile minds, it goes without saying that a SUSPECT in a crime – particularly if he is guilty – knows them better. The suspects in a crime knows well that they are in police custody for interrogation and if found guilty they are likely to be prosecuted against and punished. Therefore, they are likely to guard themselves from being caught and to this end they may employ techniques – fair or foul-including defence mechanisms to save themselves from the clutches of law.

As stated earlier, any suspect in a crime experiences frustrations or mental conflicts or both when he is being interrogated. In this regard, the suspects vary only in degrees. For instance, a first offender may experience more acute mental conflicts than a recidivist or a repeater. Because of this, a first offender may think of absconding from the scene of crime at the earliest possible opportunity. Absconding from the scene of crime is said to be an overt defence mechanism – known as *withdrawal* from a situation causing frustrations or mental conflicts – and studies and experiences with suspects tend to prove that even *Convictional Criminals* express mental conflicts when they are subjected to interrogation by police.

The author had several opportunities to observe the workings of defence mechanisms in suspects when they were interrogated by the police. When a question is asked, the suspect evaluates the *pros and cons* of his responses and he resorts to various defence mechanisms to resolve his tension in the situation. According to the author, the inner conflicts to which a suspect is put during police interrogation can be:

i) Repulsion – Repulsion Conflicts
ii) Repulsion – Attraction Conflicts

Repulsion – Repulsion Conflicts

In this case, the suspect has two options to a police question, but he is repulsive to both—in other words, he is negatively attracted to both options. Take, for instance, the classic example — 'Have you stopped beating your wife'? – asks the police interrogator.

The answer to the above question can be either is *Yes* or in *No*. Suppose, the suspect says *Yes*, it would mean that he used to beat his wife earlier and now he has stopped the same. In that case, he could be treated as guilty for having beaten his wife earlier. On the contrary, if he says *No* in which case it would mean that he continues to beat his wife. Here he feels that he is between the *devil and the deep sea.* This sort of mental conflict to which a suspect is put during police interrogation is called 'Repulsion—Repulsion (Double Repulsion) Conflict.

REPULSION – REPULSION CONFLICT

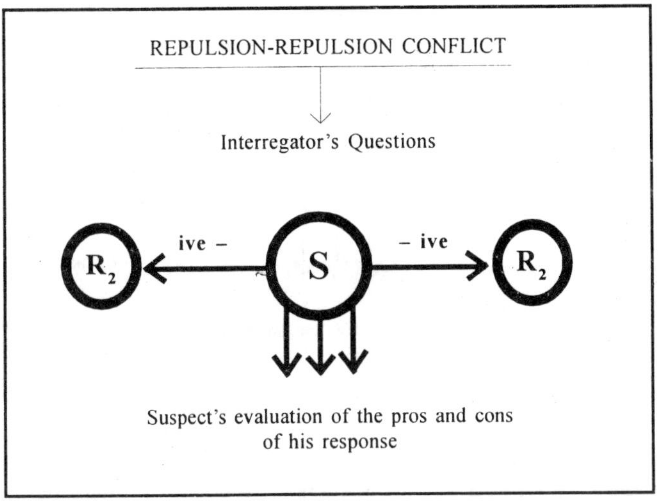

Here the suspect has only two options, but he is repelled to both —i.e., R_1 and R_2 (Responses) and he has the experience of being in between the devil and the deep sea. He cannot but chose one of the options since the interrogator is pressing for a response.

Repulsion – Attraction Conflict

It is an accepted maxim – *One cannot have the cake and eat it too.* And take for instance.

Police interrogator: "Do you know where the stolen property is"?

Suspect replies here either in *yes* or in *no*. If the suspect says *yes* he knows well that he could escape police misbehaviour – but at the same time he might be found guilty and all the possible (evil) consequences of such a response would necessarily follow. On the other hand, if the suspect says *no*, then he knows pretty well that he would be beaten up by the interrogator, but he needs not undergo prosecution and trial for a criminal case. This sort of mental conflict is called 'Repulsion – Attraction Conflict'.

REPULSION – ATTRACTION CONFLICT

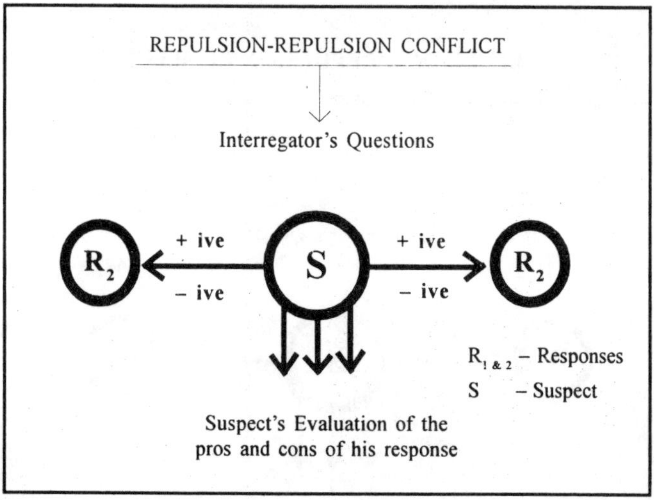

To the one and the same response, the suspect is attracted and at the same time repelled. For instance, if the suspect says 'no' to the above question, he might not be called guilty, but will be beaten up. If, he says 'yes' he will not be beaten up, but will be prosecuted and punished. He wants to *have the cake and eat it too.*

Any suspect, when he experiences mental conflicts will resort to defence mechanisms to maintain his mental balance or equilibrium. The various defence mechanisms which a suspect in a crime employs when he is being interrogated by a police officer is called 'SDMs-meaning **Suspect's Defence Mechanisms**.

Defence Mechanisms in Police Interrogators

Police interrogators are also human beings and as such a number of psychological forces are seen at work on them during the time of questioning suspects. Any police interrogator would very much desire for success in his work. He would like to avoid failures. Generally he wants speedy results as well. He tends to think – the speedier the result is, the better it is. But, during this process of achieving the end in a desired way – rather in the speediest possible way – he too experiences mental conflicts or frustrations as the case may be. In other words, frustrators stand between himself and his goal – the goal being a confession from the suspect.

FRUSTRATION IN AN INTERROGATOR

FRUSTRATION IN INTERROGATORS

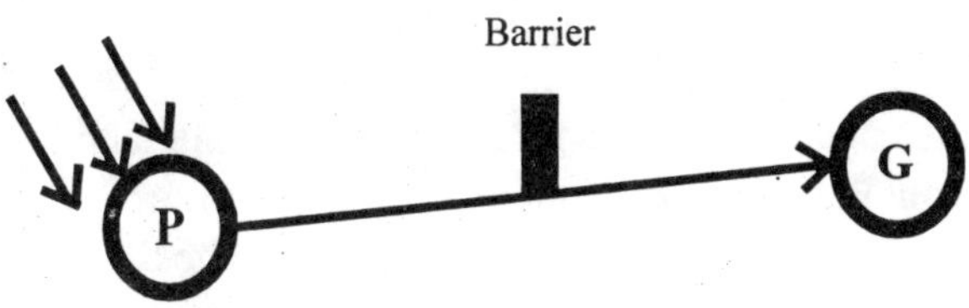

P – Police Interrogator (Individual)
G – Goal (Confession from the suspect)
Barrier, i.e., Frustrator

Here the police interogator is motivated to reach the goal in the speediest way possible. The goal here is a *confession* from the suspect regarding his involvement in the commission of crime. Frustrator is otherwise called **Barrier** and this works between the police interrogator and his goal. It can be anything from political interferecne, bribe, friendship, blood relationship, etc., to various defence mechanisms resorted to by the suspects during interrogation.

More often than not, a suspect lays down a number of *Frustrators* by means of his defence mechanisms and thereby the interrogator experiences mental frustrations. In order to resolve his frustrations, the police interrogator may resort to various types of defence mechanisms just to maintain his mental equilibrium. This is the reason why interrogation psychologists argue: "The more frustrated the police officer becomes, the more likely he is to resort to threats, to shouting at the suspects. Essentially, he has lost control of the situation when he does so.......... As he feels himself loosing control of the situations, he seeks to regain it by using more shoutings, more threats etc. This frequently makes the suspects frighten". The net result is that the suspect tries to employ more of his defence mechanisms just to counter-attack the defence mechanisms found operative in police officers or the suspect may surrender himself to the defence mechanisms of the interrogator by making the SDMs inoperative or ineffective. The Defence Mechanisms which are seen active in police interrogators during questioning of a suspect is called PDMs – **Police Defence Mechanisms.**

SDMs and PDMs During Police Interrogation

Police interrogation, in a way, is nothing but an interaction between SDMs and PDMs. Who succeeds? – The interrogator or the interrogated? This depends upon how best do the SDMs or PDMs overpower one another in a given situation. In other words:

$$PI = \frac{PDM}{SDM} \quad \text{where PI = Police Interrogation}$$

If PDMs overpower SDMs, the police interrogator wins and on the contrary, if SDMs overpower PDMs he fails. This is the reason why at every time a suspect is interrogated, the police interrogator consciously or unconsciously tries to put down the SDMs. Some Police officers may threaten, coerce or use third degree methods at the very outset – i.e., just before they start interrogating a suspect, and the purpose behind this technique is to put down the intensity of SDMs found in the interrogated. This sort of interrogation is crude and illegal and therefore is to be discouraged.

Cause and Effect Relationship

The discussions above will show that the SDMs and PDMs are found to be having some cause-effect relationship. To be more specific, the SDMs cause PDMs and in turn PDMs cause SDMs.

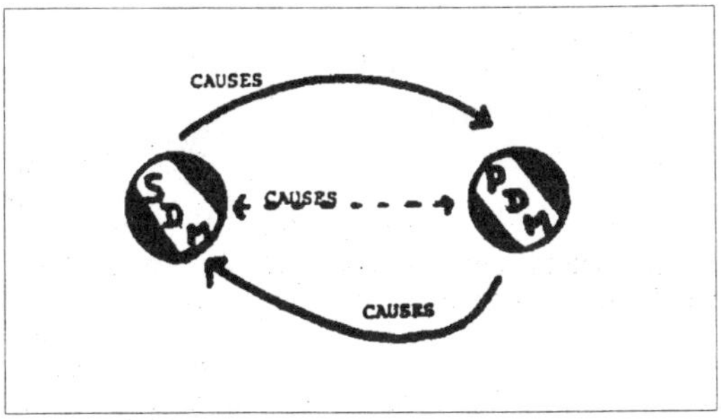

The author conducted a study to understand the working of SDMs and PDMs during police interrogation. The study on those who pleaded *not guilty* at the outset to police and later confessed their guilt revealed that in 100% of the cases, the suspects resorted to *Rationalization* and *Repression*; in 69.56% cases they resorted to *Sublimation*, in 60.96% cases – *Regression*, in 56.52% cases – *Compensation*, in 82.61% cases – *Identification*; in 78.26% cases – Tolerance; in 47.83% cases *Masochistic–Aggression*; in 26.09% cases – *Substitution* and in 86.96% cases they resorted to other types of defence mechanisms. Conversely enough, police resorted to *Rationalization* and *Compensation* in 100% of the cases; in 26.09% cases – *Repression*; in 13.04% cases – *Sublimation*; in 4.36% cases *Regression*; in 60.87% cases – *Identification*; in 69.56% cases – *Projection*; in 34.78% cases – *Tolerance*; in 21.74% cases – *Masochistic Aggression*; in 8.70% cases – *Vicarious Aggression*; in 56.52% cases – *Saddistic Aggression*; in 13.04% cases – *Substitution* and in 78.26% cases they resorted to other types of defence mechanisms[5].

It has also been found from the study that various defence mechanisms interact between the suspect and the police officer and vice-versa. In other words:

'SDM' causes 'PDM' which in turn causes 'SDM' and the process goes on until one of them is made inoperative or inactive. In other words, police interrogation will be successful if and only if 'SDMs' are made inoperative or inactive.

This theory and its application in police interrogation become very important for understanding of suspect's behaviour and for effecting self-control among investigators during interrogation.

Ego – States During Interrogation

Personality of both the interrogator and the interrogated play an important role during the questioning of suspects. Some interrogators suggest that the police officer should be the master of the situation by his dominating personality. It is disputable whether the dominating personality of the interrogator will yield success in all cases, with all types of criminals and in every situation. The author is of view that all police officers and also the criminals have three Ego States during interrogation.

EGO – STATES IN INTERROGATORS

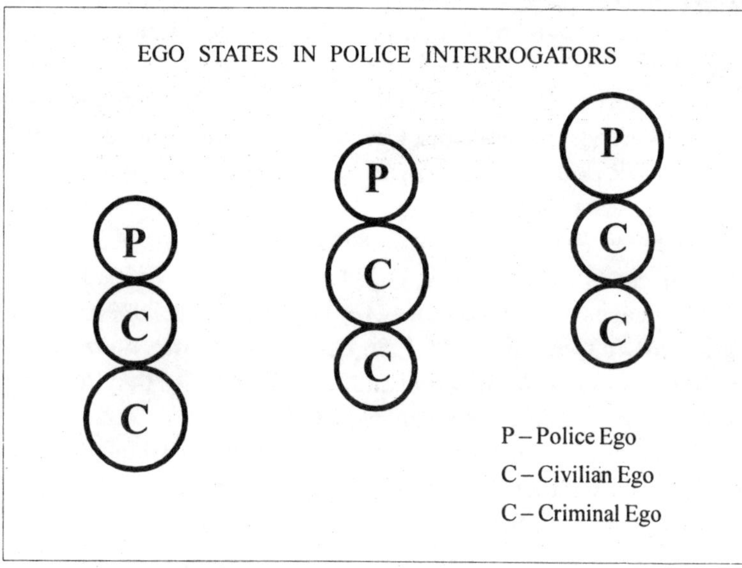

Police ego means the authoritarian personality of the police officer. No doubt, the authority of the police officer is consciously or unconsciously accepted by the suspect during interrogation. The authoritarian ego expresses itself in the words which the interrogator uses, the eyes with which he looks at the suspect, the way in which questions are asked, the mannerism with which he deals with the situation etc. *By Civilian Ego* we mean decency, politeness, sympathy, consideration, patience, honesty, perseverance etc. which a civilized person desires to possess. Some interrogators suggest that it is better if the interrogator appears in plain cloths when he is taking up the art of interrogation. This is intended to create a relation which is not hostile between the interrogated and the interrogator during the time of questioning the suspects. By *Criminal Ego* we mean the attitude of hostility, aggression, cruelty, impatience, lack of sympathy and respect etc. towards the citizen subjected to interrogation.

Some police officers have more of *Police ego* so much so that they cannot become successful in criminal interrogation and so is the case with officers who have a predominant *criminal ego.* Those who have the predominance of *civilian ego* will prove to be a good interrogator.

In other words, a successful interrogator is one who has more of *civilian ego* in his personality traits and who can alter his ego state to *police ego* if that needs be and never to *criminal ego* if and when situations demand.

Similarly, a criminal too has got three ego – states when he is being interrogated. Depending upon the type of the offender, he may assume authoritarian (police), civilian and criminal ego states. For instance, a political offender may have more of an authoritarian ego in him and a first offender may have more of a 'civilian ego' and a recidivist may have more of a 'criminal ego'. In fact, the interrogation is nothing but a transaction between the interrogator and the interrogated and the success of an interrogator depends upon how best he manages the transactions between him and the interrogated.

Type of Offenders

1. Basing on Frequency of Crime

Depending on the frequency of the commission of the offences, the suspects may be classified into *first offenders* and *repeaters*. First offenders are those who, though might have committed crimes earlier, have been detected and caught for the first time. More often than not, they might have committed the offence under sudden heat of passion, anger or revenge. They may have a feeling of remorse, mental anguish or prick of conscience. But recidivists are normally non-emotional offenders and may have no feeling of remorse, mental anguish or prick of conscience.

2. Basing on Conviction of the Need for Committing Crimes

On the basis of the mental convictions which the offender has regarding the necessity of committing crimes, the suspects may be divided into two categories – say, *convictional criminals* and *non-convictional criminals*. Political criminals, naxalites, terrorists and so on belong to the first category of offenders. And the non-convictional criminals are those who have committed the offences like theft, murder, rape, forgery etc. not because they were mentally convinced of the need for committing the offences, but because they were in such a situation that they could not but commit them. Again in the second category, there can be first offenders or recidivists.

3. Basing on the Socio-Economic Status of the Offenders

Sometimes, the interrogator will have to question persons enjoying high social and economic status. White-collar criminals, organized racketeers, syndicate criminals enjoying high political influence and so on come under this category.

4. Basing on the Sex of the Offenders

Offenders may be male or female. In the case of females, always question them in the presence of another lady.

5. Basing on the Age of the Offenders

Sometimes, juveniles will have to be questioned. There may be adolescent offenders or middle aged people or old men.

The classification is not exhaustive and also not mutually exclusive.

Requisites to Police Interrogation

The requisites for successful police interrogation are:

1. The interrogator should have collected all (at least a good many) pieces of evidence against the suspect. Here the evidence will speak louder than anything else. Usually what is seen today is to question a man and then find out the evidence against him. But the procedure is the reverse – i.e., collect the evidence and then question the suspect. In a country where civil rights are respected, it is not proper to catch hold of people, curtail their freedom and detain them in police custody in the pretext of questioning them.
2. Interrogation should be done in secret – in isolation. It should be remembered that offenders are often reluctant to make a public confession of their guilt. If interrogation room is available, then question them there only.
3. Interrogation should be conducted by an experienced officer who normally does not assume criminal ego – state during interrogation. Never allow unauthorized or unwanted people to witness the interrogation process.
4. Once the offender has started speaking out something, allow him to finish his story. Interruption while the suspect is answering a question is likely to side track the entire conversation and therefore such a procedure will never lead the interrogator to the desired destination.
5. Remember that the offender will resort to several or all sorts of defence mechanisms such as rationalization, projection, compensation etc. (as shown above). The interrogator should be able to identify and appreciate the defence mechanisms operating in the interrogated. Never react to these mechanisms in an undesirable way. The more defence mechanisms the suspect is employing, the better it is for the interrogator to unearth the truth. Never assume criminal agó – state when

QUALITIES OF A SUCCESSFUL INTERROGATOR*

1. Very strong power of observing things all around him.
2. Clarity of vision.
3. Thorough knowledge of the locality and the people residing there.
4. Good stock of patience and perserverance.
5. Zeal and energy.
6. Sound reason and power of logical reasoning.
7. Farsightedness
8. Clear and penetrating mind.
9. Good instinct and well balanced tact.
10. Accuracy and precision.
11. Expeditious and agreeable disposition, and
12. Above all,
    (a) Honesty,
    (b) Integrity, and
    (c) Sincerity of purpose.

* See *Crime Investigation,* Directorate of Police Training, Bureau of Police Research and Development, Ministry of Home Affairs, Governemnt of India, New Delhi.

the offender is seen resorting to defence mechanisms.

6. Display an air of confidence. Create an impression in the suspect that the interrogator at times believes him and at times is suspicious of his version. Whenever necessary, point out circumstantial evidence indicative to his guilt.
7. Try to establish *rapport* with the suspect. For this, taking up of the 'civilian ego state' is recommended.
8. A face to face questioning is always better-yielding than any other method as this would give him a good facility to observe the reactions, reflexes and hesitations. When interrogating, the police officer should be in a position to read the mind of the suspect, his attitudes and susceptibilities etc. The interrogator should observe:
   i) Pulsation of carotid artery.
   ii) Excessive activity of the Adam's apple.
   iii) Dryness of mouth.
   iv) Inability to look straight to the interrogator.
   v) Restlessness etc. If necessary, draw the attention of the suspect to his psychological and physiological changes indicating symptoms of his guilt consciousness.
9. Never adopt unlawful, demoralizing and objectionable means to obtain a confession. This indicates that the interrogator, in such instances, is loosing his self-control and taking up *Criminal Ego State*. In such instances, see that the interrogator comes back to the 'civilian – ego state'. To force the suspect admit the guilt by threatening, frightening, injuring him or by giving false information etc. is discreditable, unnecessary, illegal and unwise.
10. As indicated earlier, defence mechanisms will be found operative or active in the suspects as well as in the interrogator. As a result, some people will simply deny every known facts or may answer very insolently. At times they may avoid questions or grossly insult the interrogating officer. But in all such instances, the interrogator must put every restraint on himself to keep his temper. Remember that PDM causes SDM which in turn causes PDM and the process goes on until one

OBJECTIVES ON INTERVIEW AND INTERROGATION*

1. To establish facts necessary to prove the *Corpus delicti.*
2. To obtain descriptive information necessary to identify the culprit.
3. To corroborate or disprove information previously obtained.
4. To varify inferences which the investigator has drawn from other evidence.
5. To secure physical evidence which will aid in establishing the guilt of a suspect.
6. To eliminate particular persons from the suspect-set.
7. To recover fruits of the crime.
8. To identify accomplices.
9. To determine the location of a suspect; or
10. To obtain an admission of guilt from a suspect.

* Jerry L. Dowling, *Criminal Investigation,* Harcought Brace Jovanovich, Inc, New York. 1979.

of them is made inactive or inoperative. If PDM is made inoperative, naturally SDM can be made inactive.

11. Ordinary decency and fairness (civilian-ego) to a suspect demands that every chance must be given to him to explain or disprove by independent witnesses/evidence all facts which have apparently gone against him. Here, therefore, the suspect must invariably be asked whether he wants to cite any witness for his favour. If possible, the interrogator must see that his witnesses are examined.
12. In all statements made, all impossibilities, improbabilities, contradictions and gaps must be noted. The clarifications and explanations with respect to them can be sought for. The investigator can, if necessary, cross examine the suspect with an element of surprise.
13. An air of superiority (Police-Ego) will at times bring out very bad results. The police have authority and they need not project it out always. This does not however mean that the interrogator must cling to the suspect without any self respect or dignity.
14. The investigator should not form prejudices and preconceived theories about the suspect. His function is to probe into for finding out the truth.
15. As far as possible, don't bring the suspect for interrogation purposes to the scene of crime. But very rarely bringing him to the scene of crime may yield good result as it would revive in him all conditions which caused him to commit the offence. But, it shall be used only in the rarest of rare cases. In such instances, hand-cuffing should be resorted to only if and if only it is absolutely necessary.
16. Interrogate a person only when there is convincing evidence – sufficient enough to question a person. The cast, creed, status or position should not be permitted to influence the interrogator during the questioning.
17. If civilian-ego does not yield result – i.e., in spite of very decent behaviour on the part of the interrogator, still the suspect is stuborn – then the interrogator can take up the police-ego state by showing the evidence collected against him.

How to Interrogate?

Put on the *Civilian-Ego State* and try to maintain it all throughout the examination if that is possible. If the suspect takes up 'Criminal-Ego State or Police-Ego State', try to bring him to 'Civilian-Ego State'. Try to make SDMs inoperative or inactive by skillful questioning. Study the category of the offender. Be sympathetic and considerate. Let the evidences speak. Be patient and show a listening attitude. Understand the suspect fully well. Try to establish rapport. Hardened criminals should be questioned only after collecting the relevant evidence against them.*

Other Techniques

1. Lie Detection Techniques

The Lie-Detector is a mechanism by which the changes in respiration, circulation, galvanic skin response, skin temperature, pulse rate etc. are measured by the help of an instrument – to detect *the Guilt Conscience*. It cannot detect guilt as such; nevertheless a qualified examiner having education, training and experience can determine whether or not the charts provided by the instrument contain a meaningful pattern to detect the *Guilt Conscience*. The interpretation of the chart is of critical importance.

In the process of Lie-Detection, the examiner endeavours at the begining to determine the subject's *normal reaction* through a series of questions irrelevant to the issue in question. From another series in which key questions have been injected, he can observe the person's reaction to what should be a situation of stress. For instance, if a murder has been committed with a knife and the nature of the weapon is not clearly known, the examiner by skilful questioning about the weapon should be able to elicit a greater change in the respiratory, circulatory charts etc. from the suspect. If he is guilty, or has knowledge about the details of the knife, he will show

---

* Cf. *Police Interrogation : Dos which the police do not do* by James Vadackumchery, A.P.H. Publishing Corporation, Delhi, 1999.

evidence of the attempts to cover up the knowledge. The evidence will be:

i) Significant and Unusual Verbal Responses to Critical Words.
ii) Increased Association-Reaction-Time on Critical Words.
iii) Variable Association Reaction-Time on Critical Words.
iv) Change in Facial Expressions.
v) Change in Blood Pressure, Respiration, Perspiration etc.

The guilt-complex indicators can be further illustrated :

a) Word-Association

Here the suspect takes a relaxed position of sitting or in a reclining position in a quiet room and the examiner instructs him to respond to each *stimulus-word* by giving the first other word suggested to his mind. As soon as the list of 100 words are given it is once again gone through with instructions to try and recall the response made to each *stimulus word* on the first round. The evidence that the *guilt-complex* has been touched by some particular *stimulus word* is furnished by peculiarities in the responses and this is called a *Complex Indicator*. Such *Complex Indicators* can be many and an experienced psychologist can interpret them with certainty and precision.

b) Reaction-Time

Reaction-Time is the time required by an individual to get an overt response started. In other words, it is the "S-R" interval (Stimulus – Response Interval). When a *stimulus* enters the organism, it remains latent or hidden in it till it reaches the muscles and produces an observable effect on the environment. The sense receptors, nerves and muscles take their own time to move or react. It has been observed that a considerable amount of time is taken by the brain compared to other mechanisms. It is the *time* taken by the sense organs, brain, nerves and muscles to react is called the *Reaction Time*. According to Woodworth, *reaction time* is the time

A FEW DON'TS DURING INTERROGATION

1. Don't use such words as 'murder, death-penalty, sessions case, life imprisonment', etc. during interrogation.
2. Don't let the suspect know about the consequences of his offence.
3. Don't give the suspect any promise which cannot be fulfilled.
4. Don't accept as true everything which the suspect speaks and likewise don't be suspicious of everything he says.
5. Don't keep an arrested suspect for more than 24 hours under police custody. Produce him before the Magistrate strictly in accordance with the law.
6. Don't take up criminal–ego state at any time during the interrogation.
7. Don't use a language not understandable to the suspect.
8. Don't think that people react in the way in which the interrogator wants them to do; but only in the way in which they like to behave.
9. Don't try to write down everything the suspect speaks from the begining. It should be postponed until the interrogation is over.
10. Don't think that interrogation is an easy work. It is an art. It is time-consuming, laborious and painstaking.

required by an individual to get the overt response started – i.e., the S-R interval.

The Reaction-Time can be: (i) Simple, R.T. and (ii) Disjunctive R.T. In simple RT, no intervening activity is found – i.e., only one stimulus is given and as such no question of discrimination between the stimului takes place. If more than one stimulus is given and consequently a discrimination is to be made, it is called *Disjunctive R.T.* The *Disjunctive R.T.* can be either *Discriminative or Choice R.T.* In the latter case, both discrimination and a selection should be made. Experiments show that *Disjunctive R.T.* is longer than *Simple R.T.* Both the Simple and Disjunctive R.T. can be obtained through *Association Tests*. There can be *Free vs. Controlled Association* and also *Discrete vs. Continuous Association.* Combining these two, one can have a four-fold classification. They are:

1. Discrete-Free;
2. Discrete-Controlled;
3. Continuous-Free;
4. Continuous-Controlled.

In the *Discrete Free Association,* the suspect is asked to respond to the first word occurring to his mind when the interrogator gives a stimulus orally or visually. But in *Discrete Controlled*, the suspect is instructed to respond in some specific way. This can be: (i) to give the opposite of the stimulus word or (ii) naming the part of the object indicated by the stimulus. In *Continuous Free Association,* the interrogator presents a stimulus word. and the suspect is asked to respond with a series of single words as speedily as possible. In *Continuous Controlled Association*, the suspect is told to limit his association in some fashion. The rest is just similar to *Continuous Free Association.*

If the R.T. does not indicate any guilt, then it will show fairly constant *Reaction Time* to all stimulus-words. On the contrary, if the R.T. is longer than normal, it is considered to be a guilt indicator. The author has observed that the *Reaction-Time* of a murderer (who shot at the victim) to pistol has been 6.3 seconds while for words like flower, ink, radio, Srilanka etc. it has been ranging from 2.4 to 2.7 seconds. 6.3 seconds to the pistol is very significant to detect guilt conscience.

Long R.T. can be, at times, due to the effect of temporary distractions or interruptions. Like R.T., the failure to react also can be a *Guilt-Complex Indicator*. Here the person may be unable to react to the stimulus words. It can be due to the emotional shock which he has when he hears or sees the stimulus. Likewise, signs of excitement, embarrassment, meaningful smiling/laughing, stammering, whispering or shouting can be other indicators of guilt consciousness. Similarly, responses having no obvious relation to the stimulus-words or far fetched or extremely personal responses also will be *Guilt-Conscience Indicators.*

c) Circulation of Blood and Changes in Respiratory Rates

Experimental evidence shows that emotions speed up circulation. Scientists have measured the blood pressure of students before and after their examination and it has been found that the blood pressure has been higher before the examination than what it was after the examination. It has also been proved that I/E ratio (I = Duration of inspiration, and E = Duration of expiration) is high during emotions and very high in posed wonder and is very low during laughter.

d) Galvanic Skin Response

Whenever a 'tension or excitement' takes place, there will be an increase in the activation or in the energy mobilization. This is to say—when a person is experiencing an emotion, his level of activation will be higher than it is in the normal state. There are many indices to measure activation levels. But the most commonly employed index of the activation level is the electrical conductance of skin-usually of the palm of the hands. The principles underlying electrical conductance are:

i) Conductance of skin varies constantly;
ii) one can measure the level at a given time; and
iii) The rapid variations that result from stimulation can also be measured.

The rapid change in conductance has many names—P.G.R. G.S.R and E.D.R. But the term G.S.R. is most popular today. G.S.R. has been well accepted today as a good complex-indicator because of the speed and the sensitivity with which it follows stimulations. Here, two electrodes are attached to the forearm, palm fingers etc. They are connected in series with a weak source of electric current and a galvanometer. The galvanometer gives a quick deflection when the suspect is stimulated. This deflection is owing to the secretion of sweet and therefore whenever there is emotion in the suspect there will be more secretion of sweat, which in turn will be responsible for a large deflection in G.S.R.

The G.S.R., thus works on the secretion of sweats. It is found that adrenin seems to inhibit the G.S.R. Similarly, on a very hot day, even the palms participate in the general sweating and so gives a high conductance even during muscular relaxation. However they are not serious limitations for its effective use as a complex-indicator.

In Lie-Detection experiment, the person is hooked into the electrodes and asked to select one of the ten cards, remember it and return it to the pack. He is instructed to keep the interrogator from seeing which card he has actually taken. The cards are shown to him, one at a time, and he says 'no' to each. There will be a G.S.R. with each reply, but the biggest deflection will usually be to the card he has already seen. It has been observed that in 83% of the cases, it will be successful.

In practical Lie-Detection, the G.S.R. appears to be of less satisfactory because G.S.R. is too responsive even to incidental stimulus and thus observing the charges involved in deception. The G.S.R. is used in Keel's Polygraph only in conjunction with other indices. If all the indices point to a lie on the given question, the G.S.R record usually strikes enough to convince the suspect that he has been caught.

e) Other Indices of Guilt-Conscience

i) *Skin temperature :* It has been observed from experiments that the temperature of the hand and face falls during strong emotions.

ii) *Oral temperature :* The traditional value is 98.4°F. This seems plausible since increased bodily activity means more heat production.

iii) *Pupillary response :* Pain and strong emotions cause dilation.

iv) *Salivary secretion :* A sympathetic discharge decreases the flow and makes it thicker. Formerly this was used in Lie-Detection techniques because in telling a lie meant drying up the suspect's salivary secretions.

v) Gastro-intestinal activity, eye-blunking etc. are considered as complex indicators.

f) Luria Technique

An act of lying involves conflict between two responses—i.e., the true word and the lie. It is observed that the mental conflict will disorganise human behaviour. In order to obtain a good measure of the disorganization owing to mental conflicts, the suspect is asked to press a key simultaneously with the response words and keep the other hand on a duplicate key. The key measures all changes of pressure and major strokes. The strokes and key-pressures are taken as the indicators of guilt. Hints of irregularity will be seen in the pressure exerted by the hands.

g) Polygraph

A polygraph is simply a portable ink-writing instrument that records breathing, fluctuations in blood pressure and associative reaction time. A polygraph needs not be a Lie-Detector. It is a lie-detector apparatus only when the measures are good enough and when an expert can detect sings in the record which are indicative of deception. The polygraphic lie-detector records faithfully certain reactions of the suspect—blood pressure, changes in respiration, G.S.R. —which, if made under proper scientific conditions, enable an expert to distinguish truthful and untruthful responses to the stimului.

The question is are set up so that a guilty man shows an increase in level of activation (emotion) in answering a relevant question and not to a control question. Several indices are better than one and the expert by the help of these various indices attempts to:

i) determine whether the suspect is telling the truth:

ii) test and compare inconsistent statement;

iii) verify the assumptions made by the investigating officers and the statements made by the suspect before the polygraphic tests;

iv) obtain the fact when the test shows that the suspect is not telling the truth;

v) develop leads to important facts of crime.

It has been seen that in 70% of the cases, an experienced polygraph operator can decide whether the person is guilty or innocent; 20% will show little responses and 10% represent true errors. Police officers are not supposed to employ polygraphic test on suspects as they are not competent persons sufficiently qualified to conduct it. Hence they are advised to take the suspects to an expert in this matter.

In India, polygraphic lie detection test is administered in Delhi, Hyderabad etc. and the author is yet to know whether or not the result of the test is admissible in evidence in courts in India. In United States of America, the polygraphic test results were held inadmissible because the procedure had not yet gained general scientific acceptance. Again in a study conducted in United States about the validity of polygraphic test, 93% of the psychologists questioned replied that a polygraph operated by a well trained investigator had moderate or high validity; none held it to be invalid; 7% had no opinion. Again, among observers, experimenters and examiners, 95% considered the procedure had moderate or high validity; none considered it invalid; 5% had no opinion. Of examiners who actually use the technique in police interrogation, 99% rated the technique, to have moderate or high vailidity[6].

Extra Ordinary Methods of Interrogation

1. Truth Serum of the Use of Drugs

With many stimulant and depressant drugs, a transient or excitable phase in suspects can be caused. As a result, the suspect will become euphoric, talkative and sometimes emotionally responsive. Alcohol may cause loose talks during excitement phase and some people under the influence of alcohol may divulge things which they would not otherwise do. Scopolamine (an alkaloid similar to hyoscine), ether, nitrous oxide, chloroform and barbiturate drugs will produce conditions in a certain stage of anesthesia for a person to talk freely, but with a mixture of truth and falsehood. In the words of Donald B. Lindsey:

The principle involved in the so-called "truth serum" is simply that a drug may, in one of the stages of anesthesia or sedation, temporarily give rise to a condition in which certain inhibitions and obstructions to memory, and to questions consciously or unconsciously avoided, are removed. Because of the uncertainty of the truth or falsity of the statements, except as they can be susequently checked by other sources of evidence and because certain drugs may give rise to hypnotic and hallucinatory images and memories, the result cannot always be valid. The "evidence" thus revealed is not accepted in court and in general the procedure is not looked upon very favourably by the medical profession or by laymen."[7]

Hypnosis in Criminal Interrogation

The word *HYPONSIS* has never been properly defined. Some 'operational definitions' have been given by medical men and psychoanalysts. The word 'hypnosis' (etimologically, comes from Greek 'hypnos') means *sleep*. In the process of hypnosis, the patient becomes 'drowsy' and 'sleepy'—a sort of unnatural sleep. It is not a natural sleep, for the hypnotised patient is still aware of his surroundings, although in the deeper states, by suggestion he may become 'detached' from his environment and give the impression of being oblivious of things around him[8]. Harry Arons writes:

> "...the hypnotic state closely resembles the "twilight" state which immediately precedes sleep—the "transitory" state between sleeping and waking. But once a person falls asleep, he is in no sense in hypnosis and the two states are definitely not identical".

"Rapport" between the hypnotised and the hypnotist is highly required for the success of hypnosis. If this is not seen, the hypnosis will be an exercise in futility. According to noted psychotherapists, hypnosis in criminal investigation—particularly in major crimes—does not yield any good result. This is due to several factors such as:

i) Suspect's resistance to hypnosis—if the suspect seriously resists being hypnotised (particularly when he is guilty), any attempt to hypnotise him will not yield any advantageous results.

ii) Suspects may fool the hypnotist—this means that a suspect who knows how a person is hypnotised can profitably make use of his knowledge to fool the police interrogator. He may act as if he were hypnotised and may volunteer information consciously to mislead the investigator and thereby make an attempt to prove his innocence when he is otherwise guilty. Remember that there are suspects who possess good knowledge in hypnosis.

iii) Suspects may lie or may 'get sick' under hypnosis. Experts in hypnosis are of opinion that the suspects can lie under hypnosis. This, according to them, is owing to the suspect's instinctive motives of self-preservation. The guilty suspects, it has been observed, unconsciously resort to "sickness" to avoid answering questions. Hence says Harry Arons:

> "The defence mechanism of retreat into illness is not an uncommon device among humans who come face to face with some formidable impasse. Thus the suspect may become hysterical, develop nausea, asthmatic, coughing or sneezing spells, or in other ways thwart the efforts of the interrogators."[9]

iv) Defence lawyers object to hypnosis during police interrogation. Does the Indian Evidence Act admit hypnosis as an evidence to prove the confessions of an accused person? The author has not come across any rulings on the subject from the High Courts and the Supreme Court of India. In the United States of America, police interrogators do administer hypnosis to suspects in major crimes. In such instances, they take the following precautions of:

(a) getting the consent of the suspect, his counsel, the prosecutor and the police authorities. The services of a professional hypontist are used for the purpose.

(b) asking the defence counsel to be present during the entire process of hyponotic interrogation.

(c) obtaining the suspect's written consent to the hypnotic interrogation. In such cases, it is made clear that the suspect has willingly consented to undergo hypnotic interrogation and there was no compulsion, threat of punishment or promise of reward on the part of officers. A psychiatric or psychological evaluation showing that the suspect is emotionally stable is also done prior to hypnotic interrigation[10].

An experienced hypnotist can bring out important clues by a hypnotic interrogation. Nevertheless hypnosis is not regarded as a satisfactory means of obtaining a confession of guilt or innocence. The police officers are not therefore advised to use this unorthodox method of interrogation. But in unavoidable circumstances, if they use this technique, it should be done by a person having professional competence after taking all precautions before administering hypnosis. This book, however, does not make an attempt into the elaborate procedure of hypnotic interrogation. It needs elaborate study, practice and experience in hypnotic interrogation[11].

Third Degree Methods

"Interrogation in depth" which is otherwise known as 'use of third degree methods" during police interrogation is an attempt to "break" the suspect so as to get a confession. Here, no doubt the confessions are enforced. Ruler-treatment, manhandling, clipping etc. are said to be some of the notorious ways of third degree methods employed in some police stations in India and elsewhere. Legally speaking, use of third degree is not permissible however genuine may be intention of the interrogators. It should be avoided at any cost.

Interrogation of Suspects—Case Laws

1. "It is abhorrent to our notions of justice and fair play and is also dangerous to allow a man to be convicted on the strength of a confession unless it is made voluntarily and unless he realizes that anything he says may be used against him".[12]
2. " Accused was left in the magisterial lock-up which was in charge of the police. Therefore one is left only to conjecture what happened to the accused during those 24 hours."[13]
3. "In deciding whether a particular confession attracts the frown of section 24, the question has to be considered from the point of view of the confessing accused as to how the inducement, threat or promise proceeding from a person in authority would operate in his mind."[14]
4. "If the confession is made to a police officer during investigation, it will be protected under section 162 Cr. P.C. except as provided under section 27 of the Evidence Act. If the confession is made to a police officer it is invalid in view of section 25.; if confessions are sought to be brought under section 26 of the E.A., then the Magistrate should record the same as provided under section 164 Cr. P.C."[15]
5. "These discoveries are inadmissible in evidence because the police already knew where they were hidden."[16]
6. "If there is any mode of pressure, subtle of crude, mental or physical, direct or indirect, but sufficiently substantial, applied by the policeman for obtaining information from an accused strongly suggestive of guilt, it becomes 'compelled testimony.' violative of Art. 20 (3)"[17]
7. " A police officer should not insist that a woman should appear

> at the police station as this contravenes section 160 (1).......... Any person supposed to acquainted with the facts and circumstances of the case includes an accused person who fills that role because the police suppose him to have committed the crime and must therefore, be familiar with the facts".[18]

II

Interviewing of Witnesses

As shown earlier, the term *interview* goes with witnesses. This is so because; the witness is a person who is to aid the police in administration of criminal justice. Hence the mode of treatment and the manner of questioning him differ considerably from the same adopted when the suspect is interrogated. The interview is a conversation between the police and a citizen, the purpose being to find out the actual truth about the offence and the offender. It should be done in an atmosphere of mutual trust and support. A witness is a person who may be able to give either direct or indirect evidence with respect to a crime and its criminal. Section 161, Code of Criminal Procedure is about interviewing of witnesses.

Remember that the principal aim to interviewing a witness is to get a complete and accurate information regarding the whereabouts of the crime and the offender. During the interview, he will introduce the names of other persons whom when examined in turn will introduce a third lot of names. The process goes on until nobody's name is mentioned during the interview. The police have to bear in mind some statutory requirements when they interview witnesses—i.e., (i) The police are not empowered to get the signature of witness on statements recorded during an interview as such statements are made inadmissible in evidence, except for the purpose of contradiction. (ii) Whenever identification parade becomes necessary, it should be carried out before Magistrates as it amounts to statements of witnesses and is covered by section 162 Cr. P.C., 1973 if it is carried out before police. The same is applicable to identification parade conducted on property as well. (iii) Section 163 Cr. P.C., 1973 lays down that no inducement, threat or promise such as is mentioned in section 24 of the Indian Evidence Act, 1872 should be offered when statements are recorded. (iv) Every facility should be given to make free statements by witnesses.[19]

Where to Interview a Witness?

The best place to interview a witness is the place where he or she is likely to be found. But it seems that is more often violated than adhered to. The investigator, if he wants to ensure perfect co-operation and whole-hearted support from witnesses, must see that he pays adequate consideration to the many family, occupational and other social problems of witnesses. This is the reason why Police Manuals insist that "the power to summoning witnesses should be exercised only sparingly as it is desirable that the obligations of a witness are sufficiently exacting, should be lightened as far as possible. In towns, the examination of witnesses at the police station may be conducted without objection"[20]. In a study conducted by the author, it has been found that 77.17% of the police officers interviewed for the purpose of the study stated that the witnesses, as a rule, were interviewed in the Station Houses[21].This practice is to be taken in conjunction with another fact that witnesses who are summoned by police officers under section 160, Cr. P.C. 1973 are not, present, entitled to get any allowances to compensate their financial losses. The Law Commissions have repeatedly called attention to the gross disregard with which police approach the witnesses. "It is said that is not unusual for even persons who have been eye-witnesses to the commission of an offence to evade or attempt to evade giving evidence. In our view one of the reasons for the lack of co-operation is the scant regard which the police departments pays to the convenience of persons who may offer to give evidence and the general discourtesy and even suspicion with which they are treated. Witnesses should receive a far better treatment both when they appear before the police and in court than what they actually receive."[22]

Section 160 Cr. P.C. 1973 reads:

"Any police officer making an investigation under this chapter may, by order in writ'ng, require the attendance before himself or any person being within the limits of his own or any adjoining station who, from the information given or otherwise appears to be acquainted with the facts and circumstances of the case; and such person shall attend as so required:

Provided that no male person under the age of fifteen years or woman shall be required at any place other than the place in which such male person or woman resides". Of course this is the law. But the investigating officers are found to be reluctant to implement it. Again the law provides penal treatment to a witness who intentionally refuses to come to the police station in spite of written orders served to him/her.[23] If the police are going to invoke such penal provisions against citizens who are supposed to aid, support and co-operate with investigating officers, it goes without saying that very often the police will not be able to get what they need from such witnesses."

Time of Interviewing Witnesses

There is no hard and fast rule as to when the investigating officer should interview witnesses. It should be at the earliest available opportunity so that forgetfulness, influence or money will have little or no effect upon them. In any case, witnesses should be interviewed only after a thorough inspection of the scene of crime and collection of evidence.

Psychology of Witness-Testimony

Every investigating officer should have a basic understanding of the psychology of witness-testimony. Remember that witness-testimony depends much upon the accuracy and precision with which an individual makes his initial observation of an event. "The observers tend to get an overall impression of a given scene and then fill in details in sensible ways to conform to observer's meaning of the events regardless of whether the details actually did or did not conform".[24]

Professor Sutherland and Cressey think that "One remembers

what he wants to remember in many cases. Also his memory is a combination of what was actually witnessed and all other things that has been heard or imagined subsequent to the occurence.[25] No doubt, the Indian Evidence Act contains a set of rules of evidence that rests in some instances on conceptions of human nature that were the common sense views of a century or more ago, but are rejected by psychologists today. The Courts in India have, besides, evolved a set of precedents that are based on folklore assumptions about the nature of man, his perceptions and interpretations of an event. Nevertheless, in the recent past, the Courts are becoming more and more aware of the discrepancies that may be seen in witness-testimony. In the case of S.T. Shinde *vs.* State of Maharashtra, the Supreme Court of India observed: "Discrepancies in matters of details always occur even in the evidence of truthful witnesses. Such variations creep in because there are always natural differences in the faculties of different individuals, in the matter of observation, perceptions and memorization of details"[26] Yet, scientific research findings on witness-testimony in administration of criminal justice remains a field of which many judges, law enforcement officers and lawyers are still ignorant. Let us now turn our attention to factors that affect people while they witness a certain event.

1. Age of Witnesses

F.K. Berrien writes in this context: "The witness must be how many years old before reliance can be placed on his testimony? Such a question cannot be answered categorically because much depends upon the particular kind of information and the circumstances surrounding the events. There is some evidence that children are more suggestible than adults and are therefore more easily persuaded to modify their *recollections* of what occurred. The law enforcement officer must be on guard by the manner in which he approaches and questions children at the early investigation stages to make sure that he does not *put words in their mouths*. Children in situations that are uncomfortable to them are apt to accept the easiest way out for themselves and their friends, paying little regard to truth.... At this point we can merely point out that children are not necessarily less truthful as a whole than adults, but their understanding of responsibility and the consequences of inaccurate report have not matured. They are therefore less careful in distinguishing between what they know, what they guessed or fancied, and what someone else told them"[27]

2. Intelligence of Witnesses

How far does the intelligence of a person affect his observation of an incident? No noteworthy study has been conducted in this area. At the same time "the fact that persons of low intelligence are less competent and are more easily led to modify their reports by subtle suggestions, makes them less reliable witnesses."[28]

3. Education of Witnesses

Again no systematic studies have been reported on the relation between testimony accuracy and educational level of people witnessing an incident. In Boya Ganganna *vs.* State of Andhra Pradesh, the Supreme Court has given the ruling that "minor contradictions are bound to appear when ignorant and illiterate women are giving evidence. Even in case of trained and educated persons, memory sometimes plays false and this would be much more so in case of ignorant and rustic women."[29]

4. Vision of Witnesses

The interviewing officer should be thoroughly conversant with the common visual defects that may prevent or distort clear observation. A witness suffering from short sightedness (myopia) and not wearing corrective lenses cannot see events taking place at some distance away. Conversely enough, people suffering from long-sightedness experience difficulties in making fine discrimination usually at distances within arm's length.

Colour blindness may be there for years without the person knowing about his defect. It is estimated that nearly 4% of the male population and about 1% of the female-folk suffer from this defect[30].

QUESTIONS TO BE ASKED AND VERIFIED BY INTERROGATING OFFICERS DURING INTERVIEWING OF A WITNESS*

1. Has the eye-witness perceived the events with precision, accuracy and objectiveness?
2. Is he free from all types of errors in his perception or observation? If the eye-witness has been susceptible to errors in his perception or observation, what is the extent or intensity of such mistakes?
3. Are these errors in perception or observation substantial ones? In other words, how far can the discrepancies in witness testimony be treated as material ones in administration of criminal justice?
4. How did the attitudes, mental sets, experiences, motives, temperaments etc. of the witness affect his perceptual experience and subsequent interpretation of the event?
5. How far can this witness testimony be treated as the most reliable type of evidence in this case?

* See James Vadackumchery, *Reliability of Witness Testimony,* Police Research and Development, B.P.R. & D., Ministry of Home Affairs, Government of India, Quarter II, 1981.

There may be cases of individuals who, though may not be *colour blind* are *colour weak*. In this contest, says Berrien:

"Actually several types of colour blindness have been discovered, but the most common is the failure to distinguish between reds and greens. Unfortunately, such a defect has great possibilities for producting uncertainties in reading traffic signals and the like. On the other hand, most of the traffic signals are not pure colours and can also be distinguished in part by difference in brightness. A number of standard tests are available which provide a measure of colour blindness or colour weakness. Among these is the Ishahara test which consists of a number of cards covered with colour dots. Within the dotted field of a pattern of similarly coloured dots forms a numeral—at lest the normal person sees it. The colour blinded person may have difficulty seeing it, may not see the numeral at all, or may see a numeral that is different."[31]

5. Illumination on Colour Perception

The investigating officer must know that the "brightest colours in the spectrum under ordinary day light are the yellows. As illumination decreases, the reds and yellows rapidly decrease in brightness, while the greens and blues become brighter relative to other colours. Ofcourse, all colours decrease in brightness as the illumination decreases, but some drop out faster than others. It is, therefore possible to see greens when the blues and reds are invisible. For this reason, it would be wise to check closely on testimony in which the witness reported seeing certain colours when the general illumination was very low"[32] The author arranged, on one occasion, to have a person walk into a class room and interrupt the lecture by declaring that "Ha Ha Ha, I will beat him to death if anyone calls me a bastard." The incident look place most unexpectedly as it has been aimed to simulate realistically natural conditions that affect the perception of individuals witnessing an event. The person interrupted the lecture had worn a shirt red in colour and a dhoti having several squares coloured in green and several others coloured in blue. In his experiment, majority of the observers (i.e., 77. 78%) stated that the colour of the shirt had been red. Nevertheless, 18.51%

reported that the colour had been a combination of black/khaki/yellow with red. 3.70% said that he wore a black shirt. Surprisingly enough, none of the observers reported to have seen the real colours of the squares on the dhoti. Why did these discrepancies occur in the observation of colours? The author asked them the reason for it. Many of them said that they did not concentrate much on the colour. They had been keenly attending the performance and the statements uttered by the intruder in the class. Their concentration on the man and his statement, in a way, diverted their attention[33]. Hence the investigator should varify as to the things on which the person was concentrating at the time he witnessed the incident.

Remember that the colour or artificial illumination can also affect witness testimony. It can upset discriminations that are ordinary possible. Automobiles painted white are not easily distinguished from those painted yellow if both are seen under illumination by the ordinary reddish-orange neon lamps. The author selected clothes from a textile shop as he liked the colour of the cloth. He was disappointed to see a different colour when he viewed the same in ordinary day light.

It is known to all that, for a considerable period of time after one steps into a darkened room, it is impossible for him to see many things. One needs several minutes before he can see many details that are simply black at first. "The change in ability to-see-in-the dark takes place rapidly in the first three or four minutes but continues at a slower rate for at least half an hour. After a person has been exposed for as much as an hour or so to fluorescent lighting he "dark adapts" less well than if the illumination has been daylight or tungsten. The red end of the spectrum shows the least improvement in visibility under such circumstances and the violet or blue end shows the greatest improvement. This suggests that testimony concerning dim red lights at night or in darkened areas is open to more doubt than testimony concerning equally bright (in physical measurements) blue or violet lights. For example, the investigating officer should check carefully on all aspects of a report from a witness who declares that he had been sitting in a movie theatre for about an hour but failed to notice a dim blue flashing light near an exit but did see a red warning lamp. Care must be taken to establish that the lights were equal in brightness which can be done by a photometer. Wattages of the bulbs would be irrelevant to this question because the light must pass through the glass whose transmissibility affects bringtness.—says Berrien.[34]

6. Weight, Height, Size, Shape, Distance etc.

In an experiment, the author found that 85.18 per cent of the observers failed in their estimation of weight. Out of 85.18 per cent who failed in the estimation of weight, 22.22 per cent of the witnesses over-estimated the weight and 62.96 per cent underestimated it. The general tendency, it seems among people is to underestimate the weight of an individual. However, it is believed that persons affected by love, sympathy or consideration etc. usually underestimate the weight while persons having vengeance, jealously or aggression towards a particular individual, as a rule, overestimate the weight of a person seen by them. However, it needs more experimental evidence to categorically make a statement regarding the capacity of people to estimate the weight. Nevertheless, it should be accepted by all that people in general cannot make accurate estimation of weights just by observing a person or thing.[35]

Likewise, when estimating the height, people generally do not and cannot make accurate estimates. The author has seen from his experiments that when estimating of height of an individual, people have a tendency to underestimate the real height. But this depends upon from where the witness views the individual – i.e., from close quarters or from distant places. Berrien says that "Vertical lines or distances are generally overestimated such as the height of the flag pole compared with the same flag– pole laying in a horizontal position. In like manner, people have a tendency to estimate the length of a horizontal line as shorter than it really is if it is not crossed by other lines. It should be remembered that witnesses do not and cannot estimate accurately the height of vertical or horizontal lines or distances. Likewise, *unfilled space* (an open lot) is judged smaller than filled space[36]" (the same lot with a house on it).

Speed of an automobile can not be estimated accurately by people possessing no experience in assessing the speed of vehicles.

For instance, a car which produces excessive notice may seem to go slower than it really does. It is not ordinarily possible to estimate the speed of an automobile if the motion of the vehicle is directly toward or away from the observer. On the other hand, it may be possible to estimate the speed of the vehicle if the motion is across the field of view [37].

As far as the distance judgements are concerned, one must know that "small distances within reach are generally overestimated if they range between one or three inches. Lengths of four to forty inches are more apt to be underestimated. In estimating middle distances – 10 to 100 feet or greater – judgements depend heavily upon numerous cues coming from both eyes. For one thing, the mere fact that the eyes are separated by about two and one-half inches makes it impossible for both eyes to see exactly the same thing. These slight discrepancies in the images are still detectable by special means when viewing objects as far away as a mile. From these slightly different images we are able to estimate distance. Moreover, as objects move from near at hand to greater distances, both eyes turn outward, covering less and less. The convergence of the eyes controlled by the external muscles of the eyes provides signals for distance judgements as well. It is apparent, therefore, that one-eyed persons are less apt to be accurate in judging middle distance than people who can see normally with both eyes—writes Berrien .

7. Auditory Sensations

Echoing is of importance when witness testimony is appreciated. A witness said that he heard the sound of a gun shot from the west, when actually shooting took place in the east. No doubt the sound has been reflected off. But, if reflecting surfaces are not available, the location of the sound will be usually accurate.

Sometimes, the individual will not be able to say exactly from where – infront of, behind, below or above him – the sound comes from. This may be due to the fact that the sound has originated at a point in a place equidistant from each ear. The capacity of people to hear also must be tested. Some may be weak while others may be deaf. Some people may not hear the noice if he has been deeply involved in a work which needs acute concentration or meditation. Similarly if loud speakers or radios are tuned in high pitch, people may not hear the noice which they are supposed to have heard otherwise. Again, when people grow older and older, they tend to grow deaf.

VERIFICATION PRIOR TO INTERVIEWING WITNESSES

1. What is the age, intelligence level and educational status of the witness?
2. What about the vision of the witness – i.e., suffering from short-sightedness or long-sightedness etc?
3. Does the witness suffer from colour blindness? If not, is he suffering from colour–weakness? If so, what are the colours?
4. How was the illumination at the place of observation? What is its impact upon the observation of the witness?
5. Has there been artificial illumination? If so what is its impact upon observation?
6. How does the witness estimate the height, weight, size, shape, distances etc. Is there anything wrong in his estimation? Why?
7. What about the capacity of the witness in auditory sensations?
8. Any other relevant data on the capacity of other senses? If so what are they?

Classification of Witnesses

The witnesses can be broadly classified into three categories, namely:

1. Those employing acute defence mechanisms.
2. Those employing moderate defence mechanisms.
3. Those employing little or no defence mechanisms.

The author has observed that generally witnesses take up an *avoiding attitude* to police cases. Some are non co-operative while others are indifferent. Only an insignificant percentage of people take a co-operative attitude to police cases. Why are the witnesses non co-operative?[38] Several factors are responsible for the state of affairs.

According to Colaso and Sukla:

"Some of them are beyond the control of the police because they are an outcome of the situations prevailing in the society. However, there are many other factors which the police in particular, and the criminal justice system in general are responsible. Reluctance on the part of the police to register complaints, improper bahaviour, and ill treatment, corrupt and irregular practices and harassments of complainants and witnesses during police and court proceedings in criminal cases are some of the important factors mentioned in this context from time to time in published documents, including reports of police commissions, and discussions at various levels, both official and non-official. The police interviewer must therefore see that witnesses are not unduly or unnecessarily harassed if he desires co-operation from them".

In some books, witnesses are classified as: (i) *interested witnesses* –i.e., those are interested either in the administration of criminal justice or in the acquittal of the accused. The former if found to be volunturing to aid the police, and they will be doing so, more often than not, out of revenge, jealousy, personal enemity etc. towards the accused or love, sympathy, friendship or blood relation to the victim or the accused as the case may be. In such cases, they are witnesses employing maximum defence mechanisms. Likewise, those who come forward to save the accused, again for considerations like sympathy, friendship, blood relations etc. will be employing maximum defence mechanisms. They are dangerous type of people and therefore the investigating officer should be able to identify and appreciate the various defence mechanisms resorted to by them. Verification of their statements before accepting them becomes therefore necessary. (ii) *Disinterested witnesses*— i.e., those who are indifferent to the victim and to the culprit. They are people who think that do not stand to gain or lose anything as a result of their involvement. They are therefore people who will be employing minimum defence mechanisms and therefore their testimony can usually be treated as trustworthy. (iii) *Nervous witnesses*— they are timid persons who fear a lot in becoming witnesses. Usually, they are people who will be resorting to moderate defence mechanisms. (iv) *Unwilling witnesses* are those who are reluctant to advance anything as evidence. There can be a variety of causes for their unwillingness. It should be remembered that they will resort to moderate defence-mechanisms when they are being interviewed. (v) *Lying witnesses* are those who, in spite of their witnessing the entire incident, say: "We do not know anything". They are people who have moderate defence mechanisms. (vi) *Hostile witnesses* are dangerous people who do not want to tell the truth. If they are educated people, things are then more difficult. They are therefore persons who employ acute or maximum defence mechanisms. (vii) *Child witnesses* are good to give true testimony, because they have keen powers of observation, retentive memories and many a time they are incapable of exaggeration or telling falsehood. Depending upon the age, experience and consideration they have towards the victim/suspect, they may exhibit moderate or no defence mechanisms at all. Here the author has tried to classify witnesses on the basis of the defence mechanism resorted to by each one of them.

***Classification of Witnesses**

Witnesses with Acute or Maximum Defence Mechanisms	*Witnesses with Moderate Defence Mechanisms*	*Witnesses with Little /No Defence Mechanisms*
1. Hostile witnesses	1. Child witnesses	1. Child witnesses
2. Interested witnesses	2. Unwilling witnesses	2. Adolescent witnesses
3. Adolescent witnesses	3. Lying witnesses	3. Female witnesses
4. Female witnesses	4. Adolescent witnesses	4. Middle aged or old men
5. Middle aged or old men	5. Female witnesses	
	6. Middle aged or old men	

* Adolescent and female witnesses, middle aged or old men and so on can come under all the categories depending upon their attitude to police interviewing.

Manner of Interviewing Witnesses

Interviewing of witness consists of three stages: 1. getting set for the interview, 2. preparation for the interview, and 3. conduct of the interview.

1. Getting Set for Interview

As indicated earlier, the investigator may, as far as possible, go to the place where the witness is likely to be found. If that is not possible, select a place which has conducive or favourable environment for conducting the interview. Physical surroundings are of paramount importance in achieving the goal in interview. Privacy is of great importance. Hence never interview a person when he is being watched by others including police constables. Never allow the constables to interrupt the interviewer when the interview is being conducted.

The object of the interview must be to establish the best possible relation between the interviewer and the interviewed. The relationship so established must be such that interaction and exchange of ideas must flow without barriers. The barriers – physical and psychological – that are likely to interfere between the interviewer and the interviewed must be eliminated as far as possible. If barriers are not eliminated, people may resort to defence mechanisms which ultimately will prove to be harmful. Remember that barriers divide the interviewee and the interviewer and increase the social and psychological distance between them. Even the arrangement of furniture can act as a barrier. The arrangement in the office, if interview is conducted there, must suggest 'confidence, mutual trust and absence of fear".[39]

2. Preparation for Interview

Interview consists of a 'talk' between the interviewer and the interviewed. But what to talk? How to begin the talk? How to make the witness at ease? They need preparation. Remember that the success of an interview depends very much upon the planning that goes into it. Hence before interviewing a witness, it is good to know something about him – such as his occupation/profession, educational status, married or unmarried, children and their education etc. This will help the investigator to initiate the interview and to establish the needed 'rapport' without much difficulty. Always face the witness only after the preparation as to what to ask and what not to ask, what to verify and what not to verify, what to do and what not to do. About this George J. Dudycha says:

> "If a suspect or a witness is unexpectedly brought to a police captain's office for examination and questioning, the officer proceeds with the interview with little or no information, he is most likely to flounder about, create a poor impression, accomplish little or nothing and waste his and the other person's time. Because the interview was unexpected he allowed himself to be pushed into it before he was ready for it. What an officer should do at such a time is to excuse himself after meeting the person briefly and perhaps formally, retire to another office, check such records and files as are available, question other officers who may be able to give some information, and then return to his office and proceeds with the interview. It is far better to keep the interviewee waiting for 10 or 15 minutes and have a successful interview than to begin immediately without control of the situation. The delay must not be regarded as lost time, but rather as essential for success. Preparation for the interview pays off in that it increases the interviewer's prestige, enhances his control over the situation, create favourarble attitudes, secures co-operation, and even saves interviewing time".[40]

3. Conduct of Interview

The success of the interview with a witness depends considerably on the initial interviewee-interviewer contact. If the initial contact is bad, even momentarily, the success of the interview, if not defeated, will be decreased. The interviewer should therefore do his best consciously to establish a good and healthy rapport and to provide an environment that will ensure relaxation and freedom of expression.

Suppose the investigator wants to take a loan of money from a friend, how will he approach him? —If it is from a person whom he has only seen, but never had any opportunity to talk, how will he approach him? Almost this should be the approach to witnesses, for the investigator is there to collect information which the witnesses are not normally prepared to give out. Hence he should be greeted in the vernacular – as is usually done in the locality – and the greeting should be followed by the seemingly spontaneous introduction of a subject of mutual interest. This can be anything from children's welfare to the weather conditions. Next to this, the interviewer should consciously attempt to develop RAPPORT– ensuring harmonious relationship. "Anything that separates, divides or increases the social distance between the interviewer and the interviewee decreases rapport. Hence all barriers of whatever sort, must removed" — says Dudycha.

RAPPORT can be increased in very many ways. If the witness is a nervous one, put him at ease and encourage relaxation. He may be asked to sit down; or the interviewer may take a seat along with him if the interview is conducted at the residence of the witness. If tea and snacks are offered, accept it and enjoy making comments – all good about it. Likewise, if the witness is a lying one, understand the causes behind his attitude. Explain to him the need and importance of his support in the matter. In short, the attempt on the part of the interviewer should be to understand and appreciate the *defence-mechanisms* found operating in the witness and an earnest endeavour should be initiated to see that these *defence-mechanisms* are made inoperative, inactive and ineffective. Definitely the RAPPORT will be then developed and strengthened in such cases.[41]

Interviewing Techniques*

The techniques of interviewing applicable in all types are given separately in this chapter. Generally, it so happens that there is an interval of varying length between the moment a crime is committed

---

* Cf. Dr. James Vadackumchery, *Professional Police-Witness Interviewing,* A.P.H. Publishing Corporation, Delhi, 1999.

and the witness testimony is taken. "Various factors may operate during that interval to unintentionally disort testimony.......... Contrary to some legal doctrine, memory is not a unitary faculty of the mind. This assumption seems to underline a common Court rule that a witness may be examined as to his memory of events eventhough they may be unrelated to the events relevant to the case under consideration. If an individual cannot remember where he was on July 14, 1952, it is assumed that he cannot recall clearly the events of July 13, quite disregarding the effect of numerous factor which influence retention other than mere lapse of time. Among the other influences affecting memory is the prejudice existing at the time of the initial impression".[42]

Keeping in mind various factors that are likely to affect human mind, the investigator must try to unearth the defence mechanisms operating in witnesses. For instance, a nervous witness can be approached in a friendly manner. Encourage him and assure him that he is going to be only a witness and a witness alone. He may have developed an anti-police attitude and may think that policemen are always trying to put him in trouble. This must be the reason for his defence mechanisms or that he does not like to displease the accused/his family by being a witness. He may be unwilling to volunteer information, not because he does not want to help the police, but because he does not want to take up the botheration in connection with a criminal case or trial. Perhaps, explaining to him the entire case, pathetic conditions of the victim/his family, the process of law etc. may help the investigator to wipe off the defence mechanisms and ensure rapport between them. Hostile witnesses are problem-people and perhaps interviewing them with some evidence to show that they actually witnessed the incident can guarantee their co-operation. Some detection psychologists advocate that they should be questioned like a suspect and one should here employ 'friend and foe' method of interrogation. Child witnesses are said to possess *eidetic recollection or imagery* – meaning exceptional ability to describe in precise details many of their previous experiences. Their memories appear to be somewhat less selective than the same of the older folk. The interrogator should therefore question them in a loving manner by putting the questions

INTERVIEWING TECHNIQUES

1. Never boss over, brow–beat or condemn the interviewee.
2. Allow the interviewee to talk and react and keep the person talking and responding.
3. Be listening and attentive to what the interviewee speaks; take note of his gestures and body responses; never try to moralizing or lecturing.
4. Try to understand his defence-mechanisms and try to make them inactive by understanding – sympathizing and extending due consideration to what he says and does.
5. If the interviewee is found to be embarrassing, never put words into his mouth. If long pauses or periods of silence is noted, don't get embarrassed at it.
6. Ignore some of the comments made by the interviewee, for every statement the interviewee makes does not merit or require a response from the interviewer.
7. When direct questioning is resorted to for the purpose of extracting further information or for verifying facts previously presented, the questions should be stated positively. This leads to less confusion than when negatives are used.
8. 'Yes—no' questions should be avoided as far as possible. Here people may agree just for making the interviewer agreeable.
9. Avoid too rapid questioning as it causes excessive tension and emotion and these inturn produce disorganized responses.
10. Never use filthy language, third degree, threat, coercion etc.
11. Give respect and receive respect.
12. Close the interview in an orderly, definite and not too abrupt manner. Try to summarize briefly what has been said during the interview.*

* See also George J. Dudycha, '*Psychology for Interviewing*' *op. cit.*

in an understandable language. Leading questions should never be asked to little children. In the Indian cultural background, most of the women are shy and are not well educated. Hence, they should be interviewed at their homes and in all cases in the presence of a respectable lady or at least of a lady constable. One cannot deny the fact that some sort of social stigma is attached with visiting police stations by women in India. Adolescent witnesses are often emotional and have more adult personality traits in them. They should be, therefore, carefully tackled. Old people may not be able to recollect in detail things that have taken place in the recent past. Memory in them is less precise generally for recent incidents. We have a custom of respecting old people and the interviewer should offer them seats. Give them an importance more than what they actually deserve. They should be addressed with respect and consideration to their age.

Do's and Don'ts during Interviewing

1. Give your undivided attention to the person you are interviewing.
2. Don't write anything when the witness speaks. The writing should be reserved to the end of the interview.
3. Never walk around the room, talk to subordinates or colleagues when the interview is conducted.
4. Don't antagonize the witness and never try to argue with him. Arguments put each party on the defensive.
5. Don't approach a witness with prejudices or pre-conceived notions.

Witness-Testimony: Case-Laws

1. "When scanning the evidence of various witnesses we have to inform ourselves that variations on the fringes, discrepancies in details, contradictions in narrations and embellishments in essential parts cannot militate against the veracity of the core of the testimony provided there is the impress of truth and conformity to probability in the substantial fabric of testimony delivered".[43]

2. "There is no impediment in law in a conviction being based upon the testimony of a single witness provided the Courts come to the conclusion that his evidence is honest and trustworthy".[44]
3. "A witness is not like a tape-recorder. When he is giving evidence more than a year later about what happened a year earlier, his memory may not serve him completely right. He may not be able to repeat the exact words used on the occasion or all the words. Allowance must be made for these factors."[45]
4. "It is common experience that in the confusion of the moment, witnesses are prone to make such errors especially if seized by sudden fear."[46]
5. "In a melee where several people are giving blows at one and the same time, it will be impossible to particularize the blows and if any witness attempts to do it he may excite grave suspicion with regard to his veracity."[47]
6. "The question of delay in examining a witness during investigation is material only if it is indicative and suggestive of some unfair practice by the investigating agency for the purpose of introducing a got up witness to falsely support the prosecution case. The investigating officer should be asked specifically about the delay and the reasons therefor."[48]
7. "There is no hard and fast rule that simply because the prosecution witness did not explain the injuries on the person of the accused, their entire evidence should be discarded."[49]

Value of Evidence

A. Close Relations

1. "Relationship by itself is not a ground to discredit the testimony of witnesses if it is otherwise found to be consistent and true."[50]
2. "A close relative who is a natural witness cannot be regarded as interested witness."[51]
3. "Caste or neighbourhood cannot be a reason for disbelieving those who claim to be eye-witnesses of the incident and it is not necessary to look for corroboration for that reason."[52]

B. Interested Witnesses

1. "The term "interested" postulates that the person concerned must have some direct interest in seeing that the accused person is somehow or other convicted either because he had some animus with the accused or for some other reason."[53]
2. "Corroboration to the testimony of an interested witness will be necessary if they have poor moral fibre and have a load of bad anticedents."[54]
3. "However, witnesses who are not neutral may well testify to truth and need not be condemned provided in basic features their deposition is direct, probable and otherwise corroborated."[55]

C. Partisan Witnesses

1. "In a case with a communal background in which partisan witnesses depose falsely out of a mistaken or misplaced sense of a group loyalty it is necessary to scan the evidence carefully."[56]
2. "Often enough, where factions prevail in villagers and murders are committed as a result of enimity between such factions, criminal courts have to deal with evidence of a partisan type. The mechanical rejection of such evidence on the sole ground that it is partisan would invariably lead to failure of justice. No hard and fast rule can be laid down as to how much evidence should be appreciated. Judicial approach has to be cautious in dealing with such evidence; but the plea that such evidence should be rejected because it is partisan cannot be accepted as correct."[57]
3. "There is no hard and fast rule that the evidence of a partisan witness cannot be acted upon without corroboration."[58]

D. Rustic Witnesses

1. "The fact that the complainant was illiterate could not induce the Court to ignore the infirmities in his evidence or to fill in

lacunae in the prosecution case”.[59]

2. “The scene of murder is rural, the witnesses to the case are rustics and so their behavioural pattern and perceptive habits have to be judged as such. The too sophisticated approaches familiar in courts based on unreal assumptions about human conduct cannot obviously be applied to those given to the lethargic ways of our villages.”[60]
3. “But they could hardly be expected to have marked at the time the precise distance at which the person shooting the firearm was. They, therefore, gave an estimate of the distance at which he was from the victim. It is no wonder that the distances they deposed varies. Nothing can therefore turn on such variation.”[61]

E. Chance Witnesses

1. “Testimony of a chance witness although not necessarily false, is proverbially unsafe.”[62]
2. “If the witness is not a chance witness his evidence has to be carefully scrutinised from the point of view of probabilities. However, it is not a law that the evidence cannot be accepted without corroboratioin.”[63]
3. “If by coincidence or chance a person happens to be at the place of occurence at the time it is taking place, he is called a chance witness. And if such a person happens to be a relative or friend of the victim or enimically disposed towards the accused, then his being a chance witness is viewed with suspicion. Such a piece of evidence is not neessarily incredible or unbelievable but does require cautions and close scrutiny.”[64]

F. Child Witnesses

“Magistrates should always record their opinion that the child understands the duty of speaking the truth and state why they think that, otherwise the credibility of the witness may be seriously affected.”[65]

G. Hostile Witnesses

1. "When a witness, who has been called by the prosecution, is permitted to be cross-examined on behalf of the prosecution, the result of that course being adopted is to discredit that witness altogether and not merely to get rid of a part of his testimony."[66]
2. "A hostile witness may not be rejected outright but the Court has at least to be aware that, *prima facie* a witness who makes different statements at different times has no regard for truth. The Court should, therefore, be slow to act on the testimony of such a witness and normally, it should look for corroboration to his evidence."[67]
3. "While it is true that merely because a witness is declared hostile, his evidence cannot be rejected on that ground alone. It is equally well settled that when once a prosecution witness is declared hostile, the prosecution clearly exhibits its intention not to rely on the evidence of such a witness."[68]

H. Witnesses Who are Ex-Convicts

1. "In view of the huge lapse of time (43 years) between conviction and the present occurrence, his testimony cannot be discarded."[69]
2. "The witness was once convicted in a criminal case, but there is nothing brought out in cross-examination to show when he was convicted or for what offence."[70]

I. Police Witnesses

1. "The presumption that a person acts honestly applies as much in favour of a police officer as of other persons and it is not a judicial approach to distrust and suspect him without good grounds therefore."[71]
2. "The mere fact that they are police officers is not enough to discard their evidence."[72]
3. "Courts are aware of the exaggerated criticisms of the police

force as a whole and of the reluctance of the framers of the Criminal Procedure Code to trust statements recorded by police investigators, but these are, partly at least, the hangover of the British past. Today trust begets trust and the higher officers of the Indian Police, especially in the Special Police Establishments, deserve better credence."[73]

J. Raid and Trap Witnesses

1. "One cannot accede to the theory that the trapping of corrupt officials in the usual course is a polluted procedure. Excathedra condemnation of all traps, and associate witnesses is neither pragmatic nor just, nor is it fair to denounce a public servant indiscriminately."[74]
2. "There may be difficulty in detecting corruption cases and of securing conviction. Whatever be the difficulties, admissible evidence must be judged on its own merits, with due regard to all the circumstances of the case."[75]

SUGGESTED READINGS

Arsons, H., *Hypnosis in Law – Enforcement,* Hypnosis Quarterly, 7:34 – 35, 1961.

Bingham, W.V., and B.V. Moore, *How to Interview,* Harpe & Bros, New York, 1941.

Bryan, W.J. Jr., *Legal Aspects of Hypnosis,* Charles. C. Thomas, Springfield, 1962.

Erickson, C.E. *The Counselling Inteview,* Prentice-Hall, New York, 1950.

Garrelt, Annettee, *Interviewing: Its Principles and Methods,* Family Welfare Association of America, New York, 1942.

German, A.C. *Hypnosis as Related to the Scientific Detection of Deception by Polygraph Examinations: A Pilot Study,* Int. J. Clin. Exp. Hypn., 4.309 – 311, 1961.

Inbau Fred E., *Lie Detection and Criminal Interrogation,* Williams & Wilkins, Baltimore 1942.

Kroger, W.S. *Clinical and Experimental Hypnosis,* Lippincott, Philladelphia, 1963.

Larson, John, A., *Lying and Its Detection,* University of Chicago Press, Chicago, 1932.

Lee, C.D., *The Instrumental Detection of Deception,* Charles C. Thomas, Springfield, 1951.

Marston, W.M., *The Lie Detector Test,* Richard R. Smith, New York, 1938.

Mulbar, H., *Interrogation,* Charles C. Thomas, Springfield, 1953.

Weitzenhoffer, A.M. *General Techniques of Hypnotism,* Grune, New York, 1957.

REFERENCES

1. George, W.O. Conner, 'Interviewing and Interrogation' from *Criminal Investigation and Interrogation',* The W.H. Anderson Co., Cicinnati, 1962.
2. Section 163 Cr. P.C., 1973 runs thus:

(1) "No police officer or other perosn in authority shall offer or make or cause to be offered or made, any such inducement, threat or promise as is mentioned in section 24 of the Indian Evidence Act, 1872 (1 of 1872).

(2) But no police officer or other shall prevent by any caution or otherwise any person from making in the course of investigation under this chapter any statement which he may be disposed to make of his own will:

Provided that nothing in this sub-section shall affect the provisions of sub-section (4) of section 164".

Seciton 316 Cr. P.C., 1973 reads :

"Except as provided in sections 306 and 307, no influence by means of any promise or threat otherwise shall be used to an accused person to induce him to disclose or withhold any matter within his knowledge".

Section 24 of the Indian Evidence Act, 1872 is on the admissibility of confessions caused by inducement, threat, promise in criminal proceedings. Such confessions are made irrelevant and inadimissible.

Section 25 of the Indian Evidence Act, 1872 reads that confessions to police officers are not to be proved.

Section 26 of the Indian Evidence Act, 1872 says that confession by the accused while in custody of police officers is not to be proved against him.

Section 27 of the Indian Evidence Act, 1872 runs thus : "Provided that when any fact is deposed to as discovered in consequence of information received from a person accused of any offence, in the custody of a police officer, so much of such information whether it amounts to a confession or not, as relates distinctly to the act thereby discovered may be proved".

Section 28 of the Indian Evidence Act, 1872 makes relavant confessions made by the accused after removal of impression caused by inducement, threat or promise.

Section 29 of the Indian Evidence Act, 1872 is about confessions otherwise relevant not becoming irrelevant because of promise of secrecy etc.

Section 30 of the Indian Evidence Act, 1872 relates to consideration of proved confession affecting person making it and others jointly under trial for the same offence.

3. Gorber and Schrooder, *Criminal Investigation and Interrogation,* The W.H. Anderson Co., Cicinnati, 1962.

4. David E. Kerr shows how defence mechanisms are seen operative in suspects during police interrogaiton by illustrating a live example. He writes : "Shortly thereafter we arrived at his residence. He was very non-chalant and at the time of arrival has a cold can of beer in his hand. There were four or five very recent scratch-marks on his face. We asked him how he happened to obtain the cuts on his face. He replied that he had recently shaved with a bad razor. Common knowledge reveals that it is very unusual for a man to shave the lower part of his forehead, the lobes of his ears, between his eyes and along the sides of his nose. We let him believe that we accepted his explanation and started a search of his home. One of the detectives went into the bedroom where he found one shoe under the bed. Further searching resulted in the other shoe being found. We asked the suspect who owned the shoes. He stated that they belonged to his brother. "Well", we said : Just for fun, let us try them on. He tried them on and .... they fit exceptionally well. It was easy to see who owned the shoes. We later learnt that he had no brother." Here it is seen that the suspect was trying to give a rationalized explanation for every question put forth by the police detective. See how beautifully, the suspect was handled by the detectives.

5. For knowing the methodology of the study and more details read : James Vadackumchery, *Scientific Police Interrogation-Interaction of Defence Mechanisms Between Police and Suspects During the Process of Interrogation,* XVII, All India Police Science Congress, Pondicherry, 1983.

6. See Donald B. Lindsley, *The Psychology of Lie Detection,* Psychology for Law Enforcement Officers, George J. Dudycha (ed.) Charles C. Thomas, Springfield, 1970.

7. Donald B. Lindsley, *The Psychology of Lie Detectin, op. cit.*

8. Harry Arons, *Hypnosis in Criminal Investigation,* Charles C. Thomas, Springfield, 1967.

9. Harry Arons, *Hypnosis in Criminal Investigation, op. cit.*

10. Harry Arons, *Hypnosis in Criminal Investigation, op. cit.*

11. The reader is asked to go through Harry Arons, *Hypnosis in Criminal Investigation, op. cit.* and to consult professional hypnotists to know more about hypnotic interrogation.

12. Raja Khima *vs.* State of Saurashtra, A.I.R. 1956 S.C. 217: 1956 Cr. L.J. 421.
13. Tulasiram *vs.* State, A.I.R., 1954 S.C.I: 1954 Cr. L.J. 225.
14. Satbir Singh *vs.* State of Punjab, A.I.R. 1977 S.C. 1294: 1977 Cr. L.J. 985.
15. Zwing Lee Ariel *vs.* State of Madhya Pradesh, A.I.R. 1954 S.C. 15: 1954 Cr. L.J. 230; A. Nagesia *vs.* State of Bhiar, A.I.R. 1966 S.C. 119: 1966 Cr. L.J. 100.
16. Raja Khima *vs.* State of Saurashtra, *op. cit.*
17. Nandhini Satpathy *vs.* P.L. Dani, A.I.R. 1978 S.C. 1025.
18. Nandhini Satpathy *vs.* P.L. Dani, *op. cit.*; also see A.I.R. 1972 S.C. 1331.
19. According to section 132 of the Indian Evidence Act, 1872, a witness is not excused from answering a question which has a tendency to incriminate him or to expose him to a penalty or forfeiture of any kind; but a saving proviso lays down that such answers shall not be proved against him in any criminal proceedings, except in a prosecution for giving false evidence by such answer. Seciton 179 I.P.C. makes it punishable for any one legally bound to state the truth to refuse to answer a question put by a public servant.
20. Rule 788(2) of the Kerala Police Manual, 1973.
21. James Vadackumchery, *Acquittals in Administration of Criminal Justice,* Ph.D. Thesis, Kerala University, 1983.
22. 'Law Commission', XIV Report.
23. Seciton 174 I.P.C., 1860 makes a person liable to be prosecuted for intentionally refusing to come to the police station.
24. F.K. Barrien, 'Psychology and the Court' from *Psychology for Law Enforcement Officers,* Charles C. Thomas, Springfield, 1970.
25. E.H. Sutherland and D.R. Cressey, '*Prinicples of Criminology*', Times of India Press, 1965.
26. S. T. Shinde *vs.* State of Maharashtra, A.I.R. 1974 S.C. 791: 1974 Cr. L.J. 674.
27. F.K. Berrien, *Psychology and the Court, op. cit.*
28. F.K. Berrien, *Psychology and the Court, op. cit.*
29. Boya Ganganna *vs.* State of Andhra Pradesh, A.I.R. 1976 S.C. 1541: 1976 Cr. L.J. 1158.
30. F.K. Berrien, *Psychology and the Court, op. cit.*
31. F.K. Berrien, *Psychology and the Court, op. cit*
32. F.K. Berrien, *Psychology and the Court, op. cit..*
33. James Vadackumchery, *Reliability of WitnessTestimony, op. cit.*
34. F.K. Berrien, *Psychology and the Court, op. cit.*

35. James Vadackumchery, *Reliability of Witness-Testimony, op. cit.*

36. F.K. Berrien, *Psychology and the Court, op. cit.*

37. See also F.K. Berrien, *Psychology and the Court, op. cit.*

38. James Vadackumchery, *Acquittals in Administration of Criminal Justice,* Ph.D Thesis, Kerala University, 1983. A similar observation has been made by B.P.R. & D. Their study read : "Majority of police officers felt that the public of their area generally did not co-operate in the detection of crime". F.T.R. Colaso and K.S. Sukla, *Reluctance of the Public to Aid the Police in the Detection of Crime & Reporting at Police Stations,* Journal of the Bureau of Police Research and Development, Quarters I & II, Government of India, 1974.

39. George J. Dudycha, The psychology of interviewing from *Psychology for Law Enforcement Officers,* Charles C. Thomas, 1970.

40. George. J. Dudycha, *The Psychology of Interviewing, op. cit.*

41. George J. Dudycha, *The Psychology of Interviewing, op. cit.*

42. F. K. Berrien, *Psychology and the Court, op. cit.*

43. S. S. Bobde *vs.* Maharashtra, A.I.R. 1973: S.C. 2622; 1973 Cr.L.J. 1783.

44. Jose *vs.* State of Kerala, A.I.R. 1973 S.C. 944: 1973 Cr.L.J. 687.

45. Krishah Narain *vs.* State of Maharashtra, A.I.R. 1973 S.C. 2751: 1973 Cr.L.J. 1839.

46. Bharat Singh *vs.* State of Uttat Pradesh, A.I.R. 1972 S.C. 2748: 1972 Cr.L.J. 1704.

47. Baldeo Singh *vs.* State of Bihar, A.I.R. 1972 S.C. 464: 1972 Cr.L.J. 262.

48. Ranbir *vs.* State of Punjab, A.I.R. 1973 S.C. 1409: 1973 Cr.L.J. 1120.

49. Bhagwan *vs.* State of Maharashtra, A.I.R. 1974 S.C. 21: 1974 Cr.L.J. 145; Onkarnath *vs.* State of Uttar Pradesh, A.I.R. 1974 S.C. 1550: 1974 Cr.L.J. 1015.

50. Sarwan Singh *vs.* State of Punjab, A.I.R. 1976 S.C. 2304: 1976 Cr.L.J. 1751; Balwant Singh *vs.* State of Haryana, A.I.R. 1972 S.C. 860: 1972 Cr. C. J. 645: Varghese Thomas vs. State of Kerala, 1977 Cr.L.J. 343: Zuli Chand *vs.* State of Rajasthan, A.I.R. 1974 S.C. 246: 1974 Cr.L.J. 331: Labh Singh *vs.* State of Punjab, A.I.R. 1976 S.C. 83 1976 Cr.L.J. 21.

51. Dalbir Kaur *vs.* State of Punjab, A.I.R. 1977 S.C. 472: 1977 Cr.L.J. 273: Masalti *vs.* State of Uttar Pradesh, A.I.R. 1965 S.C. 202: 1965 (1) Cr.L.J. 226.

52. State of Uttar Pradesh vs. Baboo, (1978) 1 S.C. 626.

53. Dalbir Kaur *vs.* State of Punjab, *op. cit.*

54. Sat Paul *vs.* Delhi Administration, A.I.R. 1976 S.C. 294: 1976 Cr.L.J. 295.

55. S. S. Bobde *vs.* tate of maharashtra, *op. cit.*
56. Aher Bhagu vs. State of Gujarat, A.I.R. 1974 S.C. 292: 1974 Cr.L.J. 343.
57. Masalt *vs.* State of Uttar Pradesh A.I.R. 1965 S.C. 202: 1965 Cr.L.J. 226; Badri *vs.* State of Uttar Pradesh, A.I.R. 1975 S.C. 1985: 1975 Cr.L.J. 1739.
58. Tamesjwar Sahi *vs.* State of Uttar Pradesh, A.I.R. 1976 S.C. 59: 1967 Cr.L.J. 6.
59. Mahinder Singh *vs.* State of Haryana, A.I.R. 1974 S.C. 873.
60. S.S. Bobde *vs.* State of Maharashtra, *op. cit.*
61. Janak Singh *vs.* State of Uttar Pradesh, A.I.R. 1972 S.C. 1853: 1972 Cr. L.J. 1177.
62. Zuli Chand *vs.* State of Rajasthan, A.I.R. 1974 S.C.; 1974, Cr. L.J. 331.
63. Darya Singh *vs.* State of Punjab, A.I.R. 1965 S.C. 328: 1965 (1) Cr. L.J. 350.
64. Bahal Singh *vs.* State of Haryana, A.I.R. 1976 S.C. 2032: 1976 Cr. L.J. 1568.
65. Rameshwar Kalyan Singh *vs.* The State of Rajasthan, A.I.R. 1952 S.C. 54.
66. Jagir Singh *vs.* State (Delhi Administration), A.I.R. 1975 S.C. 1400: 1975 Cr. L.J. 1009.
67. Karappa Nana *vs.* State of Tamil Nadu, A.I.R. 1976 Cr. L.J. 980: 1976 Cr. L.J. 708.
68. Kishoram Bora *vs.* State of Assam 1978 (2) S.C.C. 407.
69. Arumuga Nadar *vs.* State of Tamil Nadu, A.I.R. 1976 S.C. 2588: 1976 Cr. L.J. 1998.
70. Varghese Thomas *vs.* State, 1977 Cr. L.J. 343.
71. Raja Khima *vs.* State of Saurashtra, A.I.R. 1956 S.C. 217: 1956 Cr. L.J. 421.
72. Nathu Singh *vs.* State of Madhya Pradesh, A.I.R. 1973 S.C. 2783: 1974 Cr. L.J. 11.
73. Soma Parkash *vs.* Delhi, A.I.R. 1974 S.C. 989: 1974 Cr. L.J. 784.
74. Soma Parkash *vs.* Delhi, *op. cit.*
75. The State of Bihar *vs.* Basawan Singh, A.I.R. 1958 S.C. 500: 1958 Cr. L.J. 976.

11

SEARCHES AND SEIZURES

Investigation of crimes may necessitate searching of a place for locating evidence and sometimes for finding out people who are involved or suspected to have involved in the commission of crimes. It is a well recognised principle in police work that the investigating officers should show fairness and decency while they conduct searches of people or premises, They must refrain from unnecessary hostility or militance to people when they perform their duties. There is a feeling among some sections of the society that some of the investigating officers think that they can do anything with the people and property under the cover of the their authority while they conduct searches. They fail or refuse to show respect to people and property while they perform the task of searching places and persons. There is also a complaint against some of the police officers viz., while conducting a search, they plunder property, and do not record all articles seized. If at all the seized articles are recorded sometimes, the property is damaged and becomes useless. Though these and similar allegations against investigating officers may not be true in toto, one has to subscribe to the view that there may be a grain of truth in what the public speak of the attitude and behaviour while the police conduct searches and seize articles. Admitting that the police have the power to search and seize articles, it must be borne in mind that the exercise of such powers should not call for unwanted public criticisms. People are likely to resent to a search by police,

SKILLS TO BE DEVELOPED AMONG INVESTIGATING OFFICERS WHILE THEY CONDUCT SEARCHES AND SEIZE ARTICLES

1. How to get permission to enter into the premises to conduct a search?
2. How to explain politely the purpose of visit-showing search warrant etc.
3. How to tolerate verbal abuse from people and how to answer their question politely?
4. How to explain the existing laws relating to searches to people?
5. How to show respect towards persons and property during a search?
6. How to show politeness and courtesy towards women and children and how to show regard for their privacy when conducting a search?
7. How to take care of property seized and how to interrogate/interview people during a search?
8. How to deal with the onlookers in a polite manner?
9. How to seize the property and handle it without causing any damage to it? How to record it?

for there is always some social stigma, loss of prestige and status for people when they are subjected to a search by a police officer. The public who gather at a scene of crime are interested to see what the police do there. All words, gestures and acts of the police during a search are noted by the public. Hence during a search, the police have to be minutely cautious and they should take care in showing respect to person and property. But the complaint seems to be that this attitude is not displayed by the police at the scene of crime.

People have the right to acquire, hold and dispose of property. The police officer's search during the investigation in a way affects the people's right to hold property. But, an investigator cannot but conduct a search and the search by itself is not a restriction on the right of citizens to hold and enjoy their property. The Supreme Court of India holds the view as:

"The search by itself is not a restriction on the right to hold and enjoy property. No doubt, the seizure and carrying away is a restriction of the possession and enjoyment of the property seized. This, however, is only temporary and for the limited purpose of investigation. A search and seizure, is, therefore, only a temporary interference with the right to hold the premises searched and articles seized. Statutory regulation in this behalf is necessary and reasonable restriction cannot *per se* be considered to be unconstitutional. The damage, if any, caused by such temporary interference, if found to be excess of legal authority, is a matter of redress in other proceedings"[1]

Search for a Person

Section 47 Cr. P.C., 1973 deals with the search of a place entered by person sought to be arrested and it reads:

(1) If any person acting under a warrant of arrest, or any Police Officer having authority to arrest, has reason to believe that person to be arrested has entered into, or is within any place, any person residing in, or being in charge, of such place shall, on demand of such person, acting as aforesaid or such Police Officer, allow

him free ingress thereto and afford all reasonable facilities for a search therein.

(2) If ingress to such place cannot be obtained under sub-section (1), it shall be lawful in any case for a person acting under a warrant and in any case in which a warrant may issue, but cannot be obtained without affording the person to be arrested an opportunity of escape, for a Police Officer to enter such place and to break open any outer or inner door or window of any house or place, whether that of the person to be arrested or any other person, if after notification of his authority, and purpose, and demand of admittance duly made, he cannot otherwise obtain admittance:

Provided that, if any place is an apartment in actual occupancy of a female (not being the person to be arrested) who according to custom, does not appear in public, such person or Police Officer shall, before entering such apartment, give notice to such female that she is at liberty to withdraw and shall afford her every reasonable facility for withdrawing, and may then break open the apartment and enter it.

(3) Any Police Officer or other person authorised to make an arrest may break open any outer or inner door or window of any house or place in order to liberate himself or any other person who, having lawfully entered for the purpose of making an arrest is detained therein".

Searching a house for taking a person suspected to have committed a crime should be done only if the investigating officer has definite information and reason to believe that he/she is there. The practice of searching people, if it exists, on the mere suspicion that somebody may be seen in a house should be discouraged. One's house is his castle and every one desires to have the *freedom of his home.* Therefore entry into one's house for searching a suspect by the investigating officers just for satisfying their curiosity cannot be entertained by the law and the people alike.

Search of Arrested Persons

Section 51 Cr. P.C. 1973 reads as: (1) "Whenever a person is arrested by a Police Officer under a warrant which does not provide for taking of bail, or under a warrant which provides for the taking of bail but the person arrested cannot furnish bail, and whenever a person is arrested without warrant or by a private person under a warrant, and cannot legally be admitted to bail, or is unable to furnish bail, the Officer making the arrest, or, when the arrest is made by a private person, the police officer to whom he makes over the person arrested, may search such person, and place in safe custody all articles, other than necessary wearing apparel, found upon him and where any article is seized from the arrested person, a receipt showing the articles taken possession by the Police Officer shall be given to such person.

(2) Whenever it is necessary to cause a female to be searched, the search shall be made by another female with strict regard to decency."

Section 52 Cr. P.C., 1973 empowers the police officers making an arrest to seize any offensive weapons found in the possession of the arrested and to produce the same before the Court along with the arrested.

There is an allegation against some of the investigating officers that:

1. They use undue force against the suspects just before they make the arrest and search them. The police version for the use of undue force is that it can surely cause deterrence among the suspects so much so that the latter will become submissive to police search of their person to seize offensive weapons. Whenever the suspects receive a slap from the police, suddenly and surprisingly, they are at *their wit's end* and this psychological state of mind facilitates the police to cause a thorough search of their body. One wonders whether or not this indiscriminate use of force is necessary at all for causing a search of the body of all suspects.
2. While arresting and effecting the search, the police officers at times resort to the use of filthy language. Sometimes, the arrested persons are handcuffed unnecessarily and are asked to accompany them in a humiliating way—even sometimes

PRECAUTIONS TO BE TAKEN WHILE CONDUCTING A SEARCH OF PERSONS HIDDEN IN A HOUSE OR CLOSED APARTMENTS

1. Take sufficient number of uniformed men with the investigating officer—the purpose being to guard the premises of the house as a precaution against the escape of the suspect.
2. Ask all the occupants of the house to come out. Enter the house with sufficient number of men.
3. While entering the house, expect the unexpected. Instances have been reported that the searchers were attacked with deadly weapons.
4. Have pistols/rifles for self protection as well as for detering the suspect in case he/she turns violent.
5. Never conduct the search in complete darkness or in candle light. Put the switches on and if that is not possible, take as many torches as possible for getting sufficient lights. Searching with candles of hurricane lamps should be discouraged.
6. Never search the premises alone and do it along with two or three assistants. In case, an attack comes suddenly, they will be immense help.
7. Wear protective devices, if available, as a precaution against acid throwing, explosives and attacks by deadly weapons etc.

with humiliating dresses. Many courts in India have condemned this indiscriminate use of handcuffs while the suspect is taken into custody.

3. In some western countries the police ask the suspects to raise their hands up prior to arrest and search. This practice enables the police to resort to least force when a suspect is arrested and searched. Should we not educate our people in this way so that the police are in an advantageous position to take them in custody?

Search for Persons Wrongfully Confined

Section 97 of the Code of Criminal Procedure, 1973, reads as under:

"If any District Magistrate, Sub-Divisional Magistrate or Magistrate of the first class has reason to believe that any person is confined under such circumstances that the confinement amounts to an offence, he may issue a search warrant and the person to whom such warrant is directed may search for the person so confined; and such search shall be made in accordance therewith, and the person, if found, shall be immediately taken before a Magistrate, who shall make such order as in the circumstances of the case seems proper".

Section 100 Cr. P.C. 1973 reads further as:

(1) Whenever any place liable to search or inspection under this Chapter is closed, any person residing in, or being in charge of such place, shall on demand of the officer or other person executing the warrant, and on production of the warrant allow him free ingress thereto and afford all reasonable facilities for a search therein.

(2) If ingress into such place cannot be so obtained, the officer or other person executing the warrant may proceed in the manner provided by sub-section (2) of section 47.

(3) Where any person in or about such place is reasonably suspected of concealing about his person any article for which search warrant was made, such person may be searched and

if such person is a woman, the search shall be made by another woman, with strict regard to decency.

(4) Before making a search under this Chapter, the officer or other persons about to make it shall call upon two or more independent and respectable inhabitants of the locality in which the place to be searched is situate or any other locality if no such inhabitant of the said locality is available or is willing to be a witness to the search, to attend and witness the search and may issue an order in writing to them or any of them so to do.

(5) The search shall be made in their presence, and a list of all things seized in the course of such search and of the places in which they are respectively found shall be prepared by such officer or other person and signed by such witnesses, but no person witnessing a search under this section shall be required to attend the Court as a witness of the search unless specially summoned by it.

(6) The occupant of the place searched, or some person in his behalf, shall in every instance, be permitted to attend during the search, and a copy of the list prepared under this section signed by the said witnesses shall be delivered to such occupant or person.

(7) When any person is searched under sub-section (3), a list of all things taken possession of shall be prepared, and a copy thereof shall be delivered to such person.

(8) Any person who, without reasonable cause, refuses or neglects to attend and witness a search under this section, when called upon to do so by an order in writing delivered or tendered to him, shall be deemed to have committed an offence under section 187 of the Indian Penal Code (45 of 1860).

The success of the search depends therefore considerably on:

1. The action taken before search.
2. The action during the search.
3. The action after the search.

At every stage, the search officer should act legally, ethically and should never offer any room for unnecessary criticisms.

Pre-requisites for an Effective Search

1. Never tell the colleagues and associates that a search is going to be conducted at a particular time at a particular place. It is quite likely that the news reaches the people for whom the search is made. Know the spot of search and the route earlier so that no confusion arises on the way.
2. The constables and other officers assisting the search should know the location only when the searching team reaches the spot. Give instructions to the team as to what they should do only when the team has reached the spot of search.
3. On reaching the spot, show the identity, warrant, purpose of search and authority to conduct the search to the occupants of the house. If the occupants of the house, on request, come out, ask them to gather at a particular place and instruct one or two constables to watch them closely and listen to the conversation going on among them.
4. Call two respectable inhabitants of the locality to witness the search. If people are not volunteering, explain to them the reasons for their witnessing the search. If necessary, show to them the provisions of law.
5. If women are to be searched, take sufficient number of women constables also with the team so that no accusation about indecent behaviour will be forthcoming from the public.
6. While conducting the search, the searching team should move together so that they can ensure that every place is well searched. It so happens sometimes that individual searchers make independent searches. The actual search should be made by the investigating officer himself and others should assist him and also protect him from unexpected attacks from the people who are hidden in the spot.
7. Whenever the suspect is located, ask him to raise his hands by giving the command 'Hands up'. Don't try to advance to him without taking adequate protection for self-defence/safety.
8. When the suspect has become submissive, cause a research

on his body for possessing any weapons available with him. Entrust him to the assistants and then continue the search.

9. Whenever search is conducted, show adequate respect to the person and property there.
10. Every one in the searching team and also the witnesses should offer themselves to be searched by the occupant of the house.
11. The searching team should have the search list forms, sealing wax, seal etc. and as per law, a copy of the list prepared shall be got signed by the witnesses and also shall be delivered to the occupant of the house. While conducting the search, atleast one of the occupants should be allowed to be present with the searching team. When the copy of the search memo is entrusted to the occupant of the house, proper acknowledgement of the same should be obtained.
12. The record of the search should be sent to the Magistrate at the earliest available opportunity.

Search for Property

Section 165 Cr. P.C., 1973 is about search for property and it reads as:

(1) "Whenever an officer-in-charge of a police station or a Police Officer making an investigation has reasonable grounds for believing that anything necessary for the purpose of an investigation into any offence which he is authorised to investigate may be found in any place within the limits of the police station of which he is in-charge, or to which he is attached, and that such thing cannot in his opinion be otherwise obtained without undue delay, such officer may, after recording in writing the grounds of his belief and specifying in such writing, so far as possible, the thing for which search is to be made, search, or cause search to be made, for such thing in any place within the limits of such station.

(2) A Police Officer proceeding under sub-station (1) shall if practicable, conduct the search in person.

(3) If he is unable to conduct the search in person and there is no

other person competent to make the search present at the time, he may, after recording in writing his reasons for so doing, require any officer subordinate to him to make the search and he shall deliver to such subordinate officer an order in writing specifying the place to be searched, and so far as possible, the thing for which search is to be made; and such subordinate officer may thereupon search for such thing in such place.

(4) The provisions of this Code as to search warrants and the general provisions as to searches contained in section 100, shall, so far as may be, apply to a search made under this section.

(5) Copies of any record made under sub-section (1) or sub-section (3) shall forthwith be sent to the nearest Magistrate empowered to take cognizance of the offence, and the owner or occupier of the place searched shall on application be furnished free of cost, with a copy of the same by the Magistrate."

Section 166 Cr. P.C., 1973 reads again as:

(1) An officer-in-charge of a police station or a Police Officer not being below the rank of sub-inspector making an investigation may require an officer-in-charge of another police station, whether in the same or a different district, to cause a search to be made in any place, in any case in which the former officer might cause such search to be made, within the limits of his own station.

(2) Such officer, on being so required, shall proceed according to the provisions of section 165, and shall forward the thing found, if any, to the officer at whose request the search was made.

(3) Whenever there is reason to believe that the delay occasioned by requiring an officer-in-charge of another police station to cause a search to be made under sub-section (1) might result in evidence of the commission of an offence being concealed or destroyed, it shall be lawful for an officer-in-charge of a police station or a police officer making any investigation under this Chapter to search, or cause to be searched, any place in the limits of another police station in accordance with the provisions of section 165, as if such place were within the limits of his own police station.

(4) Any officer conducting a search under sub-section (3) shall forthwith send notice of the search to the officer-in-charge of police station within the limits of which such place is situate, and shall also send with such notice a copy of the list (if any) prepared under section 100 and shall also send to the nearest Magistrate to take cognizance of the offence, copies of the record referred to in sub-sections (1) and (3) of section 165.

(5) The owner or occupier of the place searched shall, on application, be furnished free of cost with a copy of any record sent to the Magistrate under sub-section (4)".

In State of Rajasthan *vs.* Rehman (A.I.R. 1960 S.C. 210: 1960 Cr. L.J. 286), The Supreme Court of India observed:

(i) The police officer must have reasonable ground for believing that anything necessary for the purpose of an investigation of an offence cannot in his opinion, be obtained otherwise than making a search, without undue delay; (ii) he should record in writing the ground of his belief and specify in such writing as far as possible the things for which the search is to be made; (iii) he must conduct the search, if practicable, in person; and (iv) if it is not practicable to make the search himself, he must record in writing, the reasons for not himself making the search and shall authorize a subordinate officer to make the search after specifying in writing the place to be searched and so far as possible, the thing for which search is to be made. As search is a process exceedingly arbitrary in character, stringent statutory conditions are imposed on the exercise of the power".

In Gopi Mahton's case (A.I.R. 1932 Pat. 66: 33 Cr. L.J. 233), the station house officer, during the investigation got the information that a stolen bicycle was kept in the house of one of the petitioners. The Sub-Inspector told the petitioners that he was going to make a house search to take the bicycle in custody. The petitioners resisted the suggestion of the Sub-Inspector and pushed the S.I. and his constable back when they were about to conduct the search. In the meantime, one of the petitioners took the bicycle and left the house through another door. The S.I. and his constables made an attempt to arrest the petitioner who left the house with the bicycle; but were prevented by other petitioners. The Court held the view that the police procedure in the above case was not strictly legal as the police did not comply with the requirements of section 165 of the Cr. P.C. 1973. The police failed to make a record and sending a copy of the same to the Magistrate. The Court held the view that the petitioners were not guilty of an offence under section 353 I.P.C.

Again in Ram Parves Ahir's case (A.I.R. 1944 Pat. 228: 45 Cr. L.J. 802), it was held by the Court:

> "The Station Diary has not been produced and there is no evidence whatsoever on the record that the Sub-Inspector Azam ever complied with the provisions of sub-section (1) of section 165 Cr. P.C., and his own evidence clearly shows that the provision of sub-section (3) were not complied with. His omissions in this respect have necessarily led him also not to comply within another duty cast upon him by sub-section (5) of section 165."[2]

In another case (see Chander Prasad *vs.* Emperor) the Court observed.[3]

> "The recording of reason before search is provided for both under the Criminal Procedure Code and under the Excise Act and is intended to protect the liberty of citizen and avoid useless and unjustified searches. If an officer before proceeding to search has to record his reason, he will have to apply his mind to the facts and the sufficiency of the information on the basis of which he wants to search.

Section 165 Cr. P.C. 1973 – Case Laws[4]

1. A search for stolen property generally as opposed to a search for specific stolen property is not authorized by section 165 of the Code of Criminal Procedure Code. It does not authorize a general search.[5]

2. By general search is meant a search not in respect of specific documents or things which the officer considered were necessary or desirable for the purpose of the investigation in hand but a roving enquiry for the purpose of the discovering documents or things which might involve persons in criminal liability.[6]
3. Roving searches conducted without initial record regarding the places to be searched and the things for which the search should be made do not come under the provisions of section 165 Cr. P.C.[7]
4. But where a definite list of stolen articles has been given to police officer and he searches a house for those articles, his search is perfectly legal in that he is making a search for specific articles.[8]
5. An oral order to make a general search for suspicious property is not an order complying with the provisions of sub-section (3) of section 165.[9]

In Hira Lal *vs.* Ram Dulare, it was held by the Court that the search conducted by the police without making a record in writing the grounds for conducting the search could not be justified under section 165, Cr. P.C., 1973. The Court observed further that the failure of the police officer in specifying the thing for which the searching was made and also the failure to write down the reasons for requiring two subordinate officers to make the search were not justifiable. In Venkatappa Naidu *vs.* Emperor (6 Cr. L.T. 105: 17 M.L.J. 323) an inspector of police asked his constable to conduct the search and he sat down outside the house. The accused demanded a list of articles to be searched and the constable refused to show him. As a result, the accused objected to the search being carried out. He pushed the constable out. It was observed by the Court that the action of the inspector (seated outside the house) asking a constable to conduct the search without giving an order in writing specifying the things to be searched etc. was not justified in law under section 165 Cr. P.C. 1973. In another case—Satagopala Charlin *vs.* Satrughna Behara (23 M.L.J. 445), the Court held the view that Section 165 Cr. P.C. did not mean that the investigating officer who was personally conducting the search must himself make the search say, ransack the boxes, examine the roof, dig up the floor or otherwise seek for property. The section contemplated that the investigating officer should be present on the spot and should exercise a general supervision over the search.

Search witnesses should be respectable persons of the locality; otherwise it would affect the weight of the evidence (see Sunder Singh, A 56 S.C. 41). However, the fact that a person was a witness on a previous occasion does not itself make the witness unbelievable (see Nainsukh, A 1933 N. 99). A dismissed constable (Inder Dult A 1931 L. 408), a person who is convicted for a serious offence (Ram Ch. A. 1935 A. 520) a person belonging to the rival party (Pando Inderjit A 1949, A. 165) or a friend of the police officer (Md. Hiway 265 Cr. L.J. 827) are considered to be unsuitable as witnesses during a search. The witnesses, if they are respectable can belong to different locality and need not be from the same locality (Raghunath A 1932 B 160; Raji A 1967 My. 47). The absence of the search witness weakens and sometimes destroys the value of the evidence (Malak 721-A 395: A 1946 PC 16). Hence while the search is conducted, the witnesses should not be left outside rather should be present.

Section 166, Cr. P.C., 1973 empowers an officer-in-charge of a police station to have a search made within the limits of another station through the officer-in-charge of that station who will act as laid down in section 165 Cr. P.C. Nevertheless, in case of emergency, an officer-in-charge of a police station can search or cause to be searched places within the limits of another police station in accordance to the provisions and procedures contained in sections 165 and 100 Cr. P.C.

When Search-Warrant May be Issued?

Section 93 of the Criminal Procedure Code, 1973 reads as:

1. (a) When any Court has reason to believe that a person to whom a summons or order under section 91 or a requisition under sub-section (1) of section 92, has been, or might be addressed will

not or would not produce the document or thing as required by such summons or requisition, or

(b) Where such document or thing is not known to the Court to be in the possession of any person, or

(c) Where the Court considers that the purpose of any inquiry, trial or other proceedings under this Code will be served by a general search or inspection —

it may issue a search warrant; and the person to whom such warrant is directed may search or inspect in accordance therewith and the provisions hereinafter contained.

2. The Court may, if it thinks fit, specify in the warrant the particular place or part thereof to which only the search or inspection shall extend; and the person charged with the execution of such warrant shall then search or inspect only the place or part so specified.

3. Nothing contained in this section shall authorise any Magistrate other than a District Magistrate or Chief Judicial Magistrate to grant a warrant to search for a document, parcel or other thing in the custody of the postal or telegraph authority".

Section 93 – Case Laws

1. The power to issue search warrant should be exercised only when the Court finds that such a step is really necessary for the cause of criminal justice administration.[10]
2. The act of issuing a search warrant is a judicial act and the Magistrate should weigh the circumstance before they exercise their powers of search warrant.[11]
3. A telegramme received by the police is not a good ground for issuing a search warrant.[12]

Section 94 Cr. P.C. 1973

Section 94 Cr. P.C. 1973 relates to search of places suspected to contain stolen property, forged document etc. and it reads as:

1. If a District Magistrate, Sub-Divisional Magistrate or Magistrate of the first class, upon information and after such inquiry as he thinks necessary, has reason to believe that any place is used for the deposit or sale of stolen property, or for the deposit, sale or production of any objectionable article to which this section applies or that any such objectionable article is deposited in any place he may by warrant authorise any police officer above the rank of a constable –
    a) to enter, with such assistance as may be required, such place,
    b) to search the same in the manner specified in the warrant,
    c) to take possession of any property or article therein found which he reasonably suspects to be stolen property or objectionable article to which this section applies.
    d) to convey such property or article before a Magistrate, or to guard the same on the spot until the offender is taken before a Magistrate, or otherwise to dispose of it in some place of safety.
    e) to take into custody and carry before a Magistrate every person found in such place who appears to have been privy to the deposit, sale or production of any such property or article knowing or having reasonable cause to suspect it to be stolen property or, as the case may be, objectionable article to which this section applies.

2. The objectionable articles to which this section applies are:
    a) Counterfeit coin;
    b) Pieces of metal made in contravention of the Metal Tokens Act, 1889 (1 of 1889), or brought into India in contravention of any notification for the time being in force under section 11 of the Customs Act, 1962 (52 of 1962).
    c) Counterfeit currency note: counterfeit stamps;
    d) Forged documents;
    e) False seals;

f) Obscene objects referred to in Section 292 of the Indian Penal Code (45 of 1860).

g) Instruments or materials used for the production of any of the articles mentioned in clauses (a) to (f).

Section 95 Cr. P.C., 1973

Section 95 Cr. P.C. reads:

1. Where (a) any newspaper, or book, or (b) any document wherever printed, appears to the State Government to contain any matter the publication of which is punishable under section 124-A or section 153-A or section 153-B or section 292 or section 293 or section 295-A of the Indian Penal Code, the State Government may, by notification stating the grounds of its opinion, declare every copy of the issue of the news paper containing such matter, and every copy of such book or other document to be forfeited to Government, and thereupon any police officer may seize the same wherever found in India and any Magistrate may by warrant authorize any police officer not below the rank of a sub-inspector to enter upon and search for the same in any premises where any copy of such issue or any such book or other document may be reasonably suspected to be.

SEARCH AND SEIZURE	
A. Search without Warrant	
1. Section 47 Cr. P.C.	Search of a place entered by person sought to be arrested.
2. Section 51 Cr. P.C.	Search of the person of the arrested.
3. Section 165 Cr. P.C.	Search of premises within the jurisdiction of the Station House Officer in emergent cases.
4. Section 166 Cr. P.C.	Search of premises beyond the Station House Officer's jurisdiction.

B. Search with Warrant	
1. Section 93 Cr. P.C.	Search for documents.
2. Section 94 Cr. P.C.	Search for: (a) stolen property; (b) counterfeit currency; (c) forged documents; (d) false seals; (e) obscene objects.
3. Section 95 Cr. P.C.	Search for forfeited documents.
4. Section 97 Cr. P.C.	Search for a person wrongfully confined.

2. In this section and section 96 (a) "news paper" and "book" have the same meaning as in the Press and Regulation of Books Act, 1867 (25 of 1867).

(b) "document" include any painting, drawing or photograph, or other visible representation.

3. No order passed or action taken under this section shall be called in question in any Court otherwise than in accordance with the provisions of section 96.

Section 95 Cr. P.C. 1973 – Case Laws

1. The forfeiture has to be notified in the Official Gazette and therefore, there is no need for a personal service of the forfeiture.[13]
2. It is obligatory on the part of the Government to state its opinion for forfeiture of the publication.[14]

Search in Non-Cognizable Cases

Police officers are not authorised to investigate a non-cognizable case unless there is specific order to do so. Therefore, a police officer cannot make a search in non-cognizable case under the provisions of section 165 Cr. P.C., 1973.[15]

Irregular Searches — Case Laws

1. Presence of respectable witnesses (a) the witness should belong to the locality where search is conducted; (b) the occupant of the search should be allowed to be present and attend during the search and the investigating officer and the witnesses should offer themselves to be searched of their persons before conducting the search etc. are the pre-requisites of a search. If any of the conditions is violated, the search becomes irregular. The irregularity or illegality of the search here cannot vitiate the trial or effect the conviction of the accused where the accused has not been prejudiced by the defect.[16]
2. The law is well settled that the non-compliance with the provisions of section 100 Cr. P.C. 1973 is a mere irregularity.[17]
3. The emphasis is more on the word "respectable" and not on the word "inhabitant" of the locality under section 100 Cr. P.C. 1973.[18]
4. When the evidence collected through a search was believed in evidence there is no defence to say that the evidence was obtained in an irregular way.[19]
5. Because of the illegality of the search, the Court may be inclined to examine carefully the evidence seized.[20]
6. A failure to comply with the provisions of section 100 Cr. P.C. may cast doubts upon the bonafides of the officers conducting the search. There is nothing in law which makes the evidence collected by the search inadmissible. If the evidence is reliable, a conviction based on such an evidence is not invalid on the ground that the search is irregular.[21]
7. Assuming that the witnesses who actually witnessed the search were not respectable inhabitants of the locality, that circumstance would not invalidate the search. It would only affect the weight of the evidence in support of the search and recovery.[22]

Custody and Disposal of Property

Section 451, Cr. P.C. 1973 runs as:

"When any property is produced before any criminal court during any inquiry or trial, the Court may make such order as it thinks fit for the proper custody of such property pending the conclusion of the inquiry or trial, and, if the property is subject to speedy or natural decay or it is otherwise expedient so to do, the Court may, after recording evidence as it thinks necessary order it to be sold or otherwise disposed of.

Explanation: For the purpose of this section "property" includes.

(a) property of any kind or document which is produced before the court or which is in its custody.
(b) any property regarding which an offence appears go have been committed or which appears to have been used for the commission of any offence.

Disposal of Property at the Conclusion of Trial

Section 452 Cr. P.C. 1973 reads as:

(1) "When an inquiry or trial in any Criminal Court is concluded, the Court may make such order as it thinks fit for the disposal, by destruction, confiscation or delivery to any person claiming to be entitled to possession thereof or otherwise, of any property or document produced before it or in its custody, or regarding which an offence appears to have been committed or which has been used for the commission of any offence.
(2) An order may be made under sub-section (1) for the delivery of any property to any person claiming to be entitled to the possession thereof without any condition or on condition that he executes a bond, with or without sureties, to the satisfaction of the Court engaging to restore such property to the Court if the order made under sub-section (1) is modified or set aside on appeal or revision.

(3) A Court of Session may, instead of itself making an order under sub-section (1) direct the property to be delivered to the Chief Judicial Magistrate, who shall thereupon deal with it in the manner provided in sections 457, 458 and 459.

(4) Except where the property is livestock or is subject to speedy and natural decay or where a bond has been executed in pursuance of sub-section (2) an order made under sub-section (1) shall not be carried out for two months, or when an appeal is presented, until such appeal has been disposed of.

(5) In this section, the term 'property' includes, in the case of property regarding which an offence appears to have been committed not only such property as has been originally in the possession or under the control of any party, but also any property into or for which the same may have been converted or exchanged, and anything acquired by such convertion or exchange whether immediately or otherwise."

Section 457 Cr. P.C., 1973

This section deals with the procedure by police upon seizure of property and reads:

"(1) Whenever the seizure of property by any police officer is reported to a Magistrate under the provisions of this Code and such property is not produced before a criminal Court during an inquiry or trial, the Magistrate may make such order as he thinks fit respecting the disposal of such property or the delivery of such property to the person entitled to the possession thereof, or if such person cannot be ascertained, respecting the custody and production of such property.

(2) If the person so entitled is known, the Magistrate may order the property to be delivered to him on such conditions (if any) as the Magistrate thinks fit, and if such person is unknown, the Magistrate may detain it and shall in such case issue a proclamation specifying the articles of which such property consists and requiring any person who may have a claim thereto to appear before him and establish his

claim within six months from the date of such proclamation".

House Search: A Case Study[23]

On March 17, the Sub-Inspector got an information that Mr. Ravi owned an unlicenced gun. The S.I. thought of conducting a house-search and proceeded for the purpose with a party consisting of one A.S.I., one head constable and four constables. It was 6'O clock in the evening and they were in mufti.

Mr. and Mrs. Ravi were inside the house. They heard a knock at the door and simultaneously opening of the front door. On seeing 7 people entering their house, Mr. Ravi asked, "why are you coming into our house"? Since the police party were in mufti, Mrs. Ravi thought that they were burglars. She thought so because she was aware of several such incidents in recent past in the State.

The Sub-Inspector said, "We are police officers. We have information that you do possess an unlicenced fire-arm". Mrs. Ravi thought that these burglars wanted to confirm whether or not they had a gun. She, therefore, got annoyed at the statement and further asked. "What right do you have breaking into our house and accusing us of having an unlicenced fire-arm?"

The Sub-Inspector then loudly uttered: "Shut up, we know that you are having an unlicenced fire-arm. We are going to search this house." He took some papers from his pocket and said "We have a warrant to search your house". He, without showing the contents of the paper, replaced it in his pocket.

Mr. Ravi excitedly raising his voice, asked: "What kind of paper is it? How can I know that it is a warrant of search unless you show it to me. What kind of information have you got to say that I am having an unlicenced gun here? I will not let you search my house". The Sub-Inspector said: "Be quiet. Why are you getting so much excited if you do not have an unlicenced fire-arm"?

To this Mrs. Ravi replied: "How do we know you are police officers? May be that you are here to plunder us or attack us. There have been a number of incidents of this sort reported in papers these days". The police officers ignored her utterances and they were determined to conduct a house search. Seeing this, she made a hue and cry to attract people to her house.

Hearing loud cries of Mrs. Ravi people started coming to the house. Some of them understood that the people who came there were police officers. All were waiting outside. The officers inside were found to be not concerned with the people outside.

The S.I. said "We have to get on with our job and search your house". Hearing this, other officers went upstairs where they made a thorough search of bed rooms. They went through every drawer, closet and rooms. In the process, they disarranged everything. They conducted the search without taking any care for the articles kept in the room, tables, shelves, drawers, etc. They did it rather in a rude way.

After the police completed a search which brought out no evidence of having a fire-arm, the Sub-Inspector called Mrs. Ravi to a room and started interrogating her. He threatened her saying that her husband would be taken in custody unless she told where the fire-arm was kept. She pleaded innocence of everything. The Sub-Inspector then made a false promise that he would take no action against Mr. Ravi if she could show him where the fire-arm was. She repeatedly said that she did not know anything about it.

In the meantime, a family friend of Mr. Ravi came there. Seeing this, Mr. Ravi advanced towards him and wanted to say something. The A.S.I. stopped him and said: "You have no right to speak to him". Telling this, the A.S.I. took the visitor to another room and started questioning him about the unlicenced fire-arm, supposedly Mr. Ravi's.

The police could not find any evidence to show that they possessed an unlicenced fire-arm. The Sub-Inspector said "Sorry" and left the house.

But they understood the embarrassment and humiliation to which the family of Mr. and Mrs. Ravi was subjected, as a result of being falsely implicated. The public started saying that the police were trying to clean the area from illegal possession of fire-arms and that is the reason why they conducted a search there. Some others said that the police searched the house because they wanted to humiliate Mr. and Mrs. Ravi. His enemies thought that the police could get something of an unlicenced fire-arm and effect an arrest of Mr. and Mrs. Ravi.

Police Behaviour and Search

The case study above is brought to prove how do the police generally conduct searches. There is an allegation against police officers that their behaviour and attitude at the place of search to people and property are far away from being satisfactory. There is also a feeling admidst some members of the society that some police officers take the liberty to enter a house without waiting for any permission from the occupants. When the police are resisted by the occupants, some of the officers behave rudely to them. The police have to bear in mind that citizens object to have their houses searched by the police or by other law enforcement agencies. The law is clear on this point as to how should the police conduct searches. Sometimes, the police fail to adhere to the provisions laid down in the Procedure Code and their Code of Conduct. People are likely to show an arrogant and hostile attitude to police and they can be tackled properly if the police officers develop the necessary skills to handle people at the place of search. The police party intending to search a house should do everything so that any suspicion in the minds of the occupants are wipped off. They have to be considerate to the feelings of people subjected to this process. The police officers should never entertain the false notion that they can do anything with the people under the cover of their authority. Professionalism and ethics in police job will not permit any police officer to do anything which may cause damage to person, property and reputation of citizens consequent upon a search being conducted. If the police officer is objected to form conducting a search, he needs not feel abused. If he has the power and authority to conduct the search he can do his job in an acceptable way. The means adopted to reach the end also should be justifiable.

Search – More of Case Laws

[Section 103, (old section 105 of Cr. P.C.) Cr. P.C., 1973.]

1. "The irregularity in the search and the recovery in so far as the terms of section 103 had not been complied with, would not affect the legality of the proceedings but the weight of evidence".[24]
2. "If the witnesses for search are most respectable inhabitants of the locality, it would affect the weight of the evidence in support of the search and recovery. Section 103 would not apply to the seizure of shoes, which were being worn by the accused at the time he was with the investigating officer. Section 103 applies when a search is to be made of a place. It does not apply to the search of person".[25]
3. "No questions were put to the Sub-Inspector to elicit from him whether the reasons for the search were recorded or not. Regard being had to the regularity of official acts it must be presumed that the Sub-Inspector must have taken the precaution to record his reasons".[26]
4. "It cannot be !aid down as a matter of law or practice that where recoveries had to be effected from different places on the information furnished by an accused, different sets of persons should be called to witness them. The evidence relating to recoveries is not similar to that contemplated under section 103, Cr. P.C. in which search witnesses should be of the same locality".[27]
5. "In a trial for murder, the prosecution proved the panchnama prepared by the police the day the murder was committed and signed not only by the panchas but purporting to have been signed also by the accused persons. That document was a record which was a complete confession of the crime from the beginning to the end, by all the accused persons. This was highly irregular. The provisions of the E. Act and Cr. P.C. had not been observed".[28]
6. "The accused being very influential in the locality where they were residing, there was little chance of getting anyone from the locality itself to witness the search. For that reason, the certain persons, from another locality were made to accompany the raiding party. This seeming irregularity

cannot affect the legality of the proceedings. It can only affect the weight of the evidence, which it was for the Courts of facts to consider. There is also no substance in the submission that even those pancha witnesses who had the search memo were not produced. They had been prevailed upon not to give truthful evidence and therefore, they were not proceed."[29]

7. "In the case of stolen cattle, time is of the essence, because once the animal is removed and mixed up with others, it is very difficult to spot it in the big herds common in these places. Therefore, if the police officer had reason to believe that the police officer at Dankaur would take their own time because they were mixed up with the accused party, he had full jurisdiction in taking recourse to sub-section (3) of section 166 Cr. P.C. and to carry out the search himself."[30]

SUGGESTED READINGS

Aubry, Arthur, S (Jr.), *The Officer in the Small Department,* Charles C. Thomas Springfield, 1961.

Campbell, Don, *Police: The Exercise of Power,* Macdonald Evans Ltd. Estover, Plymouth, 1978.

Deinstein, William, *Techniques for the Crime Investigator,* Charles C. Thomas Springfield, 1952.

Khan, M.K.A., *Police Reports & Investigation,* Law Book Co., Lahore, 1947.

Prasad, Vindeshwari, *Criminal Investigation and Prosecution,* Supreme Court Criminal Rulings Office, Allahabad 1981.

Sinha D.N., *Powers and Discipline for Police and Security Forces,* Eastern Law House, Calcutta 1971.

Smith, Howard M. *Arrest, Search and Seizure,* Charles C. Thomas, Springfield, 1959.

REFERENCES

1. M.P. Sharma *vs.* Satish Chandra, A.I.R. 1954 S.C. 300.
2. The sections quoted in the original judgement were form the old Cr. P.C. but

were converted to the sections in new Cr. P.C. by the author.

3. A.I.R. 1937 Pat. 501: 38 Cr. L.J. 932.
4. These decisions are quoted in H.I. Capoor, *Police Diaries, Statements, Reports etc.* Law Publishers, Allahabad, 1981.
5. Bajrangi Gope *vs.* Emperor, I.L.R. 33 Cal. 304: 12 Cr. L.J. 8; Emperor *vs.* Brikhban, A.I.R. 1915 All 430: I.L.R. 30 All. 14: 16 Cr. L.J. 819; Divakar *vs.* Ramamurthi, A.I.R. 1919 Mad. 751: 19 Cr. L.J. 901.
6. Paresh Chandra Sen Gupta *vs.* Jogendra Nath Roy Chowdhury, A.I.R. 1927 Cal 93:27 Cr. L.J. 1195.
7. Gangaram *vs.* State 1944 N.U.C. 3862.
8. Paresh Chandra Sen Gupta *vs.* Jogendra Nath Roy Chowdhury *op. cit.*
9. Hiralal *vs.* Ram Dulare, A.I.R. 1935 Nag. 237.
10. Pagla Babu *vs.* State, 58 Cr. L.J. 769: A.I.R. 1957 Orissa 130.
11. Union of India *vs.* State (1971) 42 I.T.R. 703.
12. T.R. Pratt *vs.* Emperor, I.L.R. 47 Cal. 597: 55 I.C. 478: 31 C.L.J 315: 21 Cr. L.J. 313; 24 C.W.N. 403.
13. N. Veerabrahman *vs.* State of Andhra Pradesh, A.I.R. 1959 A.P. 572 at p. 576 :(1959) 2 Andhra. W.R. 269.
14. Harnam Das *vs.* State of Uttar Pradesh, 1962, S.C. R. 487: A.I.R. 1961 S.C. 1662.
15. Bhalal Singh *vs.* Traknath I.L.R. 25 Cal. 691.
16. Ali Ahamad Khan *vs.* King Emperor A.I.R. 1924 All. 214 (2) at p. 215, I.L.R. 46 Alll. 86.
17. Sunder Singh *vs.* State of Uttar Pradesh, A.I.R. 1965 S.C. 411 p. 415.
18. State *vs.* Satyanarayan Malik, A.I.R. 1965 Orissa 136: 1965 L.T. 172.
19. Indu Bhusan *vs.* State, A.I.R. 1955 Cal 129.
20. Radha Krishnan *vs.* State of Uttar Pradesh, A.I.R. 1963 S.C. 822: 1963 SCR (Supp) 408.
21. Kochan Velayudhan *vs.* State of Kerala (1961) M.L.J (Cr.) 58: A.I.R. 1961 Kerala 8.
22. Sunder Singh *vs.* State of Uttar Pradesh, A.I.R. 1965 S.C. 411.
23. *This case study is taken from* Public Relations at the Cutting Edge level, by Alphonese L. Earayil and James Vadackumchery – *National Publishing House*, *New Delhi*-1985.
24. Radha Krishnan *vs.* State of U.P., A.I.R. 1963 S.C. 822.
25. Sunder Singh *vs.* State of Uttar Pradesh, A.I.R. 1965 S.C. 411: 1956 Cr. L.J. 801.

26. 1973 Gopi *vs.* U.P. State (1970) 3 S.C. J. 116.
27. Himachal Pradesh *vs.* Om Prakash A.I.R. 1972 S.C. 975: 1972 Cr. L.J. 606.
28. Narayan Rao *vs.* State of A.P. A.I.R. 1955 S.C. 737: 1157 Cr. L.J. 1320.
29. Tej Bahadur Singh *vs.* State of U.P. 1970 (2) S.C.C. 779.
30. Gopi *vs.* U.P. State, *op. cit.*

12

ON COMPLETION OF INVESTIGATION

From registration of a case till this time the main task of the police in nothing but collection of all pieces of evidence to establish the guilt of the offender. In Sarwan Singh *vs.* State of Punjab, The Supreme Court observed. "There may be an element of truth in the prosecution story against the accused. Considered as whole, the prosecution story may be true; but between *may be true* and *must be true* there is inevitably a long distance all of which must be covered by the prosecution by legal, reliable and unimpeachable evidence before an accused can be convicted."[1] This means that the investigating officer can and should place the accused in a crime before a Court of Law for trial if and only if he is legally convinced of the involvement of the offender in the commission of crime. Dishonest and perfunctory investigation results, doubtlessly, in miscarriage of justice—i.e., the guilty will go unpunished or the innocent will be falsely prosecuted. Hence, on completion of investigation, if the investigating officer is convinced that there is no sufficient evidence or no reasonable ground to send the accused to a Magistrate, such officer, has to release the accused, if he is still in police custody, on bail and should forward his proceedings to the Magistrate. If the accused is in judicial custody, the police should request the Magistrate to order his release. Section 169 Cr. P.C.,

1973 is about this power. However, this section is employed while the case is at the process of investigation. Yet there may arise a situation in which the contingency contemplated in this section may synchronize with the completion of investigation.[2] Upon investigation of a crime, if the investigating officer is convinced about the sufficiency of evidence or reasonable grounds to prove the guilt of the offender, he should forward the accused to a Magistrate empowered to take cognizance of the offence upon a police report and to try the accused of commit him for trial. If the offence is a bailable one and if the accused is prepared to give security, he can get himself, then, released on bail unless the Magistrate otherwise directs to do. Hence, Section 170, Cr. P.C., 1973 contemplates a situation when the investigation is not complete; at the same time there exists reasonable grounds of suspicion to justify the forwarding of the accused to a Magistrate. The police officer is not directed, at this stage, by law to forward the report prescribed by section 173 Cr. P.C.

Final Report Contemplated

Under section 173 Cr. P.C., 1973.

Section 173 Cr. P.C., 1973 is about the *Report* of a Police Officer on Completion of Investigation and reads:

(1) Every Investigation under this Chapter shall be completed without unnecessary delay.

(2) (i) As soon as it is completed, the officer-in-charge of the police station shall forward to a Magistrate empowered to take cognizance of the offence on a police report, a report in the form prescribed by the State Government, stating —

(a) the names of the parties;
(b) the nature of the information;
(c) the names of the persons who appear to be acquainted

with the circumstances of the case;

(d) whether any offence appears to have been committed and if so, by whom;

(e) whether the accused has been arrested;

(f) whether he has been released on his bond and if so, whether with or without sureties;

(g) whether he has been forwarded in custody under section 170.

(ii) The officer shall also communicate, in such manner as may be prescribed by the State Government, action taken by him regarding the person, if any by whom the information relating to the commission of the offence was first given.

(3) Where a superior officer of police has been appointed under section 158, the report shall in any case in which the State Government by general or special order so directs, be submitted through that officer, and he may pending the order of the Magistrate, direct the officer-in-charge of the police station to make further investigation.

(4) Whenever it appears from a report forwarded under this section that the accused has been released on his bond, the Magistrate shall make such order for the discharge of such bond or otherwise as he thinks fit.

(5) When such report is in respect of a case to which section 170 applies, the police officer shall forward to the Magistrate along with the report.

(a) all documents or relevant extracts thereof on which the prosecution proposes to rely, other than those already sent to the Magistrate during investigation.

(b) the statements recorded under section 161 of all the persons whom the prosecution proposes to examine as its witnesses.

(6) If the police officer is of opinion that any part of any such statement is not relevant to the subject-matter of the proceedings or that its disclosure to the accused is not essential in the interests of justice and is expedient in the public interest he shall indicate that part of the statement and append a note requesting the Magistrate

to exclude that part from the copies to be granted to the accused and stating his reasons for making such request.

(7) Where the police officer investigating the case finds it convenient to do so, he may furnish to the accused copies of all or any of the documents referred to in sub-section (5).

(8) Nothing in this section shall be deemed to preclude further-investigation in respect of an offence after a report under sub-section (2) has been forwarded to the Magistrate and, where upon such investigation, the officer-in-charge of the police station obtains further evidence, oral or documentary, he shall forward to the Magistrate a further report or reports regarding such evidence in the form prescribed; and the provisions of sub-section (2) to (6) shall, as far as may be, apply in relation to such report or reports as they apply in relation to a report forwarded under sub-section.

Charge-Sheet/Final Report

The law is very clear that the police officer can dispose of the case on the completion of investigation either by submission of:

1. a charge-sheet;
2. a final report.

If the evidence is strong, necessarily a charge-sheet against the accused can be submitted. On the otherhand, if the evidence is weak, unbelievable, inadequate or absurd, a final, report can be filed. Again, a final report can be sent if the case is found to be false on investigation or to be undetectable or to be based on a mistake of fact or to be of a civil nature etc. Nevertheless, the Magistrate, on considering a Final Report, finds that the investigation is done in a perfunctory manner and there is scope for further investigation, he can order for further investigation. At the completion of this further investigation, the police can submit a charge-sheet or a final report once again depending upon the nature of evidence collected and its sufficiency to prove the case in a Court of Law. The Magistrate is not bound to accept the opinion of the police if he is satisfied that the facts set out in the final report constitute an offence. In this case, the Magistrate can take cognizance of the offence under section 190 (1) (b) Cr. P.C., 1973. Earlier it has been pointed out that a police officer (under section 169 Cr. P.C.) investigating a crime should get a bond from the accused if he is released on forming an opinion that there is no case for proceeding against the accused. Such a procedure as stated above can put the investigating officer on a safer ground even when the Magistrate refuses is expected to treat it judicially and he is not bound to act merely on the basis of the police opinion.

Charge-Sheet: The Contents

The contents of the charge-sheet are:

1. the names of the parties;
2. the names of the informants/complainants;
3. the names of persons acquainted with facts of the case;
4. details of property lost and recovered;
5. the fact that the accused has been forwarded in custody or released on bail or on his own bond;
6. the names of absconders (this is to be written in red ink);
7. facts of the case in brief along with the evidence against the accused;
8. the memo of evidence;
9. if no warrant of arrest or processes for proclamation and attachment have been obtained earlier, that fact also must be included.

Thus, it is clear that every charge-sheet sent to the Court should be accompanied by a memo of evidence. This memorandum should contain the names and addresses of the prosecution witnesses and should also specify clearly the points which are to be proved by each witness. However, it should be borne in mind that the memorandum of evidence is not a legal requirement as it is meant just to help the prosecution, the Court and superior police officers. As such, the accused is not entitled to get a copy of the memo of evidence. It is not at all a document on which the prosecution rely, its case. Nevertheless, the following documents should accompany a charge-sheet. They are:

1. All documents on which the prosecution intends to rely.
2. List of property stolen and a list of property found on the accused or otherwise recovered.
3. Bail bonds and recognizance bonds.
4. Report on previous conviction if enhancement of punishment is thought of
5. Sanction order wherever needed.

The accused is entitled under section 207 Cr. P.C., 1973 to get the copies of all documents from the Magistrate and it reads:

In any case where the proceeding has been instituted on a police report, the Magistrate shall without delay furnish to the accused, free of cost, a copy of each of the following:

i) the Police Report;
ii) the F.I.R. recorded under section 154;
iii) The statements recorded under sub-section (3) of section 161 of all persons whom the prosecution proposes to examine as its witnesses, excluding therefrom any part in regard to which a request for such exclusion has been made by the Police Officer under sub-section (6) of section 173;
iv) the confessions and statements, if any, recorded under section 164;
v) any other documents or relevant extract thereof forwarded to the Magistrate with the Police Report under the sub-section (5) of section 173.

Provided that the Magistrate may, after perusing any such part of a statement as is referred to in clause (iii) and considering the reasons given by the Police Officer for the request direct, that a copy of that part of the statement or of such portion thereof as the Magistrate thinks proper, shall be furnished to the accused.

Provided further that if the Magistrate is satisfied that any document referred to in clause (v) is voluminous, he shall, instead of furnishing the accused with a copy thereof, direct that he will only be allowed to inspect it either personally or through pleader in the court." Section 209 Cr. P.C. 1973 deals with commitment of cases to Court of Session when the offence is triable exclusively by it and reads as:

"When in a case instituted on police report or otherwise, the accused appears or is brought before the Magistrate and it appears to the Magistrate that the offence is triable exclusively by the Court of Session, he shall:

(a) commit the case to the Court of Session;
(b) subject to the provisions of this Code relating to bail, remand the accused to custody during and until the conclusion of the trial;
(c) send to that Court the record of the case and the documents and articles, if any, which are to be produced in evidence;
(d) notify the Public Prosecutor of the commitment of the case to the Court of Session."

Section 309 Cr. P.C., 1973 says:

(1) In every inquiry or trial, the proceedings shall be held as expeditiously as possible, and in particular when the examination of witnesses has once begun, the same shall be continued from day to day until all the witnesses in attendance have been examined, unless the Court finds the adjournment of the same beyond the following day to be necessary for reasons to be recorded.
(2) If the Court, after taking cognizance of an offence, or commencement of trial, finds it necessary or advisable to postpone the commencement of, or adjourn, any inquiry or trial, it may form time to time, for reasons to be recorded, postpone or adjourn the same on such terms as it thinks fir for such time as it considers reasonable and may by a warrant remand the accused if in custody:

Provided that no Magistrate shall remand an accused person to custody under this section for a term exceeding fifteen days at a time:

Provided further that when witnesses are in attendance, no adjournment or postponement shall be granted without examining them, except for special reasons to be recorded in writing.

Explanation—1 If sufficient evidence has been obtained to raise a suspicion that the accused may have committed an offence, and it appears likely that further evidence may be obtained by a remand, this is a reasonable cause for a remand.

Explanation—2 The terms on which an adjournment or postponement may be granted include, in appropriate cases, the payment of costs, by the prosecution or the accused."

Section 190 Cr. P.C., 1973 reads:

(1) Subject to the provisions of this Chapter, any Magistrate of the first class and any Magistrate of the second class specially empowered in this behalf under sub-section (2) may take cognizance of any offence.

   (a) upon receiving a complaint of facts which constitute such offence;
   (b) upon a Police Report of such facts;
   (c) upon information received from any person other than a Police Officer, or upon his own knowledge that such offence has been committed.

(2) The Chief Judicial Magistrate may empower any Magistrate of the second class to take cognizance under sub-section (1) of such offences as are within his competence to inquire into or try."

Filing of Supplemental Charge-sheet

Clause (8) under section 173 Cr. P.C., 1973 gives scope for filing up of supplemental charge-sheets. This provision enables the investigating officer to collect further evidence even after filing the charge-sheet in a case. The investigating officer, if he does so, can produce such evidence before the Court provided that the accused is given the usual facilities for obtaining the copies. If the investigating officer, after the submission of the charge-sheet, receives fresh or further information about people or things involved in the commission of an offence, he can resume investigation and file a supplemental charge-sheet even without the orders of a Magistrate. This is to say that when one investigation has been completed, another can be initiated on fresh information received. However it is not proper to resume investigation against an accused person having once laid down the charge-sheet against him.

Withdrawal of Charge-Sheet

Section 321 Cr. P.C., 1973 says:

"The Public Prosecutor or Assistant Public Prosecutor in charge of a case may, with the consent of the Court, at any time before the judgement is pronounced, withdraw from the prosecution of any person either generally or in respect of any one or more of the offence for which he is tried, and upon such withdrawal—

(a) if it is made before a charge has been framed, the accused shall be discharged in respect of such offence or offences;
(b) if it is made after a charge has been framed, or when under this Code no charge is required, he shall be acquitted in respect of such offence or offences;

Provided that where such offence—

i) was against any law relating to a matter to which the executive power of the Union extends; or
ii) was investigated by the Delhi Special Police Establishment Act, 1946 (25 of 1946); or
iii) involved the misappropriation or destruction of, or damage to any property belonging to the Central Government, or
iv) was committed by a person in the service of the Central Government while acting or purporting to act in the discharge of his official duty.

and the Prosecutor in charge of the case has not been appointed by the Central Government, he shall not, unless he has been permitted by the Central Government to do so, move the Court for consent to withdraw from the prosecution and the Court shall, before according consent, direct the prosecutor to produce before it the permission granted by the Central Government to withdraw from the prosecution".

Final Report/Charge-Sheet — Case Laws

1. A charge-sheet is hardly a complete and accurate thesis of prosecution case.[3]
2. The Magistrate is not bound to accept the police report as it is; he can take a view that the facts appearing in the final report constitute an offence.[4]
3. The Magistrate can certainly disagree with the opinion of the police. In that case the Magistrate can either direct further investigation if he sees that the investigation is unsatisfactory and improper or he may take cognizance of the offence if the final report sets out facts constituting the oftence.[5]
4. The chief Judicial Magistrate can disagree with the report of the police officer or any other person whom the matter has been entrusted for investigation and take congnizance.[6]
5. Once cognizance is taken by a Magistrate, he really takes cognizance of an offence and not of the offenders. The Magistrate here has a duty to find out who the offenders really are. Magistrate comes to the conclusion that there are persons other than those sent up by the police also have involved in the commission of the offence it is his duty to proceed against those persons. Hence the summoning of additional accused is a part of the proceedings initiated by the Magistrate.[7]
6. The accused to be furnished with the statements of P.W.S. does not apply to a trial for a non-cognizable offence. The right which the accused has of obtaining copies of the statements made by witness during investigation is a very valuable right and that the wholesale refusal to grant the same will be a serious irregularity which would vitiate the trial.[8]

7. Failure to furnish statements of witnesses recorded in the course of investigation may not vitiate the trial. It does not affect the jurisdiction of the Court to try a case nor is the failure by itself a ground which affects the power of the Court to record a conviction, if the evidence warrants such a course. The provision relating to the making the copies of statements recorded in the course of investigation is undoubtedly of great importance, but the breach therof must be considered in the light of the prejudice caused to the accused by reason by its breach.[9]
8. When a person is arrested in suspicion, it is the duty of the police to carry out prompt investigation without unnecessary delay. It is the duty of the police to collect evidence to satisfy the Court that there is sufficient evidence to raise a suspicion that the arrested man may have committed an offence.[10]
9. Before parting, I would like to observe that there has been undue and unexplained delay in putting the case in the Court against the accused. The case, so far as the prosecution is concerned, is very simple as it depends entirely on the speech made by him on 16th, August, 1961. The prosecution claims to have taken down the speech and recorded the statements of the witnesses; in support of it. I fail to see why it has been necessary for the prosecution to withhold the challan for all these days when no further investigation is needed and nothing further has been done. Such a course is apt to leave an impression in the mind of the accused that the challan is being delayed in order to punish him before he is convicted or to ensure that he would not escape punishment by detention in prison even if the court ultimately finds him not guilty.[11]
10. The following three courses are open to the Magistrate before whom a final report is submitted.
    a) Agree with the report of the police and file the proceedings;
    b) Not agree with the police report;
    c) Order further investigation or hold that the evidence is sufficient to justify the forwarding of the accused to the Magistrate and take cognizance of the offence, complained of."[12]

Final Report: How to Prepare it?

The investigating officer can close the investigation in many ways. If he is unable to collect more evidence, in spite of his earnest attempts to do so, and he is convinced that he can do nothing more in the case, he should then submit a final report treating the case as *undetectable*. He can as well treat the case as: (i) mistake of fact or mistake of law; (ii) civil nature, (iii) non-cognizable. If the investigating officer sends the final report of a case stating that the case is a false one, he should specifically say in the report whether or not he intends proceeding against the complainant. If he is not intending to proceed against the complainant, the reasons for it must be clearly stated in the final report. The Magistrate should approve the report of the police officer if the latter's report states that the case is a false one.

If the investigating officer writes in his final report that the case is undetectable or is due to mistake of fact/law etc. he should briefly state the evidence on record and the circumstances demanding such an action by the investigating officer. He should get the proceedings of the Magistrate on the final report. The investigating officer should then incorporate the same in the F.I.R. order for verification by the supervising officers.

The Magistrate can definitely order further investigation of the case if he is not satisfied with the reasons adduced by police to prove that the case is false, undetectable or is based on mistake of fact/law etc. The Magistrate can call for the Case-Diary and statements recorded under section 161 Cr. P.C. and read them to satisfy himself about the facts about the investigation. If, on perusal of the records, he feels that the police has unjustly omitted some persons as accused, he can issue summons against such persons. The case against such accused persons would come under section 190 (1) (b) Cr. P.C., 1973. The Public Prosecutor, if on perusal of all the records, finds that the police has unjustly left out some persons who ought to have been included in the list of accused persons, he can move the Magistrate to summon them on the basis of the records available and other documents referred to in section 173 Cr. P.C., 1973 even without examination of witnesses in court. Again, sub-section (2) of section 173 Cr. P.C., 1973 empowers superior police officers to direct further investigation even after submission of a final-report under sub-section (1) of section 173 Cr. P.C. When the superior police officer directs further investigation after the submission of a final report and subsequently on investigation he finds that the accused has committed an offence, he would be bound to submit a charge-sheet against the final report already filed by the investigating officer. In Sharma *vs.* State, it was held by the Court that the Superintendent of Police who is an officer superior to the rank of the Sub-Inspector is competent to supervise investigation and as such he has the power to direct the submission of a charge-sheet even when the investigating officer has already submitted the final report under section 173, Cr. P.C., 1973. Such a subsequent charge-sheet which supercedes the final report already submitted is a perfectly valid document and the Magistrate is bound to take cognizance of the offence[13]. The Court can not quash investigation of a cognizable case before the completion of investigation. The Court interferes only when the case is investigated and a report under section 173 Cr. P.C. is filed before it. Before that stage, not even the High Court which enjoys certain inherent powers under section 482 Cr. P.C., 1973 will interfere with police investigation. However, the High Court may interfere and order the police to stop investigation if it finds that the F.I.R. does not contain any facts constituting an offence under the law.

Penalty for Submitting False Report

A police officer who submits an incorrect report of an investigation negligently or improperly, can be punished under section 29 of the Police Act. He can be punished under section 218 of I.P.C. and cannot be proceeded against under section 211, I.P.C.

Charge-Sheet and Period of Limitation

When the charge-sheet is filed, the Court is bound to consider the question of limitation. In this case, the Court has to see as to whether or not it is competent to take cognizance and whether or not the limitation prescribed by section 468 Cr. P.C., 1973 has expired. If limitation has expired, the Court can not take cognizance. If the Court, disregarding the period of limitation under section 468 Cr. P.C. takes cognizance, then the order of the Court will be without jurisdiction.

If the court finds that the period of limitation has expired, it can condone the delay if it is satisfied that there are sufficient and justifiable grounds for condonation of delay or for extension of the period of limitation. Here, there is no need for the prosecution to make an application under section 473 Cr. P.C., 1973 for condonation of delay. The prosecution can explain the grounds for the delay in the charge-sheet itself. Of course, the prosecution can also make an application accompanied by an affidavit or documents in support of the same. However, the Court can not condone the delay and extend the period of limitation once it has taken cognizance of the offence. In Panney Singh *vs.* State of Rajasthan, a Magistrate took cognizance of the offence on presentation of the charge-sheet beyond the period of limitation. It was later held that the order taking cognizance is not sustainable in law and is bad and without jurisdiction.[14] Again in Jagmohan *vs.* State, it was held by the Court that: "in the present case not only that delay was totally unjustified and unexplained, interest of justice could never require that peace of mind of petitioners which had been bestowed due to lapse of period of limitation should be snatched away. On the other hand it will be abuse of process of law if the petitioners are made to suffer harassment of prosecution for stale alleged infractions of law after months together of expiry of period of limitation. In such cases of wrong exercise of discretion, the High Court has to exercise revisional as well as inherent jurisdiction to redress the wrong. The application of the prosecution for condonation of delay is accordingly dismissed.[15]

To wind up, it may be reiterated here that investigation of crime from registration of the F.I.R. to the filing of final report/charge-sheet is a laborious process which calls for initiative, enthusiasm and intelligence. While investigating a crime, the police has to keep in mind that the justice is not one-sided, the purpose of investigation is to determine whether or not the accused has committed the offence alleged of. The Courts of law can pronounce its judgement only on actual and credible evidence on record. The police has to remember that the accused is always entitled to get the benefit of every reasonable doubt in a criminal trial and therefore honesty and credibility should be there in police investigation *ab initio*.

SUGGESTED READINGS

B.P.R. & D., *Educative Material on the Basic Course for Sub-Inspectors of Civil Police.*, Vol. II, Directorate of Police Training, M.H.A., New Delhi, 1981.

Capoor, H.L., *Police Diaries, Statements, Reports etc.*, Law Publishers, Allahabad, 1981-82.

Khan, M.K.A., *Police Reports & Investigation*, Law Book Co. Lahore, 1947.

Pisolkar, S.M., *Supreme Court on Crimes,* Chandrakant Chimanlal Vora, Ahmedabad, 1978.

REFERENCES

1. A.I.R. 1957 S.C. 637 at p. 645; 1957 Cr. L.J. 1014.
2. Kali Charan *vs.* State, A.I.R. 1955 All. 462.
3. R.K. Dalmia *vs.* Delhi Administration A.I.R. 1961 S.C. 1821.
4. Siddappa Gurappa *vs.* State of Mysore, A.I.R. 1960 Mys. 237; Lumbaran *vs.* State of Rajasthan, 1957 Cr. L.J. 231 (Raj); A.K. Roy *vs.* State of West Bengal, A.I.R. 1962, Cal. 135 (F.B.).
5. State of Gujarat *vs.* Shah Lakhamshi Umarshi, 1966 Cr. L.J. 1420.
6. Rampratesh Rai *vs.* Bishun Mandal, 1981 Cr. L.J. 139.
7. State *vs.* Ganesha, 1968 Cr. L.J. 648: A.I.R. 1968 Raj. 116.
8. Purushottam *vs.* State of Kutch, A.I.R. 1954 S.C. 700: 1954 Cr. L.J. 1751.
9. Noor Khan *vs.* State of Rajasthan, 1964 Cr. L.J. 167: A.I.R. 1964 S.C. 286.
10. Sehhat Khan *vs.* State A.I.R. 1965, Tripura, 27.
11. Vidya Singh *vs.* State 1962 Cr. L.J. 633: A.I.R. 1962 Punj. 487.
12. Kamalapati Trivedi *vs.* State of West Bengal, 1979 Cr. L.J. 679: A.I.R. 1970 S.C. 1777.
13. 1963 (2) Cr. L.J. 42 Pat.
14. 1980 Cr. L.J. 339 (Raj.)
15. 1980 Cr. L.J. 742 (Delhi) and the extract is taken from H.L. Capoor, *Police Diaries, Statements etc.*, Law Publishers, Allahabad, 1981-82.

13

INVESTIGATOR BEFORE THE BAR

The investigating officer's task continues till the case is presented before a Court of Law. He should therefore bear in mind, right from the time of recording the F.I.R., that some day he will be summoned to the court to give testimony. The acquittal or the conviction in a case will considerably depend on the investigator's ability to present the facts, explain the actions taken, and convincing the Court on the decisions taken etc. Hence, when the investigating officer is informed that the case is posted for trial, he should:

i) review all the facts, reports and data concerning the occurrence of the case as well as the Case-Diary;
ii) study the role played by him (his predecessors, if any), his colleagues and others who participated or aided the investigation work;
iii) make a revisit of the scene of crime and once again ascertain the distance, measurements, location or things of this kind;
iv) necessarily arrange a pre-trial conference with the Assistant/Public Prosecutor. This will surely help the prosecutor and the investigator as to how best the case can be conducted;
v) collect as much data and background information as possible about the witnesses of the defence;

vi) before going for the pre-trial conference with the prosecutor, ask the following questions to himself and once again try to find out an answer to each question.

Questions

1. In Relation to Persons Connected with the Offence:

WHO
- are the accused persons?
- is the first accused and why?
- is the first informant and the reason for his preferring an information in this case?
- who is the victim? or victims? their role in becoming the victims? The motive of the accused for committing the offence?
- is an accessary? How?
- are the prosecution witnesses? How are they going to help the prosecution?
- are the defence witnesses? their background? etc.

2. In Relation to Officers Participating in the Investigation:

WHO
- responded to the first information? and why?
- questioned the first informant? and why?
- recorded the first information? and why?
- were taken to the scene of crime?
- guarded the scene? conducted the inspection? and why?
- questioned whom at the scene of crime? – and the information collected?
- collected physical clues?
- were the scene witnesses?
- took the photographs? and why?
- marked and preserved the material evidence?
- were called to the scene of crime? and why?

WHO – visited the scene of crime? – superior police officers? scientific experts? finger print experts? dog-squad?
– took the custody of the evidence? who carried the evidence to Forensic Science Laboratory/ Finger Print Bureau/Chemical Examiner etc.?
– dusted the finger prints?
– checked out possible leads?
– identified and located the perpetrator?
– obtained a warrant for arrest, if that was necessary?
– made the arrest? and whom? and when?
– granted bail? if not by the investigating officer, why?
– brought the accused to the police station?
– questioned the culprits and why?
– questioned the witnesses? and why?
– recorded the statements of the accused and witnesses?

3. In Relation to the Offence:

WHAT – has actually happened?
– is the offence? is the section of law?
– damages were done? – to the person (accused and victim), to the property?
– injuries were done to the victim/accused? and why? how?
– was the condition of the victim/accused immediately after the commission of the offence?
– statements were made by the accused initially? – then later? by the victim? by informers? by witnesses?
– news appeared in the press?

4. In Relation to the Evidence:

WHAT – material evidence were obtained from the scene of crime?
– physical clues could be collected in such a case? Why were they not collected?
– oral and documentary evidence were collected? How do they help the prosecution?

5. In Relation to Police Action:

WHAT – police action was initiated? why?
– information was received? why?
– agencies were notified? why?
– further actions (subsequent to the initial action) were taken?
– is the delay between recording the F.I.R. and commencement of inspection? why?
– is the delay between commencement of inspection and arrest of the suspects? why?
– is the delay between registration of the case and questioning of witnesses? why?
– is the delay between registration of the case and submission of final report? why?

6. In Relation to Offence:

WHEN – was the offence committed? hour? day? date? month? and year?
– was the offence reported? hour? month? date and year?
– was the offence investigated? hour? day? date? month? and year? If delay has taken place between the registration of the case and the commencement of actual and serious investigation, then why?

7. In Relation to Persons Connected with the Offence:

WHEN

- was the victim last seen alive? and by whom?
- did the victim arrive at the scene?
- did the victim leave the scene?/was he removed from the scene and by whom?
- was the accused seen at the spot of the occurrence of crime? and by whom?
- did the accused leave the scene?
- did the accessory arrive at the scene? leave the scene?
- did the witnesses see the incident? observe the scene? arrive and leave the scene?
- was the witnesses questioned? If delay has taken place, the reasons?
- was the accused arrested? granted bail? detained in custody? questioned?
- was the expert opinion received? If delay has taken place, why?
- was the investigation completed? If undue delay is seen, why?

The hour, day, date, month and year may be written against each question.

8. In Relation to Police Action:

WHEN

- did the investigation commence?
- did the investigator arrive at the scene of crime?
- did the investigator get in touch with the victim and obtain his statements?
- did the investigating officer contact the accused? arrest him/them? take his/their statements? question him/them? did the officer contact each witness and record his statements?

WHEN – did the investigator check out other possible sources of information? when did he get each item of evidence?

– did the investigator receive expert opinion? or when did the scientific experts/medical officer/finger-print expert/photographer etc. arrive at the scene of crime?

– was the warrant obtained if that was necessary? and when was the charge-sheet made?

The answers to these questions should be answered with respect to hour, day, date, month and year whenever possible to ensure accuracy.

9. In Relation to the Offence:

WHY – was the offence reported?

– was the offence committed? If there was some lapse of time between the commission of the offence and reporting of the same, then why?

10. In Relation to the Accused:

WHY – did the accused commit the offence?

– did he use a particular *modus-operandi*? use the particular means of entry? use the particular tools or weapons?

– was the victim injured? What was the role of the victim in the commission of this offence?

11. In Relation to Others Involved:

WHY – was a particular witness seen at the place of occurrence?

- was a particular witness interested in giving information?
- was a particular informant interested in lodging an information to police?
- was the victim moved from the scene of offence?

12. In Relation to the Offence:

HOW
- was the offence committed?
- was the accused provoked?
- were the tools and weapons employed for the commission of the offence?
- was the offence planned? where? when?
- was the offence discovered and reported?

13. In Relation to Persons Connected with the Offence:

HOW
- did the accused arrive at the scene of crime?
- did the accused secure the tools and weapons used?
- did the accused leave the scene of crime?
- did the witnesses happen to see the incident?
- did the informant come to know of the offence?
- did the victim happen to be at the scene of crime?

14. In Relation to Police Action:

HOW
- did the investigator identify the victim? obtain evidence? identify the accused? locate the offender? arrest the culprit?

15. In Relation to Offence:

WHERE
- is the scene of crime?

– was the offence discovered?
– was the offence reported?

16. In Relation to Persons Connected with the Offence:

WHERE – was the culprit residing at the time of committing the offence? where is he now?
– did the accused obtain the tools and weapons from?
– were the tools and weapons hidden after the commission of the offence by the accused?
– were the tools and weapons discovered from?
– were the witnesses at the time of committing the offence? are they now?
– was the informant at the time of committing the offence? is he how?
– was the victim residing at the time of committing the offence? is he now?

17. In Relation to Police Action:

WHERE – was the Station-House Officer (if he was absent) when the information was lodged?
– was the evidence obtained from? marked? stored?
– were the victims, witnesses and informers interviewed?
– was the accused questioned and his statements were recorded?
– was the accused arrested from?
– was the accused detained initially? and later?

The answers to these and similar questions will surely give all information that the prosecutor would like to know. Remember that ours is an accusatorial system of criminal justice and the prosecution has to prove everything beyond any shadow of doubt. Andre Evans writes: "Unlike an atheletic event or a card game, where the winner is one making the most points, the outcome of a lawsuit depends on the evaluation of many intangibles, most of them subtle and subject to a difference of opinion........... In a criminal case, the defendant is presumed to be innocent".[1]

The Investigator Before the Bar

Giving testimony before a Court of Law is a noble and imprortant duty of any civic-minded man—and especially of a police investigator. Judges are also human beings and therefore like other people, they too make their first impressions of the investigating officer at the first sight – i.e., when he walks into the court-room and take the oath. Hence the invetigator's walk and appearence, especially his actions and uniform, should make the Judge to feel that the officer is there to perform a dignified job. The investigating officers, therefore, should bear in mind the following *do's:*

i) approach the witness – stand in a dignified manner – i.e., in a deliberate and unhurried way;
ii) do not glare at the accused or the defence counsel;
iii) stand erect and salute the Chair;
iv) don't be over-confident;
v) give an impression to the Judge that the officer is taking things with due seriousness and sincerity;
vi) take the oath seriously, pronouncing each word in a clear and audible way;
vii) look at the Judge and wait patiently for the proceedings to begin;
viii) don't make sounds or movements which are distracting. Clearing of throat, frequent crossing and uncrossing of arms, wiping of the face always with towels and similar nervous mannerisms should as far as possible be avoided;
ix) be truthful. Tell the truth and nothing but the truth. "Every relevant fact should be readily admitted, even if it is not to

the advantage of your side of the case. Do not stop to figure out whether your answer will help or hurt. Just answer the question to the best of your ability. To try to colour or shade testimony to help your side only invites troubles. By so doing, you give the appearance of taking sides and lose credibility. Sticking to the truth is the best defence against cross-examination. No matter, how skillful a lawyer will be, he will be unable to trap you up if you stick to the truth".

x) answer the questions slowly and specifically using normal language. Do not try to be wiser than the Judge and never use a word or jargon that is not clearly known to the Judge;

xi) look always and every time at the Judge. Answer all questions looking at and looking at the Judge only. The defence counsel may make attempts to confuse and may show signs and facial expressions to fool the officer. Therefore do not look at him so that his attempts will not have any impact. The officer need is only his ears to hear him and needs not see how he acts in the court;

xii) never answer the questions without understanding the full meaning and implications. If the question is not clearly understood, ask the counsel to repeat it. An officer is not an encyclopaedia;

xiii) if the lawyer is asking lengthy questions, ask him to repeat it. The same procedure can be adopted if he is asking questions in an angry tone. In such instances, more often than not, the lawyer will not be able to repeat the question with the same vigour he had when he asked earlier. This will, perhaps, put him in a confusion as to the question itself;

xiv) answer the questions in a loud tune but with due politeness and courtesy;

xv) asking the counsel to repeat long and confusing questions is found to be good. It does not mean that every time, this technique proves to be rewarding. Remember that repeatition is at times annoying to any body – and the Judge may not be an exception to this. At the same time, if questions which are calculated to confuse the investigator is deliberately put, then ask the counsel to explain what he actually means by that question. It is likely to confuse the lawyer himself;

xvi) think before answering. A pause before answering proves to be always good. Slow answers give the impression that the answers are believable. "If you respond slowly enough to consider your thoughts before speaking, your testimony is enhanced. Speaking hurriedly can result in the misunderstanding of testimony because words were slurred, answers were improperly phrased, or the question was misinterpreted. Before replying, wait until you are sure that the question has been completed. Answering before the question is completed may be perceived as eagerness to help your side of the case or, on cross-examination an attempt to avoid a difficult question. Adopt a deliberate pace, but avoid speaking so slowly as to cause your listeners to doubt your testimony. Body gestures with hands or nods of the head must be avoided, since the Court reporter or recording device cannot record them."[2]

xvii) do not volunteer information unless called for. If it is very necessary, then only it should be done. But an information which is not asked for is almost certain to be objected to;

xviii) hearsay evidence is not admitted in Indian law. Hence, in replying to questions, never say things that someone else said to the officer or the officer heard from somebody else speaking to another. State only those facts and information about which the officer has personal knowledge. Such phrases like, *I like to say, I am to think, I must believe* or *I am of opinion* etc. must be avoided. What the officer know is more important than what he thinks or believes. The officer is not summoned to give an opinion in the court;

xix) **errare humanun est-to err is human**— is a well accepted dictum. Hence, if a mistake, is committed it does not matter. Recognize the mistake at the earliest and acknowledge the same. This is the reason why Andre Evans writes, "The simple statement that you have made a mistake and would like to correct it is better than having your entire testimony discredited later. If you have not recognised your mistake, but it becomes apparent perhaps, during cross-examination admit it. It is better to acknowledge an error than to adamently maintain a position that is plainly wrong and thereby discredit your entire testimony.[3]

xx) no one will be able to make accurate estimates about height, weight etc. unless he has actually measured the same or verified through measuring instruments. The same is the case with time, speed, depth, slope etc. Being not exact in such matters proves that the officer is honest in his testimony;

xxi) When the prosecutor conducts Examination-in-Chief, it is likely that he is objected to or unnecessarily interrupted by the defence counsel. This may be a calculated attempt to distract the prosecutor or the investigator or both. In such instances, wait until the matter is ruled on and instruction is given to officer testimony by the Judge. No doubt, cross-examination is really *'torturous'*. Politeness and calmness here will be rewarding. Never get upset and do not try to be wiser. "Telling the truth and remaining pleasant and courteous will assure your credibility. Answer these questions as you would to any others. Information honestly given cannot cause trouble. Only when you contradict yourself can your testimony be shown as unworth of belief. Your courtesy will require courtesy in return or reveal the cross-examiner's tactics as being unfair to you and therefore resented by the Jury. You should testify deliberately on cross-examination rather than hurriedly so that your attorney can offer an objection."[4]

Cross-Examination in Court

After the Examination-in-Chief, the cross-examination follows. During cross-examination "it is difficult indeed to keep cool when all sorts of attacks are made about one's character, efficiency and even integrity. The only way a police officer can train himself to this situation is to remember that the defence counsel has nothing against him and is only trying his best to shatter prosecution evidence to the best of his ability. A quiet, clear and concise answer, given by calm, pleasant and well composed witness in an impersonal manner will contribute much to the weight of his testimony given. The ability to maintain such an attitude when under attack is an art that every competent witness must learn."[5]

How best can a cross-examination be faced? For this, one show know the various types of defence lawyers and their tactics.

Defence Lawyers – Types[6]

Sl. No.	*Types*	*Mode of Approach*
1.	Professional Defender	Adopts more or less a legal approach. He does not indulge in personal attacks on the investigator.
2.	Subtle Defender	Puts questions in such a manner that the answer given will be suggestive of something which the investigator never meant. He combines two or three questions in one question.
3.	Explosive Defender	Puts questions initially in a calm manner and then would suddenly raise his voice and simulate emotions to confuse the investigator.
4.	Dramatist	Plays to the gallery and by gesticulations at the end of each question tries to give an impression that he has got an important point when he has no point at all. He may employ insulting remarks mainly against the intelligence and efficiency of the investigator.

One cannot say that a defence counsel can be clearly classified strictly in one or the other types shown by Krishnamurthi. One and the same counsel may exhibit all modes of approach to win his case. Hence there is scope for the mixed type among defence lawyers. Therefore, it is better if the investigating officers understand the common tactics of cross-examination employed by lawyers and adopt an attitude that is best suited to handle each situation. Besides what has been said above, the following guidelines may also be kept in mind during cross-examination:

1. be short in your answers;
2. wherever possible say "yes or no";
3. be precise and specific in replies;
4. think thrice before responding to questions;
5. speak only the truth;
6. don't get upset, be self-confident;
7. don't be emotional;
8. don't be over-zealous and extra-zealous;
9. remember that you are answering questions before intelligent people who are accustomed to this. Hence don't try to bluff;
10. give respect and get respect back.

COMMON TACTICS DURING CROSS- EXAMINATIONS*

Sl. No. (1)	Counsel's Tactics with Example (2)	Counsel's Purpose (3)	Investigating Officer's Response to Counsel's Tactics (4)
1	*Rapid - Fire Questions* : e.g., one question is followed by another with very little time to answer. In other words, questioning before the answer is completed.	This is a calculated attempt to confuse the witness. The court-craft helps to compel inconsistent answers from the investigator. The investigator becomes at his wit's end and feel defident.	Advised to take a pause - i.e., *Reaction-Time* to counsel's question should be longer. Take sufficient time to evaluate the pros and cons of the question and be deliberate in answering. Ask the counsel to repeat the question. Never look at him, look at the Court and remain calm and collected.
	Condescending Counsel : e.g., adopts a benevolent approach and appears to be over-sympathetic in questioning to the point of redicule and humiliation. This craft may at times irritate the witness.	This is a calculated attempt to simulate emotions to confuse the investigator and to confuse the investigator and to give an impression to the Court that the witness is incapable and lacks self-confidence or may not be wholly reliable and trustworthy.	Think that the lawyer has no reason to be over-sympathetic towards the investigator. Hence give firm and decisive answers. If too much benevolence is shown, ask him to repeat the question. He cannot be that benevolent then. If redicule is sensed, or the question is improperly phrased, the counsel should necessarily be requested to repeat the question. Never become angry or loose self-confidence when rediculed.

* See also the *Common Tactics During Cross-Examination* prepared by Association of Chiefs of Police, Inc. for types and classification, purpose of counsels and responses to their questions.

(Contd.)

(*Table Contd.*)

(1)	(2)	(3)	(4)
3.	*Friendly Counsel :* e.g., shows undue courtesy and politeness and decency. The questions tend to take witnesses into counsel's confidence. It may enhance rapport as well.	To give the witness a false sense of security and to develop an unduly important ego-consciousness in the investigator. He may feel elevated in such situations and resultantly may try to side with counsel.	Undue courtesy is not expected from defence lawyers. Stay alert bearing in mind that the purpose of the counsel is to discredit or diminish the effect of witness testimony. Benevolence for benevolence sake is not benevolent at all.
4.	*Badgering, Belligerent Counsel :* He stares at the investigator right in his face. He comes close to the witness box, fists at times and shouts *that it is not so? isn't it?* etc. He may dramatise his actions also. With women witnesses, the dramatisation may be more. In such instances, they become confused and feel humliated.	To cause anger in the witness and thereby to make him/her confused. This is more seen among women-witnesses. The witness may lose logic of thinking. Generally here rapid-fire questions also may be included.	Don't look at the counsel; look at the Court; turn your body towards the Court. Stay calm and speak in a deliberate manner. Pause after each question if that need be. Give the prosecutor sufficient time to make appropriate objections to the Counsel's behaviour. Show to the Court that you do not like the peculiar behaviour of the counsel. Let the Court rule on it.*
5.	*Mispronouncing Officer's Name or Using Wrong Rank :* e.g., The officer may be a Circle Inspector of Police but he is addressed as S.I. Again, the officer's name may be Madhu, but he addresses him as Mandan.	To distract the attention of the officer and to draw the same to the error rather than the question asked. This may cause the witness to make inadvertent errors in testimony. The witness feels humiliated when his rank is reduced to a lower one.	Ignore the error in the rank. Concentrate on the question the counsel is asking. The Court knows the rank of the witness and the rank has nothing to do with witness-testimony.

* It is not easy for an investigator to assess the counsel and his tactics. Experience will make this task easier.

(*Table Contd.*)

6. *Restrictive Questions :* e.g., 'Did you discuss this case with anyone? Did you visit the scene of crime prior to the recording of the F.I.R? Have you stopped harassing the prosecution witnesses and then insisting for a *yes* or *no* answer.	To confuse the investigator and then to feel that he is in *between the devil and the deep sea*. For instance, a 'no' answer will put the investigator in a position of denying to have had pre-trial conference. On the other hand a 'yes' answer would mean that the officer was told how of testify. So is the case with the second and the third questions.	Hence answer should not be in 'yes' or 'no'. The officer should say : "I have discussed the case with the Assistant / Public Prosecutor and other officers working on the case. No one has told me how to testify". Again, in the third question, he should say : "The question of harassing witnesses does not arise here. It was never resorted to".*
7. *Insisting Questions :* e.g. If the restrictive question is answered not in *yes* or *no,* rather by an explanation, lawyers may insist the witness to say *yes* or *no*. The counsel may get angry at times if answer is not given in *yes* or *no*.	To cause mental tension in the investigator. The investigator gets confused and does not know how to answer. He may become pale and sometimes may get angry.	Attempt to give an explanation. If the defence counsel insists on *yes* or *no* answer, pause until the prosecutor intervences and raises his objection. The matter will be ruled on by the Judge. Then give your answer in a calm and collected manner. Never loose your temper.
8. *Leading Questions :* e.g., 1. was the colour of the car yellow? 2. was the time dark? 3. was he 24 years of age? 4. were you absent on the day? etc.	This is to lead the witness —i.e., putting the answer to the mouth of the witness so that the witness may vomit the answer put to his mouth.	Concentrate carefully on the facts; disregard the suggestion and answer the question truely.

* See also Andre Evans, *The Investigator in Court, op. cit.*

(*Table Contd.*)

(1)	(2)	(3)	(4)
9.	Insisting for a *Yes* or *no* answer to the question that needs explanation. Here, even without restrictive question being asked, lawyers may insist on getting a *yes* or *no* answer.	To prevent all pertinent and mitigating details from being considered by the Judge. This is also meant to cause confusion in the mind. Sometimes, the witness may become angry.	Explain the answer to the question. If stopped by the counsel demanding a *yes* or *no* answer, pause until the Court gives a ruling or the prosecutor intervenes.
10.	*Reversing Witnesses' Words* : e.g., The investigator says : "The accused was located and arrested by H.C. 8040". The counsel asks : "you say that the accused was located and arrested by H.C. 4080?" 2. "It was at 8 p.m." and the counsel says "It was at 8 a.m.?".	To confuse the witness and show the investigator's lack of confidence in what he testifies. The witness may become defident in such occasions.	Listen carefully to the questions and say : "I have just answered that question". If necessary, repeat the answer already given.
11.	*Assessment Questions* : The counsel asks "where was the victim from the accused when the crime took place?" Before answering the question, he says: "It is 3 yards, 5 yards or was at a distance from you and the Court (meaning the Judge)?	To confuse the witness and to show the investigator's inability to make assessment of distances, speed etc.	Don't he led by the suggestions made by the counsel. Answer the question correctly. If necessary, look the Case-Dairy and tell the answer. It is quite natural that one cannot recollect all the measurements without referring to the documents.

(*Contd.*)

(*Table Contd.*)

12. *Repetitious Questions :* The same question asked several times slightly rephrased.	To obtain inconsistent or conflicting answers from the investigator or to cause confusion in the mind.	Listen carefully whenever counsel repeats something you have already said. Correct if any error is uttered by the counsel. If necessary, ask the counsel to repeat his questions.
13. *Conflicting Answers :* e.g., "but S.I. Ram, the Inspector Tom said:" .... and so on". or "but S.I. Gopi told that.......... and so on"	To show inconsistency in the investigation. The tactics is normally used on measurements, time, speed etc.	Remain calm. Conflicting statements have a tendency to make a witness extremely nervous. Be guarded in your answers on measurements, time etc. Unless you have exact knowledge of them use the term *"approximately"*. Refer the notes if that need be.
14. *Staring Posture :* After the witness has answered, the counsel just stares as though there were more to come.	To have at long pause that one normally feels must be filled thus saying more than necessary. To provoke the witness into offering more than the answer called for.	Wait patiently for the next question to follow.
15. *Quotings :* The Counsel quotes authorities to show the ignorance of the investigator.	To feel "less" in front of the Judge. To confuse the investigator.	Say politely that you are not there to make opinions, rather you are stating the facts in the case.*

* One and the same lawyer may show any or all the tactics shown above. Hence the investigator has to be conscious about it.

SUGGESTED READINGS

Jayasimha Rao and K. Bhimiah, *Law on Sessions Trials*, Bharadwaga Publications Ltd., Bangalore, 1968.

Mitter V. *Confession and Evidence of Accomplices*, Law Book Co., Allahabad, 1967.

Malik B. *Criminal Trials*, Law Publishers, Allahabad, 1977.

Malik B. *Practical Hints on Cross-Examination*, Delhi, 1975.

Ramanatha Aiyer, P. and P. Raghava Aiyer, *The Principles and Precedents of the Art of Cross-Examination*, Law Book Co., Vols. I & II, Allahabad, 1971.

Venkatarama Aiyer, T.L. *et. al.* (Revised) *Field's Law Relating to Witnesses and Art of Cross-Examination Along with Law Relating to Accomplices and Approvers*, Law Publishers, Allahabad, 1914.

REFERENCES

1. Andre Evans, *The Investigator in Court from Criminal and Civil Investigation Hnad Book,* by Joseph J. Grau ed., Mc Graw Hill Book Co. New York, 1981.
2. Andre Evans, *The Investigator in Court, op. cit.*
3. Andre Evans, *The Investigator in Court, op. cit.*
4. Andre Evans, *The Investigator in Court, op. cit.*
5. K. Krishnamurthi, *Police Diaries, Statements, Reports, Investigations and Arrests etc.* Law Book Co., Allahabad, 1973.
6. K. Krishnamurthi, *Police Diaries, Statements, Reports, Investigaitons and Arrests etc. op. cit.*

INDEX